# you were not expected to do this

d|u|p

# materialisierungen 5

Andrea von Hülsen-Esch, Ricarda Bauschke-Hartung, Vittoria Borsò,
Reinhold Görling, Hans Körner, Achim Landwehr, Roger Lüdeke,
Eva Schlotheuber, Timo Skrandies, Jürgen Wiener (Hg.)

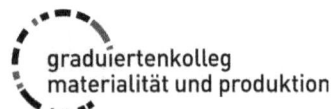
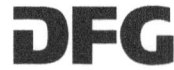

Daniel Blanga-Gubbay and Elisabeth Ruchaud (eds.)
# you were not expected to do this
## on the dynamics of production

HEINRICH HEINE
UNIVERSITÄT DÜSSELDORF

d|u|p

**Bibliografische Information der Deutschen Nationalbibliothek**
Die Deutsche Nationalbibliothek verzeichnet diese Publikation in der
Deutschen Nationalbibliografie; detaillierte bibliografische Daten sind
im Internet über http://dnb.dnb.de abrufbar.

© düsseldorf university press, Düsseldorf 2017
http://www.dupress.de
Lektorat: Sven Ondrazek
Redaktion: Daniel Blanga-Gubbay, Elisabeth Ruchaud
Titelbild: https://fr.fotolia.com/id/83216908, Broken Glass © Pink Badger – Fotolia.com
Satz, Layout und Umschlaggestaltung: Hannah Reller
Herstellung: docupoint GmbH, Barleben

Der Fließtext ist gesetzt in Adobe Garamond Pro
ISBN: 978-3-95758-040-5

# Table of Contents

Daniel Blanga-Gubbay and Elisabeth Ruchaud
Five Figures of Resistance.
An Introduction Through the Images of Erdem Gündüz,
Rosa Parks, Matthew Barney, Bartleby and Zinedine Zidane ............................ 9

Claudio Rozzoni
Creation Needs Interference.
The Five Obstructions ................................................................. 17

Veronica Peselmann
Rupturing Backgrounds.
Production as Resistance in Courbet's "The Artist's Studio" ............................ 31

Akos Hermann
The Resistance of Language.
Translation and Nomination in Walter Benjamin's Philosophy ........................... 51

Nicole De Brabandere
Inhabiting the Thick.
The Affects of Erosive Surfacing ........................................................ 63

Noémie Chardonnens
Dynamics of Medieval Production.
The Grail Motif in the Roman de Perceforest ...................................... 81

Joseph S. Freedman
The 'Unexpected' in the Context of Philosophy and the Arts
as Taught at 16th- and 17th-Century Academic Institutions ............................ 95

Dawid Kasprowicz
The Hidden Space of Production.
Virtuality in Henri Bergson and Gilbert Simondon ............................................. 111

Francesca Valentini
Tino Sehgal's "Constructed Situations".
The Tension of Immaterial Production ................................................................ 127

Katharina Thurmair
'Organisme d'art'.
Evolution and Artistic Production in the Work of Odilon Redon ...................... 143

Claudia Mongini
Aesthetic Mechanisms of Bio-Production .......................................................... 163

Louis Schreel
Empty Time.
The Temporality of Self-Affection in Kant's Analytic of the Sublime ................. 179

Ralph-Miklas Dobler
Working Traces in the History of Art ................................................................. 199

Berit Callsen
Traces in Sight.
Aesthetic Production Dynamics by Nathalie Sarraute and Alain Robbe-Grillet .. 217

Friederike Sigler
The (Im-)Possiblity of Tracing Labour.
On Jean-Luc Moulène's Objets de Grève ............................................................ 235

Katja Gentric
Labour and Its Aftermath, or:
On the Difficulty of Catching Oneself in the Act of Doing ................................ 251

About the Authors ........................................................................ 269

# Five Figures of Resistance.
## An Introduction Through the Images of Erdem Gündüz, Rosa Parks, Matthew Barney, Bartleby and Zinedine Zidane

Daniel Blanga-Gubbay and Elisabeth Ruchaud

On June 17, 2013, while crossing Taksim Square in Istanbul, Turkish choreographer Erdem Gündüz suddenly stopped, freezing himself in a standing position and without pronouncing a word. Minutes went on and he kept staying in position, staring at the Cultural Centre in front of him, with the picture of Mustafa Kemal Atatürk – the father of the modern state of Turkey – and the national flag. In the middle of the weeks of contestations against Erdogan and his government and the consequent ban on public demonstrations, his gesture produced an unexpected reaction: Some people approached him, at first to understand the reasons behind his mute standing position. Then the police came in an attempt to stop him, as far as an already motionless man could be stopped.

One might say that he was not expected to do this. Even if his gesture could not be defined as explicitly prohibited, he was not expected to stand still in a public space. Even though mute, his gesture was disturbing; or maybe it was disturbing precisely because of its non-evident nature. It was a clear protest, and still it was a mute protest, which was probably even more dangerous because, with no slogans, everything was potentially put into question by his gesture. That is why the response created by the counter-protesters of the governmental AKP party, with similar standing men wearing T-shirts saying 'Standing men facing against the standing man' did not have the same impact, responding to the 'silent call' with a narrowed political intention.

After some hours news of this vulnerable protest went viral and a hundred men and women joined the silent call of the protest, following the unique rule of standing still in the middle of the square, ignoring everything around. Suddenly the standing body of Gündüz became as strong as a stick inserted into the gearing of an entire society.

The gesture of Erdem Gündüz enters the tradition of silence in passive resistance, echoing in examples that range from history to fiction, from Gandhi to the *Silence of the Sea*, a novel by Jean Bruller[1], published in occupied France in 1942 and describ-

---

[1] Vercors, *Le silence de la mer*, Paris 1991. Cf. also Nathalie Gilbert-Joly, La bibliothèque dans le Silence de la mer. Un espace symbolique, in: *Conserveries mémorielles*, vol. 5 (2008), p. 166–173; Sabine Halbach, *Die Personenkonstellation in*

ing an uncle and his niece's resistance to German occupiers through the constant neglecting of the presence of the occupiers and the production of an unbearable silence. A question emerges: Should we consider these gestures as actions, or should we start considering them rather as the interruptions of an action? While standing still in the middle of Taksim, is Edem Gündüz accomplishing an action or is he interrupting one, namely the one of simply walking through the main square?

Sixty years ago, on December 1, 1955, while sitting in the front row of a bus in Montgomery, Alabama, and backed by months of protests of the African-American fight for civil rights, Rosa Parks refused to obey the bus driver's order to give up her seat to a white passenger. She kept sitting in the front row, mute and still, and her gesture – like Erdem Gündüz' – seems to have been first of all a gesture of disobedience. However, while reading what she wrote in more recent years, before dying in 2005, there clearly emerges a theoretical perspective on resistance:

> People always say that I didn't give up my seat because I was tired, but that isn't true. I was not tired physically, or no more tired than I usually was at the end of a working day. I was not old, although some people have an image of me being old then. I was 42. No, the only tired I was, was tired of giving in.[2]

It is no coincidence that these same words are incorporated within a political reflection on the notion of resistance, which arose out of a dialogue between Athena Athanasiou and Judith Butler in 2013, published under the title *Dispossession: the Performative in the Political*.[3] Therein, Athena Athanasiou refers back to the African-American fight for civil rights and the figure of Parks by showing how, while refusing to move and claiming her right to stay there, she induced a resistance within the social flux in which she was placed. "In this sense, staying in place may require some movement".[4] Athanasiou points out the resistance as something that takes place within a flux of movement, which, in the case of Rosa Parks, can be easily considered the application of the law: There is a law which calls for its application, its production.

---

*Le Silence de la Mer (Vercors)*, Munich 2004; Colum Kenny, *The Power of Silence*. Silent Communication in Daily Life, London 2011; Jérôme Meizoz, Ce que l'on fait dire au silence. Posture, ethos, image d'auteur, in: *Argumentation et Analyse du Discours*, vol. 3 (2009), https://aad.revues.org/667 (12/05/2016).

[2] Ruth Ashby, *Rosa Parks. Freedom Rider*, New York 2008, p. 62.

[3] Judith Butler / Athena Athanasiou, *Dispossession. The Performative in the Political: Conversations with Athena Athanasiou*, Cambridge 2013.

[4] Ibid., p. 23.

We imagine us collectively living on a surface where any pre-determined flux of movement (from the application of a law to the automatism of a production) is similar to an inclination of a surface, which predetermines our movements on it. That is why resistance is not an action but the interruption of an action, the one of sliding on the inclined surface. That is why, on this inclined surface, staying in place may require some movement. Yet, while resisting a pre-given form of production, we cannot say that the gesture of resistance is not a form of production at all: What does resistance produce and what is eventually the relation between these two forms of production?

Between 1987 and 1989, while being a student at Yale, Matthew Barney staged a series of performance events entitled *Drawing Restraint 1–6*. The primary intention of Barney addressed the implementation of some pencil drawings in a condition of impairment of the drawing itself: Barney proceeds by hanging the white sheet on the wall in a position nearly impossible to reach so that he can leave some marks on it only through an extremely high effort of his body. Matthew Barney seems to recover an artistic approach that focuses more on the process than the object, pioneered among the first by Yves Klein's conception of his well-known *Anthropometries* as ashes of his art. Nonetheless, in the *Drawing Restraint* series, the signs appearing on the sheet at the end of the performance are not to be conceived just as ashes of an effort: Rather than bearing a relation with the past, they are traces of a 'not yet'. By opening towards a conception of art as a conflictual relationship between creativity and resistance, the *Drawing Restraint* series fixes a movement that refuses to be exhausted in the object, in which the artistic tension must be kept as such. It is only by giving up the realisation of the creation from which it is attracted that the artist can keep himself in a creative tension towards the very object. In a text focusing on *Drawing Restraint*, English art critic Neville Wakefield[5] use the words "desiring machines" for the body of Barney: Barney in this performance presents himself as the one – or the "machine" – able to maintain this physical distance in which the desire keeps itself as still-desiring and never satisfied desire. In order to prevent himself from what seems to be an unavoidable absorption, Barney tenaciously tries to preserve this unfolded distance and he materializes a physical strength that allows him not to yield to the attraction. Hence, if in one of the last *Drawing Restraints*, he places the sheet to the bow of a boat and

---

[5] Neville Wakefield, *Matthew Barney. Drawing Restraint*, vol. 5, London / Cologne 2007.

ties himself to the opposite side with some partially elastic ropes, it is hard not to think that through the ropes – which will slowly become the most significant tool of these performances – and the set of this *Drawing Restraint* Barney establishes a very strong relation to the episode of the sirens in Odysseus, keeping himself from falling for something that loudly calls him. Hence, Barney's gesture is anything but idle: It is already headed for the 'object', but crystallizes in this half-way between an opening towards the creation and a refusal of it, in an interstitial space where the creative forces are not exhausted, where the desire is not reabsorbed in satiety.

To understand the possibility of reading this resistance of Barney we should take a look at how Emmanuel Lévinas, in his whole body of philosophy, set a dialectic relation between two terms which – even though they largely overcome the act of speaking – are defined as *le dire* ('the saying') and *le dit* ('the said'), which can be useful in understanding the consequence of realising the 'object'. If the 'saying' would actually be the same act of saying, the 'said' would mark an already realised moment, as a completely pronounced word would be. Lévinas openly underlines how, even though I personally contribute to realise the 'said', once it comes to light, it manifestly settles its independence from me. This is in strong analogy with the 'object' of artistic creation: Once separated from the work he creates, the artist has no longer the option to 'say' anything, since the object reached its autonomy.

And yet, it is not an independence that leaves these two terms without relation. Indeed, in realising the task, the realised task turns to me not to reveal how all efforts of 'saying' were for nothing but to let the 'said' appear. It turns to me to reveal the body as its instrument, as that in which all movements were previously and precisely designed starting from the aim to be realised. We can now understand Barney's refusal. While breaking the linearity of production, Barney freezes himself in an uncertain position where he is no longer simply the one who is conceived by the instrumental relation with the creation that he realised.

In *Bartleby, the Scrivener: A Story of Wall-Street* (1853), Melville tells the story of a copyist in an office near Wall Street, who is completely efficient in a brand new world turning towards complete inefficiency. Melville does not randomly choose the profession of Bartleby: The role of the copyist shows us scrupulously how in human activity the end to be realised always precedes the process, the latter being almost subordinated to and neglected in the former. What might be interesting in our gallery of portraits of resistance is that, through the short story, the same body of Bartleby is described as transparent and inconsistent. When 'production' is a bodily activity that takes into account the effort of a process, the world described by Melville seems to be a context in which frictions and gaps in realising the end have already evaporated. For this reason, after some months of daily working in the office, Bartleby one day suddenly refuses to work and pronounces his well-known and sibyllic sentence: "I would prefer not to." Bartleby tries to put up resistance to his condition: he 'prefers not to'; he prefers not to start an action since he lives in a world where any production is reduced to an identification with the task, in an adherence that admits no variation.

We may say that the body is usually an instrument in the production of specific actions, and, as clearly described by Martin Heidegger in *Sein und Zeit*, any instrument shall be described as an item that disappears in the realization of its end. As long as it is good for its use, the tool is invisible in front of the work it produces: While writing, I do not perceive the pen with which I write, precisely because I am already projected into the dimension of 'what' I write; and I would focus on the pen only if it suddenly refused to continue to write. If, while continuously realising actions and movements, the body is constantly projected into the production of things he has to do (actions and situations), by refusing to do something he simply exposes the simple presence of the body itself. In this sense, the gesture of Rosa Parks, like those of Bartleby and Erdem Gündüz, underlines the body.

While refusing to be an invisible instrument in the application of the law, Rosa Parks brings attention to her own body, producing her presence as a human being reclaiming specific rights. As in the act of striking, the interruption of the body produces a presence of the body: For this reason we might describe each resistance as a 'production of presence'. Derived from Hans U. Gumbrecht[6], this term speaks about the existence of two elements during the act of perception: a meaning effect – the projection towards an epistemological dimension – and a presence effect that brings to mind the materiality of the perception.

And still, is not this body that appears in resistance and interruption emerging with more than its materiality, namely with its freedom? What is this link between body and freedom that emerges here?

---

[6] Hans Ulrich Gumbrecht, *Production of Presence. What Meaning Cannot Convey,* Stanford 2004.

Not in many cases does the 'presence' of the body appear so loudly as in the frames shot by artists Douglas Gordon and Philippe Parreno in *Zidane: A 21st Century Portrait*[7], a 2006 movie in which the worldwide celebrated French football player is captured by dozens of cameras during ninety minutes of the match between Real Madrid and Villareal, held on April 23, 2005. The movie opens up a new dimension of vision to the match. It is not seen in its entirety or following the game, but the cameras rather mark Zinedine Zidane's body regardless of where the ball is. The body of Zidane is given back to the spectators in all these moments when – even on the football field – he does not strictly play; in all the instants when he is not necessarily in action. A collection of attempts, failures and intimacy is captured from afar and given back isolated from the match. A living body is present between the task and its accomplishment. If we already perceive him as an instrument in something he has to do while in action, his bodily dimension while failing comes out as full of gestures and possibilities. By bringing attention to the body, Gordon and Parreno remind us of its non-obligation to produce a specific action, and these traces of production inform us about the contingency of production itself. In *L'Être et le Néant*, Jean Paul Sartre wrote:

> Common sense will agree with us that a being, which is to be considered free, is one that can realise its projects. But to have the possibility to realise these, the simple projection of its purpose needs to be distinguished *a priori* from the realisation of the same. If it were enough to conceive in order to realise, I would be immersed in a world similar to that of dreams, in which the possible does not differ from reality.[8]

And that is why we can consider resistance to be charged with freedom, as it presents the body not simply in its materiality, but rather in the different possibilities that a body has.

Zidane, like Bartleby, is able to reveal the different forms of 'production' existing within production: If we go back to the character created by Melville, one can say that during his daily activity Bartleby was within a line of potential. Before copying a document, he had the means to do it, and, once done, he constantly had the option to create new possible action to be realised. This form of possibility may be identified as 'producing something', the power to realise something, and the possibility of constantly displacing the horizon in order to produce and reproduce new possibilities within

---

[7]   Douglas Gordon / Philippe Parreno, *Zidane. A 21st Century Portrait* (DVD), France 2006.

[8]   Jean-Paul Sartre, *L'Être et le Néant*, Paris 1943, pp. 562–563. Transl. by the authors.

the same line. But by refusing to work he opens up a different form of possibility. Bartleby does not simply ask for a pause and he does not simply quit his job to apply for a different one either. He tries to rationally put up a resistance to his condition of invisible efficiency: he 'prefers not to' start copying since, in the era of the technical reproduction, he feel the narrowness of the space of production between the original and the copy, a space in which he cannot produce himself or be present in his work.

Refusing to be the instrument in an already given production, the body emphasises production as a process full of uncertainty. The distance existing between the body and its task is full of variations, uncertainties, failures, and different possibilities. If any interruption of the process sheds light on the process itself, by preventing himself from achieving something and suddenly freezing himself in the middle of the process, Bartleby calls attention to the process too, suddenly disclosing how it is made of uncertainty, friction, possibilities of failures, and variations that can open up different directions at any moment. And with his resistance he eventually shows us that in the end any production includes another form of production within.

This text introduced four questions that were at the core of the conference *You Were not Expected to Do This*, organised by the postgraduate school "Materiality and Production" at Heinrich Heine University Düsseldorf in April 2014. This book, collecting some of the contributions that enriched the three-day conference, essentially follows the same four main points: 'On the Necessity of Resistance', 'Virtual Failures', 'Spaces of Accident', and 'Working Traces'.

As organizers of the conference, we would like to thank all participants for their rich contributions in developing this reflection on the notion of resistance and failure.

Above all, however, we would also like to thank all members of the postgraduate school for their help and support during the scientific as well as practical organisation of the conference; the professors for their advice and remarks when we were trying to define the theme of the conference throughout our workshops; the PhD students for two very rich years, especially those who were more particularly engaged in the conference; as well as Miriam Fick and Anna-Lisa Langhoff, our scientific coordinators, for their help and support during the process of organizing the conference and the subsequent publication of its proceedings.

Without all of the above this conference would not have been possible.

# Bibliography

Ashby, Ruth, *Rosa Parks. Freedom Rider*, New York 2008.

Butler, Judith / Athanasiou, Athena, Dispossession. *The Performative in the Political: Conversations with Athena Athanasiou*, Cambridge 2013.

Gilbert-Joly, Nathalie, La bibliothèque dans le *Silence de la mer*. Un espace symbolique, in: *Conserveries mémorielles*, vol. 5 (2008), p. 166–173.

Gordon, Douglas / Parreno, Philippe, *Zidane. A 21st Century Portrait* (DVD), France 2006.

Gumbrecht, Hans Ulrich, *Production of Presence: What Meaning Cannot Convey*, Stanford 2004.

Halbach, Sabine, *Die Personenkonstellation in Le Silence de la Mer (Vercors)*, Munich 2004.

Kenny, Colum, *The Power of Silence. Silent Communication in Daily Life*, London 2011.

Meizoz, Jérôme, Ce que l'on fait dire au silence. Posture, ethos, image d'auteur, in: *Argumentation et Analyse du Discours*, vol. 3 (2009), https://aad.revues.org/667 (12/05/2016).

Sartre, Jean-Paul, *L'Être et le Néant*, Paris 1943.

Vercors, *Le silence de la mer*, Paris 1991.

Wakefield, Neville, *Matthew Barney. Drawing Restraint*, vol. 5, London / Cologne 2007.

# Creation Needs Interference.
# The Five Obstructions
*Claudio Rozzoni*

Destroying the Theme

In the film *The Five Obstructions* (2003), Lars von Trier 'forces' his friend and fellow director Jørgen Leth to remake a short film, which Leth had shot in 1967, five times: *The Perfect Human*. From that coercion, a game arises between the two directors, and the film can be seen as a match where the possibility of creation is at stake. My proposal is that we consider this 'exercise', this 'game' – or maybe we should call it a 'play' –, as a particular way in which cinema shows itself as able to think and, in particular, to think of the relationship between ideas and creation: This film does so by overturning some of the more classical points of view regarding this relationship.

First, there is the outlook that considers the process of creation above all as both an active and voluntary process, for which the most important thing is the idea that the artist sees and 'only' has to express in order to show it to the audience. From this point of view, matter is a 'low' obstacle, and every obstruction along the way during the artistic process is merely an accident that must simply be removed. According to this way of thinking, we have the primacy of the idea compared to its physical presentations, namely its copies, which are supposed to reproduce it and which are at the same time supposed to be endowed with lesser quality than the idea itself, given the lowness of matter.

In our case, it is significant that the 'opening theme', the original short, which Leth has to shoot again, is not presented to us in whole before we see its 'variations', as with a musical 'opening theme' that comes before its variations. We initially see it appear on a TV screen, then in full-screen. These two ways of presentation come before other fragments, which follow one another throughout the film. We only see parts of it, we hear some 'notes' of it.[1] It is as if it was dismembered: As Leth puts it, it seems von Trier aims to "destr[oy]" the theme "from the start". With its own "pedagogy", *The Five Obstructions* aims to overturn such a supremacy working from the

---

[1] On this point, cf. also Paisley Livingston, Artistic Nesting in *The Five Obstructions*, in: *Dekalog 1: On The Five Obstructions* (2008), ed. by Mette Hjort, London, pp. 59–61.

very process of creation, 'obstructing' it in every possible way. In the following series of variations, the issue at the heart of the matter seems to be the very Platonic – better: 'Platonistic' – idea of human being: *The Perfect Human*. The crucial point is that it can do that only through 'interference'. After all, on closer inspection, every variation is already an obstruction. There is no gesture without obstacle, no creation without interference, there is no idea which does not get itself involved with an encumbrance. It is not by chance that I speak in terms of a 'match' (Leth himself speaks about this film in terms of a tennis match[2] or a football match).

Indeed, for the notion of 'obstruction', he has recourse to the former Danish football player Michael Laudrup, thus making us think about a rhythm of the hindrance, without which a 'perfect action' cannot be carried out. Facing the third obstruction, a paradoxical 'complete freedom', Leth affirms: "I don't like it, I'd rather have something to hang onto. [...] It's bad", and so he finds himself imagining a narration that unfolds as a "dialogue": a "playing back and forth across the net. He [von Trier] serves hard and we return as hard as nails. That's the way it is". In other words, facing freedom, Leth has to imagine an opponent. In order to find a 'perfect shot', Leth seems to need a 'lethal shot' from von Trier: Then "he serves hard again. A deadly serve, and we have to pull our best shot out of the bag to return his serve". It is a matter of 'waiting', 'observing', 'describing the right moment' when, as we will see, one can 'feel' the idea.[3] At that very moment, Leth finds out that he needs interference to create, that the idea is not metaphysically hidden behind a veil, but rather virtually suggested, as yet to be created, in the sinuous imperfections of matter. This reference to tennis, as well as the one to football, works well together with the observations Gilles Deleuze devotes to tennis in his *Negotiations (1972–1990)* as well as in the posthumous interview *Abécédaire*. Furthermore, such observations can certainly be compared to what Deleuze said in his well-known conference on *Qu'est-ce que l'acte de création?*[4]

---

[2] Leth devoted an experimental film *(Motion Picture)* about a Danish tennis player (Torben Ulrich) to the very same tennis dynamics in 1970.

[3] Jørgen Leth, Manifeste de Jørgen Leth. Le moment vient (Paris, le 11 Avril 2000), in: *The Five Obstructions*, production dossier, Brussels 2003, p. 5.

[4] Deleuze held the conference for the students of FEMIS (École nationale supérieure des métiers de l'image et du son) on May 17, 1987. I refer here to the text drawn from this conference and published in Gilles Deleuze, What is the Creative Act?, in: Gilles Deleuze, *Two Regimes of Madness. Texts and Interviews 1975–1995*, ed. by David Lapoujade, Semiotext(e), transl. by Ames Hodges and Mike Taormina, New York 2006.

In *Abécédaire*, the space reserved for the letter T is saved for tennis. Here, the French philosopher almost takes an idea of a 'qualitative' history of tennis into account in order to speak of creation. It should be noted that this comes right after Deleuze's reflections devoted to the notion of 'resistance' and of 'style', developed for the letter R and S respectively. It is helpful to keep that in mind because, through the letter R, Deleuze tells us "to create is to resist". First of all, to create is to resist prejudice, to resist stupidity. Philosophy, for example, is resistance. To philosophize, Deleuze says, is to "resist stupidity". As far as the artist is concerned, to resist is "to free life". In the conference on *The Act of Creation*, which, just as the *Abécédaire*, is from the second part of the 1980s, he specifies that "no one has an idea in general", that "an idea is already dedicated to a particular field".[5] There is no such a thing as an abstract idea: "Ideas have to be treated like potentials already *engaged* in one mode of expression or another and inseparable from the mode of expression".[6] This means ideas are always committed with obstructions, but – on the other side of the coin – a possibility arises from this constraint. In a paradoxical way, we have here the possibility of a necessity. In order for an idea to be produced, "there has to be a necessity".[7] If we refer to the pages about tennis in *Negotiations*, which anticipate the letter T of *Abécédaire*, in words which echo those of Leth's, "McEnroe's an inventor, that is, a stylist", who has "brought into tennis Egyptian postures (in his serve) and Dostoyevskian reflexes ('if you insist on banging your head on the wall all the time, life becomes impossible')".[8] It is not that it comes to a triumph of these inventors; rather, there are "imitators" of these inventors "who can beat [them] at their own game".[9] What matters in creation is the qualitative leap, the gesture which calls something new into question, something that was virtually there and that needed to be 'created' in order to come to light:

> [T]he history of sport runs through these inventors, each of whom amounts to something unforeseen, a new syntax, a transformation, and without them the purely technological advances would have remained quantitative, irrelevant, and pointless.[10]

---

[5] Deleuze, Act (see note 4), p. 312.
[6] Ibid.
[7] Ibid., p. 313.
[8] Gilles Deleuze, *Negotiations, 1972–1990*, transl. by Martin Joughin, New York 1995, p. 132.
[9] Ibid.
[10] Ibid.

## Am I Supposed to Create?

Let us return to *The Five Obstructions*. In this particular context, it becomes immediately clear that, as it has been noted[11], the 'paternity' of this work of art is not easily definable: who actually is the author?

First of all, if we look at the title of the film, *The Five Obstructions,* our attention is directed to the obstructive character of the variations von Trier imposes on his victim, who every time has to face a specific hindrance. Von Trier's obstructive rules are as follows:

Obstruction #1: Twelve frames, answers, Cuba, no set
Leth has to shoot without exceeding twelve frames for each shot; the questions that the voice-over of the 'original' film poses have to be answered in this first variation; Leth has to film in Cuba and he cannot make use of a set.

Obstruction #2: A miserable place, don't show it, Jørgen Leth is the man, the meal
Leth has to shoot in a miserable place without showing it; Leth will be the man, the actor, without the woman who was there in the 'original' film; he has to shoot the meal scene of the original film in this very miserable place.

Obstruction #3: Complete freedom or back to Bombay
Von Trier imposes on Leth whether to shoot the film in "complete freedom", without rules, without obstructions, or to go back to Bombay (that is, the miserable place of the second obstruction).

Obstruction #4: Cartoon
Leth has to shoot *The Perfect Human* as a cartoon.

Obstruction #5: Lars von Trier will make the last obstruction, Jørgen Leth will be credited as director, Jørgen Leth will read a text written by Lars von Trier

---

[11] Pietro Montani, *L'immaginazione intermediale. Perlustrare, rifigurare, testimoniare il mondo visibile,* Rome / Bari 2010, p. 43. This question arises in particular through the alternating shifts of sense, which occur in the fifth obstruction, in which Leth is forced by von Trier to read a text as if he had written it himself.

In this variation, Leth and von Trier intertwine. We may ask at this very point: Who really is the author of this film?

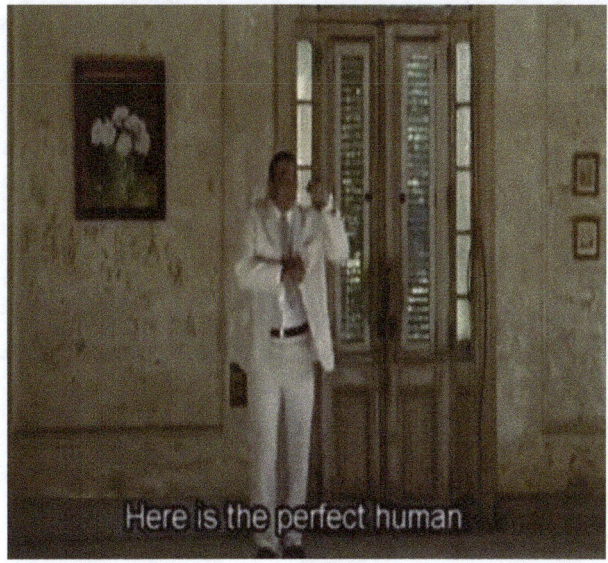

Fig. 2.1: Obstruction #1 from *The Five Obstructions* (2003)

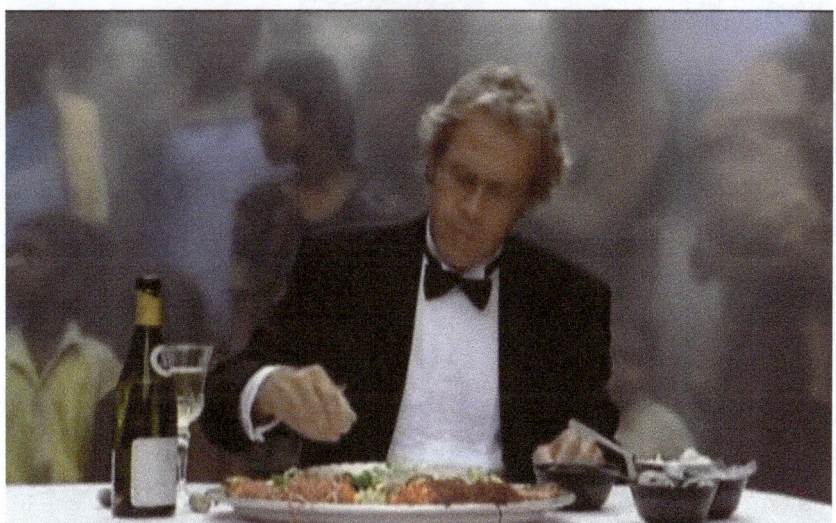

Fig. 2.2: Obstruction #2 from *The Five Obstructions* (2003)

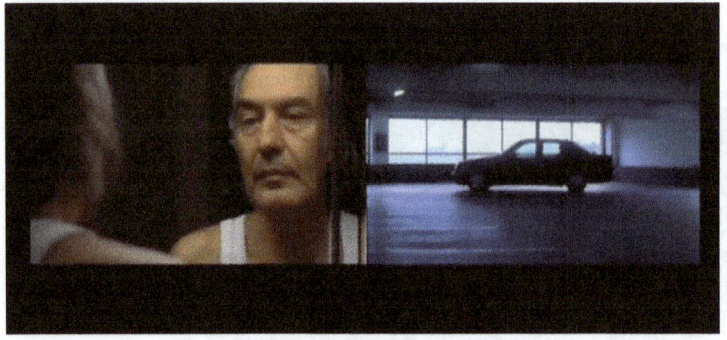

Fig. 2.3: Obstruction #3 from *The Five Obstructions* (2003)

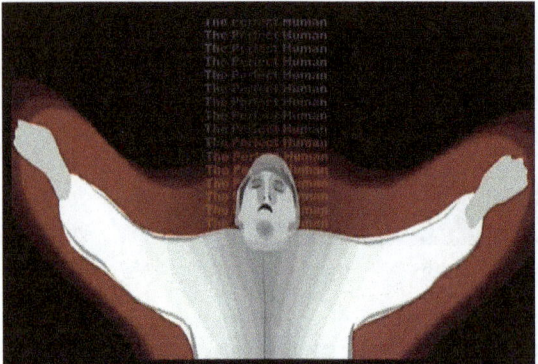

Fig. 2.4: Obstruction #4 from *The Five Obstructions* (2003)

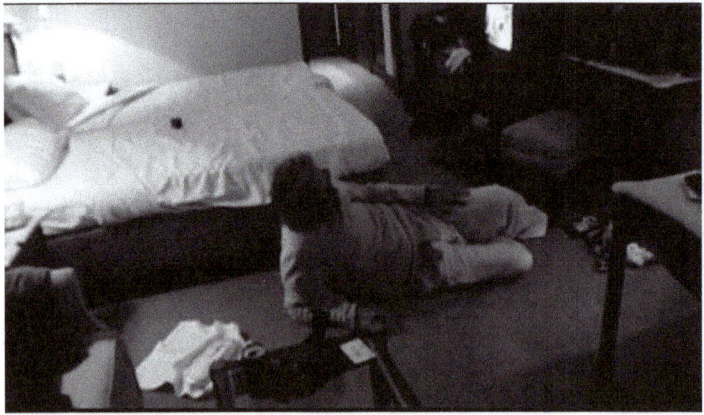

Fig. 2.5: Obstruction #5 from *The Five Obstructions* (2003)

One might think that even from the first variation, the extreme obstructions von Trier imposes are going to tie Leth's hands and accordingly prevent him from adequately expressing the "Idea of the Perfect Human". Nevertheless, it seems that Leth is able to respond to von Trier's shots precisely because he knows very well that he has to fail. However, he will have to fail in a 'perfect' way, that is, he must "dodge" the shots.

Once again it is worthwhile to recall how Leth, in order to explain this very concept of "dodging", calls on athletic gesture. Here is what he states on the subject before the film's shooting. Inspired by his reflections on football, which we have already evoked, he comes to speak of his own "dodges": "Obstruction", he says,

> it's a word stemming from football terminology. I once made a movie about the great Danish football player Michael Laudrup *[Michael Laudrup – A Football Player (1993)]*. He was a virtuoso with lots of unpredictable moves. He attracted obstructions, he pushed to tough play, but nevertheless always elegantly avoided falling or injuring himself. Michael Laudrup will be my role model. I will invite Lars to put in all his dirty tricks and ways to make life difficult for me. I will be full of inventiveness in my responses, in my dodges. I will defend my movie while trying at the same time to remain open, trying to see where these obstructions will lead me.[12]

According to Merleau-Ponty[13], there is a "secret transcendental loss" in human gestures, and by responding to von Trier's provocations Leth wants us to feel this loss of the present time.[14] There is a 'leak' in the present that is not a 'lack' but rather becomes an inexhaustible resource, because in it lies the very possibility to make the idea felt through images, a possibility that subsists even when the images consist of twelve-frame shots, as the first obstruction requires. Thus, Leth's responses do not stop 'dodging' the idea, but precisely 'by dodging it' allow us to feel it: by dodging it and not simply 'missing it'. Always early, always late with respect to the present[15], his responses, as it were, know they can never be an adequate image of the perfect human. But this is the very transcendental richness. The perfect human, like Deleuze's Alice – like the

---

[12] Jørgen Leth, Note d'intentions (Toronto, le 3 mai 2001), in: *The Five Obstructions*, production dossier, Brussels 2003, p. 6. Transl. by the author.

[13] Maurice Merleau-Ponty, *Notes des cours au Collège de France 1958–1959 et 1960–1961*, Paris 1996, p. 209: "Donc, il n'y a pas la ligne ou la série du temps, mais un noyau transtemporel – Visible ou Monde, – une sorte d'éternité du visible qui, comme un récipient 'perd' secrètement, et par là est toujours en avance et en retard sur le présent, jamais à l'heure."

[14] For example, cf. Leth, Manifeste (see note 3), p. 5.

[15] On these simultaneous directions of time as *aion*, see Gilles Deleuze, *The Logic of Sense*, transl. by Mark Lester and Charles Stivale, London 1990, p. 79.

19th century philosopher, according to Merleau-Ponty[16] –, does not know yet what he thinks of. That is why he says:

> Today, too, I experienced something I hope to understand in a few days. Around my left hand was shining a ring of hazy white flames. And I peered closely at the left side of my own dark coat. In the middle of my heart there was a small white spot. I don't know what it's supposed to mean [The Perfect Human].

## The 'Sixth' Obstruction

These productive failures are constantly threatened by von Trier's restrictions. It is not enough to miss the event for it to be felt, it must be 'dodged'. If Leth did not dodge the obstruction, he would not have 'failed the right way', and we would not be able to hear one variation resound with another. Leth makes us feel this idea through differences, replying to the solicitations of the differences. There is no easy way to the 'sediment' of this secret leak. At first, one might be tempted to connect this secret 'place' to the neutral space of the 'initial film': an aseptic white, almost an 'in-itself colour', an empty room, in which nothing is there, which "is boundless and radiant with light", as the voice-over says. Nevertheless, in the 'first' *Perfect Human* as well, in its fragments which are spaced out between the five variations, we can see that Leth needs concrete elements – even if essential, minimal ones – with which to complete his short, his portrait-study. An eye, a foot, a bed, in a space that starts filling up with human gestures which seem to bring about an impersonal echo.

Here we are dealing with the possibility of making someone feel what 'cannot be', that is, this 'leak' of time in the present. The interference game between von Trier and Leth takes this relationship to the limit with a leak that we start to think may be an origin that is always late, always early, but never present: always 'dodged'. In this way, even the original version that the film started with, Leth's 1967 *Perfect Human*, that is, the alleged theme of the variations, was indeed a 'repetition'. By playing on the limit of the obstruction and the intensity of difference, as Deleuze would put it, we are forced to think of an idea that can never be directly presented, but which can only be given through a repetition, which is always essentially obstructed. In every hindrance von Trier imposes on him, Leth has to make sensible the 'blow' of what his images secretly dodge and, in doing so, make us feel the idea, that is, that event

---

[16] Merlau-Ponty, Notes (see note 13), p. 163: "Nous ne savons pas ce que nous pensons: depuis 100 ans, il y a une pensée fondamentale qui n'est pas toujours 'philosophie' explicite."

which usually cannot be seen, in the same way that, as Merleau-Ponty recalls, we do not see grass grow.[17]

The paradoxical result of such constraints is the discovery that creation 'needs' obstruction, that only through the passive-active rhythm articulated by the confrontation with obstacles can 'creation' arise, which then turns into a 'response'. As we have said with Deleuze, to create is to resist. Talking of possibility, Deleuze loved to recall, inspired by Danish philosopher Kierkegaard, the formula "the possible or I shall suffocate".[18] Here, in the game between von Trier and Leth, the former seems to say to the latter: 'I suffocate you so that you can create'. This is the "pedagogy" evoked in the letter with which the film ends, and Leth creates by resisting and responding to von Trier. Indeed, here it seems there is no longer the possibility for a creation without interference. There is no variation, nor is there repetition, without obstruction. To create is to give rise to a "coherent deformation"[19], as Merleau-Ponty would put it, and the best way we have is to cope. To create is a peculiar way, the perfect way, to dodge the idea we can make sensible. The idea is dodged. Only this way it is found: By falling down, as the perfect human falls in the variations, which are presented to us. The secret loss of the 'now' is a drop which resounds in the receptacle without measure of *aion*, the time which dodges the present, the time which finds no place on the timeline but rather "pull[s] in both directions" – past and future – "at once"[20]: *après coup* and *avant coup*.

The five obstructions produce a constellation and do so also thanks to von Trier's persistence on the differences and obstacles in his playing with Leth: Through this series, through each variation, there is a flash[21] which sheds light on them and binds them, even when between them there seems to be the height of difference. The image of the perfect human is not that which reproduces its "eternal" essence but rather that "in which new creations are produced", the image "endowed with a capacity for innovation or creativity".[22]

---

[17] Merlau-Ponty, Notes (see note 13), p. 215.
[18] Gilles Deleuze / Félix Guattari, *What is Philosophy?*, transl. by Hugh Tomlinson and Graham Burchell, New York 1994, p. 177.
[19] Merlau-Ponty, Notes (see note 13), p. 52.
[20] Deleuze, Logic (see note 15), p. 1.
[21] Gilles Deleuze, *Difference and Repetition*, transl. by Paul Patton, London 1994, p. 118.
[22] Gilles Deleuze, *The Fold. Leibniz and the Baroque*, transl. by Tom Conley, London 1993, p. 79.

Of course, these variations are actually "incompossible"[23]: "From the point of view of the presents which pass in representation, the series are certainly successive, one 'before' and the other 'after'. It is from this point of view that the second is said to *resemble* the first"[24], and – we add – one could affirm that the first is the 'origin' of the others. However, what this film shows is the possibility – on which Deleuze insisted so much – of the coexistence of series in an intersubjective virtuality through which "what is originary [...] is not one series in relation to the other, but the difference between series in so far as this relates one series of differences to another series of differences, in abstraction from their empirical succession in time".[25] Series echo one another inasmuch as they are different. In a relationship where none of them can be considered the first with regard to their resemblance to the others, it is no longer possible "to regard one as originary and the other as derived, one as model and the other as copy".[26] The 'origin' is repeatedly dodged: It is at the same time 'no-where' and 'now-here'.[27] As Deleuze famously puts it: "only differences are alike".[28]

How does the *Five Obstructions* constellation end? In the last variation, Leth has to face a very eccentric imposition. He 'must not' film anything and 'must' be accredited as the film's director: there is apparently no chance of any response whatsoever. Nevertheless, this is not completely true. This is the 'four-handed' variation, once again unleashed from a hand-to-hand combat. Leth must read a letter written by Lars, and the film must be edited "illustratively vis-à-vis the words". How can Leth still find a way to create under these conditions? (Perhaps, for example, by accentuating some particular words, as von Trier suggests? "You're doing everything you can to evade the text! [...] You are really wriggling"). Whatever the answer may be, the last image we see in the film is Leth falling on the ground (which repeats and varies that of his 1967 *Perfect Human*). This act of letting himself fall down seems to be the extreme Leth/von Trier response, which evokes this transcendental failure we must under-

---

[23] Ibid., p. 61.
[24] Deleuze, Difference (see note 21), p. 124.
[25] Ibid., p. 125.
[26] Ibid.
[27] Ibid., p. xxi.
[28] Ibid., p. 116. Deleuze borrows this formula from Claude Lévi-Strauss, *Totemism*, transl. by Rodney Needham, Boston 1963, p. 77: "If we may be allowed the expression, it is not the resemblances, but the differences, which resemble each other".

take in order to create. "Hopefully we captured something human", von Trier finally states. The human side of the idea, the sensible side is that which is 'needed' to give the essence of the man: Leth – even when played by Lars – answers this way, letting us feel the *Perfect Human* idea by dodging it perfectly, even, and above all, when he falls down in the last scene.

In this sense, we do not choose to create either, but rather participate in a creative recognition as a result of a process full of constraints (a process starting from material questions as well: whether they be questions of colour, of sound, and so on, as in the case of the obstruction of the cartoon). We could say we 'recognize' the idea only by creating it, as a 'familiar stranger'. After the last variation we can go 'back' to see the 'original' *Perfect Human* from a new point of view, because now even Leth's 1967 short film – which was supposed to be 'the veritable theme' – has become a 'variation', the 'sixth'. It can thus be said that the idea of the Perfect Human has become a familiar stranger that goes through 'all' the 'original' responses Leth (and Lars) 'was (were) not expected to give'.

# Bibliography

Deleuze, Gilles, *Difference and Repetition,* transl. by Paul Patton, London 1994.

Deleuze, Gilles, *The Fold. Leibniz and the Baroque,* transl. by Tom Conley, London 1993.

Deleuze, Gilles, *The Logic of Sense,* transl. by Mark Lester and Charles Stivale, London 1990.

Deleuze, Gilles, *Negotiations, 1972–1990,* transl. by Martin Joughin, New York 1995.

Deleuze, Gilles, What is the Creative Act?, in: Gilles Deleuze, *Two Regimes of Madness. Texts and Interviews 1975–1995,* ed. by David Lapoujade, Semiotext(e), transl. by Ames Hodges and Mike Taormina, New York 2006.

Deleuze, Gilles / Guattari, Félix, *What is Philosophy?,* transl. by Hugh Tomlinson and Graham Burchell, New York 1994.

Leth, Jørgen, Manifeste de Jørgen Leth. Le moment vient (Paris, le 11 Avril 2000), in: *The Five Obstructions,* production dossier, Brussels 2003.

Leth, Jørgen, Note d'intentions (Toronto, le 3 mai 2001), in: *The Five Obstructions,* production dossier, Brussels 2003.

Lévi-Strauss, Claude, *Totemism,* transl. by Rodney Needham, Boston 1963.

Livingston, Paisley, Artistic Nesting in *The Five Obstructions,* in: *Dekalog 1: On The Five Obstructions* (2008), ed. by Mette Hjort, London, pp. 59–61.

Merleau-Ponty, Maurice, *Notes des cours au Collège de France 1958–1959 et 1960–1961,* Paris 1996.

Montani, Pietro, *L'immaginazione intermediale. Perlustrare, rifigurare, testimoniare il mondo visibile,* Rome / Bari 2010.

Von Trier, Lars / Leth, Jørgen, *The Five Obstructions* (DVD), Denmark 2003.

**Image Credits**

Fig. 2.1: Obstruction #1, still from Lars von Trier / Jørgen Leth, *The Five Obstructions* (DVD), Denmark 2003.

Fig. 2.2: Obstruction #2, still from Lars von Trier / Jørgen Leth, *The Five Obstructions* (DVD), Denmark 2003.

Fig. 2.3: Obstruction #3, still from Lars von Trier / Jørgen Leth, *The Five Obstructions* (DVD), Denmark 2003.

Fig. 2.4: Obstruction #4, still from Lars von Trier / Jørgen Leth, *The Five Obstructions* (DVD), Denmark 2003.

Fig. 2.5: Obstruction #5, still from Lars von Trier / Jørgen Leth, *The Five Obstructions* (DVD), Denmark 2003.

# Rupturing Backgrounds.
# Production as Resistance in Courbet's "The Artist's Studio"
*Veronica Peselmann*

Current art history considers French painter Gustave Courbet as a key figure of the 19th century. The reasons are manifold. His reputation was earned not only because of his extremely acclaimed oeuvre, or its leading role in the overthrow of the Vendôme Column during the Paris Commune, but also because of the famous advice that he gave to his students. The advice reads as follows: "[D]on't do what I'm doing, nor what the others are doing, nor what the old masters once did."[1] With this advice, Courbet calls for resistance against traditional conventions of painting and tries to free the production process of the image of its characterisation by traditional expectations. However, the advice also implies that students should resist the temptation to imagine their picture from already existing products. They should not orient their way of painting and producing a picture on what other famous painters did. Nor should the product of others be decisive to them. What matters instead is their individual impression of adequacy during the production processes.

Courbet's famous painting "The Artist's Studio"[2] shows such a production process. It depicts an artist sitting in front of an easel, surrounded by an audience. At first glance, it appears that Courbet's image takes place in the canon of a traditional genre, the so called 'studio visit'. Traditionally, the participants express their interest and curiosity in the proceedings of the image production. In contrast, Courbet chooses an arrangement and an embodiment that opposes the standards and traditions of that particular topic[3] – the majority of the depicted audience is turned away from the main scene: the image formation process. Although physically present, the visitors of the studio seem little interested in the different steps of producing a painting. Courbet

---

[1] Martin Schieder, "Ne fais pas ce que je fais." Dans l'atelier de Gustave Courbet, in: *Apprendre à peindre. Les ateliers privés à Paris 1780–1863*, ed. by France Nerlich and Alain Bonnet, Tours 2013, pp. 333–353, especially pp. 338–341.

[2] The title varies in French as well as in English between "The Painter's Studio" and the "The Artist's Studio". I refer to the official title of the Musée d'Orsay in Paris, which owns "The Artist's Studio".

[3] Matthias Winner had interpreted the painting being a result of many traditional influences, e.g. as a "studio visit"; cf. Matthias Winner, Zu Gustav Courbets "Allégorie réelle" und der Tradition, in: *Jahrbuch der Berliner Museen*, vol. 4 (1962), p. 178.

presents the visitors as inward looking, or gazing into the distance as if they already knew what the product of a classical academic painting in the 19th century was going to look like. The image contrasts against the traditional composition of how a 'studio visit' should be arranged.

Courbet resists meeting the expectations of an artistic end product in a twofold way: in terms of the chosen image scene as well as in terms of the painting technique. This relationship between image composition and technique reveals particularly how Courbet combines the image format with materiality. "The Artist's Studio" consists of seven individual canvases that are sewn together. As we know nowadays, he successively added particular parts one after another, depending on the development during the image formation process; the image size he left up to the course of the manufacturing process. As the composition progressed, he would add another canvas fabric.[4] In addition, we also know that Courbet did not try to hide his mode of production. From the beginning the seams were visible – it is not a result of material ageing of the canvas. The seams become part of what one could call a 'rupturing background'. Through this vivid, ruptured background and the way he treats the canvas, Courbet resists the idea of painting on a smooth surface by not hiding his own materiality.

The aim of this essay is to answer the question of how "The Artist's Studio" breaks conventional expectations of paintings of that time. The argument unfolds in four parts. The first part explains the material basis of contemporary image production. The second part considers formats and choice of subject. The third part regards the background design as a rupturing picture plane. Finally, the materiality of the painting is discussed in a fourth step. The general thesis is: The material support and the background assemble the resistance to conventional image production. In both a material and a compositional way, Courbet uses the contemporary conventions of image production. However, he stands aloof from these standards in the way he integrates these traditions by presenting them as a citation of a former time.

---

[4] For this and much other information, I would like to thank the conservators Daniel Cheron (Paris) and Bruno Mottin (C2RMF, Paris), who examine Courbet's "The Artist's Studio" as part of a major restoration project by the Musée d'Orsay.

## Materials and Preparations

19th century painting was subject to significant and profound changes, particularly from a material point of view. New industrial material supplies had an impact on the painting process. Industrially produced and pre-primed canvasses increasingly dominated the market of artists' materials. Due to this material innovation, production and preparation of the support, such as paper or canvas, was now outsourced and not necessarily done by the artists themselves. These new industrial forms of canvas production interfered in centuries-old methods of craftsmanship and transformed the artistic profession. Up until then, artists had to pre-prime their canvasses with different types of coatings. The first application of paint required the canvas to be well prepared through different layers of groundings with long lasting drying times. The use of pre-primed canvasses meant it was no longer necessary to attune the primer to the pigments of colours. As the artist did not need to ponder chemical reactions of primer and colours as he had to before, work in the studio focused more and more on the image composition.

In earlier times, an artist's studio was organised as a workshop. In workshops, every single step in the production chain of a painting was covered: from washing the linen to varnishing the completed composition.[5] The preparation of each single canvas took a large amount of effort. Working with pre-primed canvasses, the painting process begins immediately with the colour of the composition, thus freeing the artists of time-consuming prerequisites. However, these transformations undermine the firm and rigid structure of a handicraft that was manufactured from previous centuries. A traditional workshop was turned into an artist laboratory. The decline of the workshops provided artists with increasing leeway when producing a picture. The alteration of material conditions had an impact by affecting change on long enduring traditions.

A market for pre-primed canvasses was already raised and established in the 17th century. However, these canvasses were made manually and were therefore more expensive.[6] It was commercial production that opened a broader market for ready-to-paint-canvasses. However, this broadening did not only address trained artists. The ready-to-paint-surface allowed a freer, less academically influenced painting and as a

---

[5] Albert Boime, *The Academy and French Painting in the Nineteenth Century*, London 1971, p. 1.
[6] Pascal Labreuche, *Paris, capitale de la toile à peindre, XVII<sup>e</sup> – XIX<sup>e</sup> siècle*, Paris 2011, pp. 33–35, 71–72.

result these canvasses also permitted laymen a painterly work. In previous times, only regulated admission to the Academy or to a master's studio qualified an artist with handling skills for different pigments and supports.[7] In the 19th century, painting was now accessible even to a less educated clientele. The ready-made canvasses encouraged artistic activities beyond a strictly hierarchical or structured curriculum, whether in the Academy or in the masters' studios.

Nevertheless, commercial canvasses incorporated the academic system. They were produced in standardised dimensions – dimensions that corresponded with traditional academic genres – and were manufactured in three motivic formats: portrait (*figure*), landscape (*paysage*) and sea pieces (*marine*).[8] This system of fixed and normed sizes also applied to France from the middle of the 17th century and was valid for all common supports. Numbered sizes ranging from 12 to 130cms in height and 22 to 195cms in width were offered.[9] It is striking that the genre of historical painting, highly respected at that time, is not reflected in the standard sizes. This may be attributable to the fact that canvasses for the usually large-scaled history paintings were mostly individually custom-made, and, furthermore, this genre was mainly realised by well-trained artists with appropriate skills to prepare, prime and stretch their supports.

It seems that regulations concerning the measurement of the support, in length and width and its relation to the subject, tried to ensure that the category of the depicted subject and the dimension of the canvas were set in proportions that were harmonious and compliant to academic rules. Nevertheless, this correlation led to a paradox. On the one hand, the standardised system was linked to genres according to the regulations of the Academy. On the other hand, this material transformation provided a lesser skilled clientele the opportunity to paint without extensive prior technical knowledge. This illustrates a special dual function of the canvas. As the academic regalia were inscribed by naming the different genres, painting was still situated in a highly professionalised context. Simultaneously, the new canvasses eased access into art for untrained people. This antagonism underlined the central position of the material support at that time; the material support assembled both traditional aca-

---

[7] Eva Mongi-Vollmer, *Das Atelier des Malers. Die Diskurse eines Raumes in der zweiten Hälfte des 19. Jahrhunderts*, Berlin 2004, pp. 90–91.

[8] David Bomford, *Art in the Making. Impressionism*, exh. cat., London 1990, p. 44.

[9] Anthea Callen, *The Art of Impressionism. Painting Technique and the Making of Modernity*, New Haven / London 2000, p. 18.

demic standards and the possibility to open up to non-academic processes of picture production. With new material supports, painting was able to enlarge its position beyond academic restrictions in the 19th century.

Formats and Subjects

The new canvas production methods enabled an open range of possibilities that were less influenced by considerations of painting techniques. Until late in the 19th century, encyclopaedia entries or statements and instructions in educational books stressed the necessity for a coordinated relationship between canvas, priming and motif. The 'success' of the image relied on skilful technical expertise that was able to link the adequate priming to the depicted subject. In this regard, at the end of the 18th century, Academy member Claude-Henri Watelet (1718–1786) described that the quality of the painting was dependent on the thoroughness of the priming. The more elaborate, the more it influenced the quality of a painting and therefore either increased or diminished the value of an artwork.[10] In later texts, too, as in a lexical entry from the French Universal Lexicon by Marie-Nicolas Bouillet (1854), the necessity of a well-considered correlation between priming and subject is described in nearly the same way.[11] Yet, when pre-primed canvasses were already established and widely available, lexicon entries still described traditional methods by explaining every single step of how to prepare a canvas. These texts did not only address laymen, but also students of the Academy, who consulted these entries as teaching material and theoretical supplement, as they were often written by Academy members.[12] These theoretical teaching texts allow us to draw conclusions on the significance of the canvas in general. Detailed presentations of priming methods and procedures in texts from the 18th century lead to the assumption that the ready-made canvasses were not very widely used, probably due to their high price. Therefore, detailed written instructions of painting techniques concerning priming and stretching were still necessary.

---

[10]  *Dictionnaire des Arts de Peinture, Sculpture et Gravure*, vol. 2, Paris 1792, p. 333. Watelet was a member of the academy. His work was continued and finished after Watelet's death in the year 1786 by Pierre-Charles Lévesque as well as other, not specified or named authors. It was published in 1792 and consists of five volumes.

[11]  Marie-Nicolas Bouillet (ed.), *Dictionnaire universel des sciences, des lettres et des arts*, Paris 1854, p. 688.

[12]  Michel Roland, *Marianne. Die Zeichnung im 18. Jahrhundert*, Munich 1987, p. 50.

In the mid to late 19th century, encyclopaedic entries still discussed issues concerning painting techniques, although less detailed. The fact that even in the late 19th century technical issues were still described, implies, on the one hand, that the texts did not react to the changing of material conditions or, on the other hand, that instructions were not willing to promote new industrial products as they stood in opposition to the 'official'[13] education of young artists. Either the texts responded to material shifts in delay, as descriptions on painting technique only diminished by the end of the 19th century, or the instructions stuck to fixed and traditional methods on purpose. In any case, it seems that both interpretations undermine the unique significance of new canvasses for the dynamics of production during the 19th century.[14]

Dictionaries and encyclopaedias often described and discussed the relationship between painting technique and composition. This relationship is also reflected through pre-primed canvasses. However, when working with pre-primed canvasses, it is not necessary to consider the priming anymore. Instead, consideration shifts rather to the relationship between subject and support, i.e. the size of the support. These industrial products abolished rigorous and fixed processes of painting technique, although they still adhere to the academic coordination of format and subject.

## Courbet's View on Production Processes

Within his oeuvre, Courbet uses different canvas materials. His manifold techniques and materials indicate how his time was characterised by a transitional disposition. Trained by a former teacher at the Academy, Courbet gained knowledge of traditional priming and stretching methods. However, he often uses pre-primed canvasses too.[15] Being trained in different methods enabled him to select freely among different modes of production and among a wide range of different materialities. Courbet was perfectly trained in both traditional and new ways of picture production. In certain works, he

---

[13] Concerning the debate about an "official" artists education, cf. Monique Segré, *L'École des Beaux-Arts. XIX<sup>e</sup> et XX<sup>e</sup> siècle*, Paris 1998, p. 129.

[14] Until 1863, the École des Beaux-Arts has been integrating practical studios in their official curricula and triggering a debate about the role and importance of the painting technique and its practice. Concerning the reform of the École des Beaux-Arts in 1863, cf. Alain Bonnet, *L'enseignement des arts au XIX<sup>e</sup> siècle*, Paris 2006, pp. 10–113, 116–117.

[15] For Courbet's painting technique, cf. Bruno Mottin, A Complex Genesis. Courbet in the Laboratory, in: *Gustave Courbet*, exh. cat., Paris / New York 2007, pp. 70–82.

did not follow that distinction but transgressed the traditions of proper picture production. It is unlikely that these transgressions were the result of a lack of skills. The inappropriateness was not a technical failure but a means to convey a certain view on the way that art should be produced beyond academic restrictions. His academic and non-academic way of dealing with supports designates a difference that was impossible to be anticipated at times without the commercial canvas production. The rupture of conventions required that conventions were noticed and identifiable as such. However, this could only occur if alternative modes of production already existed. If new methods exist, the usage of an old method generates meaning, for instance, as a citation of a passed time or a satirical statement about out-dated traditions. Through such a switch between material production processes, Courbet was able to establish a subtle border; a border that differentiates between traditional academic standards and alternative positions.

In a fulminant manner, Courbet's painting "The Artist's Studio" counters expectations regarding the relationship between subject and recommended academic format.[16] The large-scale work with a height of 3.61m and a length of 5.98m[17] provides space for a fictitiously assembled circle of figures. Courbet represents himself in the centre of the painting in the form of a self-portrait, as a painting artist before an easel, surrounded by different figures. The figures on the right side show clearly individual traits while those on the left are schematised representatives of various social groups.[18] In a famous and frequently quoted letter to his friend Jules Champfleury, Courbet designates the depicted figures. The group on the right, showing individual features, is reserved to friends, colleagues and supporters, such as, for example, Champfleury, Max Bouchon, who was one of Courbet's supporters, or the poet Charles Baudelaire. The group on the left side depicts formalised representatives of everyday life, for example

---

[16] Eugène Fromentin discusses the relation between composition and dimension using an example of genre painting in 1845; cf. Salon in 1845. Cited in: Barbara Gaethgens, *Genremalerei. Geschichte der klassischen Bildgattungen in Quellentexten und Kommentare,* vol. 4, Berlin 2002, pp. 391–393.

[17] Official data from the Musée d'Orsay.

[18] The painting "The Artist's Studio", its figures and their potential meanings have frequently been described and interpreted in various and controversial directions. These interpretations shall not be repeated here in full. For a summary of corresponding literature, cf. Werner Hoffman, *Das Atelier. Courbets Jahrhundertbild,* Munich 2010.

citizens, a hunter, a priest and a rabbi as well as an unemployed man or a 'tomfool'.[19] Painted in an indifferent brown tonality and positioned side by side, all figures meld into a homogenous inactive group. A lifeless mannequin is arranged among them in a pose that reminds one of a crucifixion. Similar to this lifeless mannequin, the depicted figures degenerate to accessories and decoration. The visitors of the studio remain lethargic and firm in their assigned positions in a way that does not allow one to anticipate any dynamic or movement. Their tired, empty gazes are directed towards the floor or to an unspecific point in the distance.

The way Courbet characterises the figures forms a contrast to the numerous studio visit pictures that came out at that time, where the visitors usually observe the painting process with great enthusiasm and interest.[20] The only figures who concentrate on the artist's work are a little boy and a female nude. Traditionally, the female nude was the object of inspection as well as observation and the counterpart to the lifeless mannequin. Contrary to the motivic tradition, the woman leaves the motionless ranks behind her and emerges as a visitor who occupies the position of an active viewer.[21] The posture of the naked woman still belongs to the canon of classical model poses while the bright tone of her skin and the gleaming white and tender rose cloth on the ground highlight the female figure and reinforce her special role in the painting. The female figure being specifically expressed in this way evokes a motivic focal displacement and forces a reinterpretation of this specific and classic academic motif.

The dwindling importance of academic image issues is also reflected in Courbet's unconventional combination of different genres. "The Artist's Studio" assembles diverse genres side by side, without giving one genre a dominant position. In addition to the bare model and, along with it, nude painting, a white skull, embedded on white fabric, can be interpreted as reminiscent of a classical Vanitas still life. The plumed hat with the guitar on the ground is known from genre paintings and depictions of

---

[19] Gustave Courbet, *Correspondence de Gustave Courbet,* ed. and transl. by Petra ten-Doesschate Chu, Paris 1996, pp. 121–123.

[20] Winner, Courbet (see note 3).

[21] The role of the female figure has been discussed in different and manifold manner; cf., i. e. Linda Nochlin, Courbet's Real Allegory. Rereading "The Painter's studio", in: *Courbet Reconsidered,* exh. cat. The Brooklyn Museum, ed. by Sarah Faunce and Linda Nochlin, New York 1988, pp. 26–40; Marcia Pointon, *Naked Authority. The Body in Western Painting 1830–1908,* Cambridge 1990, pp. 113–134.

musicians from the 17th century. In addition, on the easel in the centre, a landscape can be seen. The figures on the right side – some among them prepared by individual portraits – add the genre of 'portrait painting'. These diverse genres are equally gathered on the large format, akin to an assemblage. A large-scale size was usually reserved for the genre of history painting. By choosing such a large-scale format, Courbet includes history painting as well – at least indirectly. Thus, all genres are represented thematically via content, except for the history painting, which is suggested by its format.

History painting was considered to be the most prestigious genre at the time.[22] However, Courbet only uses its frame and fills it with the so-called 'genres mineurs'.[23] He repeatedly underlines the loss of academic form specifications. The format only serves as an empty shell without providing it with a traditional motif of history painting, for instance a narrative such as a battle scene. By emphasizing format and downplaying content, Courbet historicises a certain period of academic requirements, which have lost their validity for him. With "The Artist's Studio", he presents a résumé and a review of its own history and summarises seven years of his artistic work, as the full title of the painting explicitly indicates.[24] His "Studio" demonstrates not only a disruption in his biographical career, that is, in his 'personal history', but also demarcates an estrangement of his own stand towards academic requirements and rules. Herewith, Courbet transfers the traditional genre of history painting into a modified version, depicting the history of this turning point as a motif. Still unnoticed by his impassive visitors, Courbet breaks with the conventions of contemporary painting with regards to his unconventional use of conventional motifs and genres.

---

[22] Rudolf Preimesberger / Hannah Baader / Nicola Suthor, *Porträt. Geschichte der klassischen Bildgattungen in Quellentexten und Kommentaren*, vol. 2, Berlin 1999, p. 373.

[23] Félibien, cited in: Nicolas Pevsner, *Die Geschichte der Kunstakademie*, Munich 1986, p. 103.

[24] The complete title is called: "L'Atelier du peintre. Allégorie réelle déterminant une phase de sept années de ma vie artistique et morale."

## Resisting Grounds

In addition to the temporal aspect of historicising academic conventions, the arrangement of figures implies another disruption with existing conventions. In a particularly striking manner, Courbet deals with the well-known and commonly accepted compositional prescription to divide a picture into foreground, middle ground and background. The relation of this scheme was well defined by numerous guidance and teaching pamphlets in encyclopaedias, often written by members of the Academy. In these texts, a background was supposed to be in harmonious accord with the major scenes depicted in the foreground. The background was meant to stay behind, as the proposition of 'back' indicates. Its role was to be nearly invisible and supportive in order to create an atmosphere, not to 'act' like a depicted figure. Academy member Claude-Henri Watelet, for instance, had a clear idea of the function of a background and how it should be depicted adequately in a proper painting. In Watelet's guidelines, the background was indicated to be responsible for the atmosphere and for the 'impression'. The foreground, on the contrary, is the narrative area where the central action takes place.[25] This classification was maintained until the late 19th century and accepted as a valid and binding instruction. An example is given by an entry in the encyclopaedia *La Grande Encyclopédie* from the years 1886 to 1902: "Le fond doit rester absolument neutre pour laisser tout l'intérêt se porter sur le sujet principal du tableau ou faire valoir ce sujet d'une manière plus active, par un habile contraste de lignes ou de tons."[26]

Furthermore, through the painting of "The Artist's Studio", Courbet also reverses a classical narrative hierarchy: At first glance, he divides the pictorial space into different layers and sticks to the traditional tripartite of foreground, middle ground and background. However, he varies this scheme in an innovative way. The foreground, traditionally reserved for the main events, is emptied, except for the discarded clothes of the bright female figure. In the middle ground, behind a pink pile of clothes, a group of three is formed by the figure of the artist, the female nude and the little boy. All other figures are dispersed over the entire width and depth of the painting. They appear as cutouts, which are arranged in front of a stage set and form a backdrop by

---

[25] Dictionnaire (see note 10), pp. 339–340.
[26] *La Grande Encyclopédie*, ed. by H. Lamirault et C$^{ie}$, Paris 1886–1902, p. 710.

themselves, framing the artist, the boy and the woman. Framed as such, the group of three is highlighted and moves visually into the foreground, even though the group is in fact placed in the middle ground. This arrangement forces a multi-layered impression of staggered areas.

High above the heads of the various figures, the background is towering over the scenery, subtly dominating the whole event. The background consists of a wall, on which a delicate landscape is sketched in a gentle manner. This landscape, with its thin contours and its oscillating texture, is opposed by the landscape painting on the easel in front of the painter. In vibrant colours and striking brushstrokes, the painter works on a rocky landscape with a river. The canvas on the easel and the landscape sketched on the back wall frame the depicted figure groups and divide the painting into extra layers. While the landscape in front of the painter is clearly marked as an oil painting, as the colours on the palette indicate, the technique of the landscape in the background is not clearly identifiable. The wall irritates with its ambiguous appearance and is hardly classifiable in terms of materiality and structure within the composition. Fragments of a thin and gentle sketched landscape seem to be visible. The landscape varies with regards to the applied drawing technique: It appears either as a fresco or as a painted picture on canvasses that lean against the wall. The landscape is interrupted by some pillars almost like a trompe-l'oeil painting. Remarkably, the landscape outline continues, disregarding the spatial gaps of the pillars. The mural painting oscillates between being a backdrop or scenery and being a perspectival space. Courbet's manner of depicting this wall abandons the strict directions of a clear structure and composition with well-defined backgrounds. In "The Artist's Studio", the wall is no longer only a highlighting background but an independent plane with independent aesthetic significance.

The significance of the background reveals itself both in its size and its compositional ambiguity.[27] The ambiguous background is presented with different aesthetic functions. The landscape on the wall in the background serves as a background in order to highlight the figures in front of it. However, the wall could also be interpreted

---

[27] It is not possible to make a conclusive assessment whether this ambiguity is a result of multiple revised versions, whose traces become more visible during time, or whether the artist has worked with this ambiguity by then. These various steps within the working process are the topic of a major conservation project by the Musée d'Orsay.

as a material medium within the composition, as the depicted wall serves as a support for the outlines of a landscape that is applied directly onto the wall. This double structure becomes apparent due to the partially continuing contours of the landscape disregarding the interruptions of the depicted pillars. Furthermore, the landscape appears as consisting of different individual canvasses that lean against the wall. Each panel presents slight fragments of a landscape drawing. This particular appearance of the background might just be a result of different stages in the production process. Yet, the specific presence of the background underlines the fact that for Courbet the design and texture of the background constantly mattered, particularly as its massive size dominates the whole arrangement.

The aesthetic of this spacious area alternates between transparency and opacity: If the landscape scenery was directly applied onto the wall, the wall would appear in terms of a trompe-l'oeil painting, as a permeable level, which overcomes the density of the brickwork and forwards the view to an outside. Should the wall rather be interpreted as a support that serves as a counterbalance to the individual canvasses leaning against the depicted masonry, the wall would appear as an opaque and impenetrable level. The background, which is hard to identify precisely, evokes presumptions on how the artist experimented with the composition during his working process. Traces of these experiments are inscribed in the painting's aesthetic. However, not every single experimental move was planned and intended. Instead, it seems that during the production process non-expected turns occurred. Some traces led to unexpected results that have become manifest in the composition, without having been planned beforehand.

The connection between the landscape in the background and the landscape on the easel additionally suggest a comparison between two different working techniques of artistic methods. The landscape in the background appears in gentle sketching and diffuse contours. In contrast, the landscape on the easel is a well defined and framed painting that corresponds to the genre of landscape painting. This classification results from the choice of the format, as well as from the compositional design. The landscape on the easel follows a clear configuration and its preparation and painting technique is precisely marked by presenting the working process. In comparison, the arrangement in the background is mainly characterised by an appearance that allows one to anticipate a variety of possible techniques and potential compositions. It seems as if the background must not necessarily be characterised by distinctive delineation.

Regarding official teaching pamphlets, the background is an area, which does not attract the same attention and accuracy as the foreground. The development of the foreground is subject to more fixed regulations concerning the composition of figures or the way the main issue of the painting is supposed to be presented in general. The composition of the background is less regulated; therefore, the image plane provides ample scope for unusual and unexpected compositions and creations. In the case of "The Artist's Studio", the structure of the background remains undetermined; various possible explanations are presented next to each other simultaneously. Due to the fact that the background was generally attributed to be of lower relevance, it arises as a field where various experiments in composition become possible and where various attempts of its production can be seen. As traces of experimentation are still visible in the painting, Courbet stresses the background in general and shifts the attention of the observers more and more from the foreground to the background. The background moves further to the surface and, with it, creates the supportive meaning and enters the level of visibility.

In contrast, the landscape painting on the easel rather follows the rules of decisiveness. The presentation of the painting not only indicates how the paint was applied, but also how the materiality of the support was disclosed. Through a slightly diagonal presentation, the texture and character of the support becomes visible. A canvas materialises the landscape in front of the depicted artist, covered by thick impasto. In stark contrast to the impasto, the material support of the landscape in the background remains undetermined. Because of the diffuse identifiable materiality and composition, potential paths emerge that exceed the limits of the material support and lead to areas beyond the linen. Thus, the landscape on the wall oscillates between opacity and transparency, between materiality and immateriality. Being applied on a material carrier though, the way it is composed enables it to overcome the prominence of the material and to deny identification of a concrete support within the composition.

The two opposing landscapes contrast two possibilities of how the material support can be integrated as part of the composition. Simultaneously, they confront two options of artistic working methods concerning the wide range of compositional styles and painting techniques – ranging between powerful oil colours and delicate contour drawing. On two spatial levels, lying one after another, "The Artist's Studio" visualises different major preconditions of artistic work and creation.

In "The Artist's Studio", Courbet intensively deals with the categories of foreground, middle ground and background and keeps this scheme as a rough framework for the picture construction. However, he detaches the construction from its traditionally assigned functions and connotations. Due to the fact that the foreground is mostly held empty, the validity of the composition method has been reduced to a minimum. The middle ground inheres all figures and central motives and the background is more than a setting or a framework, as all the possibilities of artistic production are visible on this plane. These shifted accents reveal themselves in the distinctive shape of the background. With its diffuse landscape painting, the background dominates the painting and appears increasingly as an independent aesthetic image plane. Through this evident scheme, Courbet subverts the traditional hierarchy of image composition. The acting figures are still in the centre, situated in front of a backdrop; though the scenery – the background – is set in motion, while the figures remain motionless in their postures and gestures.

The classification of foreground and background does not only concern questions of narrative significance, but is also crucial for the creation of perspective. Neither the division into levels of relevance nor the creation of space seems to be a salient criterion for Courbet. Although he uses the traditional division, he opposes academic traditions as he works with the image planes in an unexpected way. The traditional construction scheme – foreground, middle ground, background – turns into a move of resistance, a resistance against conventions. This modification causes a shift in meaning, and, by means of resisting grounds, he transforms the gradation of importance and goes beyond the creation of perspective. As the background is set in motion, the observer is forced to look at the background, the ground and even further, on walls and canvasses. Without demonstrating and delineating the bare linen, Courbet integrates the materiality of a painting as an internal part in the composition.

## Material in Action

In the 19th century, production processes were considered something that should remain invisible by all means.[28] While the studio of an artist was a popular motif during that time – with the artists presenting themselves at work –, the thought should be avoided that the observation was disturbed by obvious reminders that painting was handmade and produced by men. The material was considered as a necessary condition helping the idea to appear. The attempt to cover the material underneath the imagery was still in practice in the 19th century, as the smooth varnished surfaces of the Academy pictures demonstrate.[29] Courbet's "Studio" breaks with these regulations to redeem production processes and presents a lively structured surface by intertwining inseparable intersections and interdependencies of material, workmanship and image.

Thus, the production process in the "Studio" is not just a topic, but is incorporated and still visible as traces in the surface of the painting. Like the majority of contemporary artists, Courbet often used industrially pre-primed and stretched canvasses, but "The Artist's Studio" is an exception. The large-scaled painting shows visible traces and seams of different panels. Seven pieces of fabric are sewn together to achieve the desired size. The final size was not intended from the beginning[30], but was enlarged successively due to the different stages of the production process and the development of the image composition.

Starting with the central group of figures, Courbet added successive pieces during the painting process and sewed them onto each other in a quite rough and crumpled manner. One result was a long horizontal seam that cuts almost through the entire painting. This trace of the production process is still visible. Courbet did not try to cover it. The trace is not a result of material ageing after centuries either. Courbet somehow left a visible scarf. This method, however, was not due to Courbet's incapability concerning his technical knowledge. Conservation studies testify Courbet's competence in dealing with a wide variety of supports and painting methods in gen-

---

[28] Richard Shiff, He Painted, in: *Cézanne's Card Players*, exh. cat., ed. by Nancy Ireson and Barnaby Wright, London 2010, p. 88. Shiff describes the handling as a production of a "transparent medium".

[29] Ibid., pp. 88–89.

[30] Daniel Cheron (Paris) and Bruno Mottin (C2RMF), in discussion with the author.

eral.[31] It seems that Courbet was able to skilfully deal with both; being attentive to priming processes, as some of his letters indicate[32], and wasting little effort concealing traces of the working process. His disregard considering the way to prepare the canvas 'properly' underlines how he opposed academic care and accuracy in the production process. In "The Artist's Studio", traces of unforeseen production processes are included and staged. The unforeseen additions and modifications are not hidden and neglected but are represented as traces. The material appears as an autonomous entity of the painting and for its perception.

This heightened focus towards backgrounds and materiality can be interpreted as an attempt to initiate change. In their visibility, they oppose their ascribed functions to disappear and become invisible. Furthermore, their visibility has been intensified by time.[33] Furthermore, these working traces are testimonies of the past[34], as the seam does not only refer to the duration of the working process, but also takes account of the time after completion. Thus, material traces do not only point to a single and closed moment in the past, but rather mark the progress of time and continually materialise this course of transformation. This process is also mirrored in the depiction and in the title, which points to 'seven years of his artistic life'. This duration of time has continually left new traces over and over again, shaping Courbet's working process and having been incorporated into the composition. Materiality and composition are inseparable from each other, since the composition does not follow the requirements of the material, nor does the canvas remain just a materialised idea. Composition and materiality are related to each other in a mutually interdependent dynamism, which arises in the course of production and does not end with the last brushstroke.

On several levels, Courbet's "Studio" revolts against academic regalia. The revolt lies less in the fact that he breaks with all academic conventions, but rather in his integration of them in his composition by citing and altering them. Courbet refers to the correlation of the three different image planes: foreground, middle ground and

---

[31] Mottin, Genesis (see note 15), p. 76. Courbet also used already painted canvasses as supports, which were not necessarily painted only by himself but also by others not always identifiable painters.

[32] Courbet, Correspondence (see note 19), letter 50/6, August 5, 1850.

[33] Daniel Cheron (Paris) and Bruno Mottin (C2RMF), in discussion with the author.

[34] Sybille Krämer, Was also ist eine Spur? Und worin besteht ihre epistemologische Rolle? Eine Bestandsaufnahme, in: Spur. Spurenlesen als Orientierungstechnik und Wissenskunst, ed. by Sybille Krämer et al., Frankfurt am Main 2007, p. 15.

background. On the one hand, he cites this scheme; on the other, he disbands this strict structural principle. While formally positioned according to academic conventions, Courbet undermines them on two levels: by the arrangement of image planes and by assembling contrasting motifs and formats. Regarding the handling of the canvas, Courbet contradicts the prevailing principle that tries to make the working process and material disappear beyond a smooth and flat surface. Seams and stitches of the separate pieces of canvas remain significantly visible. As traces, they refer to the time of the production process and simultaneously to the period after its completion through the increasing visibility of the stitching. The material stands out as an element of a historical event, which itself becomes an element of historicisation by indicating the 'seven years of an artistic life' as a historic turning point.

In a paradigmatic way, "The Artist's Studio" presents the relationship between materiality and production. Courbet situates his subject in the classical artistic production site – the artist's studio – and emphasises the importance of materiality. Materiality is not presented as a means to an end; instead, it is portrayed as a fundamental ground in order to produce. The image production is not shown as a purposeful, linear imaging process, but implies dynamics that lead to unexpected and unpredictable results.

# Bibliography

Boime, Albert, *The Academy and French Painting in the Nineteenth Century*, London 1971.

Bonnet, Alain, *L'enseignement des arts au XIX$^e$ siècle*, Paris 2006.

Bomford, David, *Art in the Making. Impressionism*, exh. cat., London 1990.

Bouillet, Marie-Nicolas (ed.), *Dictionnaire universel des sciences, des lettres et des arts*, Paris 1854.

Callen, Anthea, *The Art of Impressionism. Painting Technique and the Making of Modernity*, New Haven / London 2000.

Courbet, Gustave, *Correspondence de Gustave Courbet*, ed. and transl. by Petra ten-Doesschate Chu, Paris 1996.

*Dictionnaire des Arts de Peinture, Sculpture et Gravure*, vol. 2, Paris 1792, pp. 333–343.

Gaethgens, Barbara, *Genremalerei. Geschichte der klassischen Bildgattungen in Quellentexten und Kommentare*, vol. 4, Berlin 2002.

Hoffman, Werner, *Das Atelier. Courbets Jahrhundertbild*, Munich 2010.

Krämer, Sybille, Was also ist eine Spur? Und worin besteht ihre epistemologische Rolle? Eine Bestandsaufnahme, in: *Spur. Spurenlesen als Orientierungstechnik und Wissenskunst*, ed. by Sybille Krämer et al., Frankfurt am Main 2007, pp. 11–33.

Labreuche, Pascal, *Paris, capitale de la toile à peindre, XVII$^e$ - XIX$^e$ siècle*, Paris 2011.

*La Grande Encyclopédie*, ed. by H. Lamirault et C$^{ie}$, Paris 1886–1902.

Mongi-Vollmer, Eva, *Das Atelier des Malers. Die Diskurse eines Raumes in der zweiten Hälfte des 19. Jahrhunderts*, Berlin 2004.

Mottin, Bruno, A Complex Genesis. Courbet in the Laboratory, in: *Gustave Courbet*, exh. cat., Paris / New York 2007.

Nochlin, Linda, *Courbet's Real Allegory. Rereading "The Painter's Studio"*, in: *Courbet Reconsidered*, exh. cat. The Brooklyn Museum, ed. by Sarah Faunce and Linda Nochlin, New York 1988, pp. 17–41.

Pevsner, Nicolas, *Die Geschichte der Kunstakademie,* Munich 1986.

Pointon, Marcia, *Naked Authority. The Body in Western Painting 1830–1908,* Cambridge 1990.

Preimesberger, Rudolf / Baader, Hannah / Suthor, Nicola, *Porträt. Geschichte der klassischen Bildgattungen in Quellentexten und Kommentaren,* vol. 2, Berlin 1999.

Roland, Michel, *Marianne. Die Zeichnung im 18. Jahrhundert,* Munich 1987.

Schieder, Martin, "Ne fais pas ce que je fais." Dans l'atelier de Gustave Courbet, in: *Apprendre à peindre. Les ateliers privés à Paris 1780–1863,* ed. by France Nerlich and Alain Bonnet, Tours 2013, pp. 333–353.

Segré, Monique, *L'École des Beaux-Arts. XIX$^e$ et XX$^e$ siècle,* Paris 1998.

Shiff, Richard, He Painted, in: *Cézanne's Card Players,* exh. cat., ed. by Nancy Ireson and Barnaby Wright, London 2010, pp. 73–92.

Winner, Matthias, Zu Gustav Courbets "Allégorie réelle" und der Tradition, in: *Jahrbuch der Berliner Museen,* vol. 4 (1962).

# The Resistance of Language.
# Translation and Nomination in Walter Benjamin's Philosophy
*Akos Herman*

In Walter Benjamin's linguistic writings, human language, understood in its representational and communicational function, finds its condition of possibility in 'pure language', a negative linguistic dimension that is inaccessible and unsayable as such. It is thus when language stumbles, when 'pure' linguisticity comes to resist in speech and halts this latter for a fleeting second, that language becomes aware of its potential, of the performative force it holds. As we will see, this affirmation is not without a number of paradoxes. It is in fact when language renounces saying or doing that it gains in power.

Paradigmatic examples of such an advent of the transcendental dimension of language in Benjamin's writings are the naming of a newborn and translation. Before getting to the heart of the matter, it seems necessary to contextualize these examples in Benjamin's general theory of language.

In the very first lines of his widely-commented essay "On Language as Such and on the Language of Man", Walter Benjamin extends the linguistic phenomenon to every entity of the created world: "There is no event or thing in either animate or inanimate nature that does not in some way partake of language, for it is in the nature of each one to communicate its mental contents. This use of the word 'language' is in no way metaphorical".[1] In fact, brought into existence by the Word of God, every creature takes part in the linguistic movement (*Sprachbewegung*) of Genesis.

Even though the world in its entirety is thus caught in a universal *panlogue,* this latter should not be understood as a homogenous linguistic medium. Benjamin distinguishes between the 'language of things' and 'human language'. This latter is indeed a "language of language"[2], or a language of the second degree. Its task consists in receiving the silent language of things and allowing it access to the articulated and sonorous name. Through this gesture, which we will ultimately understand as an act

---

[1] Walter Benjamin, *Selected Writings*, vol. 1, 1913–1926, ed. by Marcus Bullock and Michael W. Jennings, Cambridge 1997, p. 62.

[2] Ibid., p. 65.

of translation, human language allows for an accomplishment of creation: It echoes the creating word and therefore ends language by reverberating its origin.

"To whom does the lamp communicate itself?"[3] Benjamin asks in order to shed light on the cyclical character of the *Sprachbewegung* in question. It communicates itself to man, who, in the name, pronounces the spiritual essence of things. Human language must then also be interrogated: "To whom does man communicate himself?"[4] Benjamin's response is somewhat less clear. He simultaneously asserts that the language of man knows "no addressee of communication" and that "*in the name, the mental being of man communicates itself to God*".[5]

How can one comprehend such an address (of God) that is at the same time the absence itself of all addressees? In order to gain a better grasp of the nature of the language of paradise that Benjamin describes in his treatise on "Language", let us refer to an article by Emile Benveniste, entitled "Subjectivity in Language". The French linguist explains that every discursive act depends on a series of indicators of enunciation and foremost on the personal pronouns 'I-you'. These do not refer to "a concept or to an individual". Benveniste writes:

> There is no concept 'I' that incorporates all the *I*'s that are uttered at every moment in the mouths of all the speakers, in the sense that there is a concept 'tree' to which all the individual uses of *tree* refer. The 'I', then, does not denominate any lexical entity. Could it then be said that the *I* refers to a particular individual? If that were the case, a permanent contradiction would be admitted into language, and anarchy into its use. How could the same term refer indifferently to any individual whatsoever and still at the same time identify him in his individuality? We are in the presence of a class of words, the 'personal pronouns', that escape the status of all the other signs of language. Then, what does the *I* refer to? To something very peculiar which is exclusively linguistic: *I* refers to the act of individual discourse in which it is pronounced, and by this designates the speaker. It is a term that cannot be identified except in what we have called elsewhere an instance of discourse and that has only a momentary reference.[6]

The pronoun 'I' indicates the discourse in its own 'taking place'. It can only be understood in the context of an individual enunciation – deprived of its 'actuality', it is no more than an empty word. On the other hand, there can be no act of discourse without this basic indicator of enunciation – "the 'personal pronouns' are never missing from the signs of language".[7]

---

[3] Benjamin, Writings (see note 1), p. 64.
[4] Ibid.
[5] Ibid., p. 65.
[6] Émile Benveniste, Subjectivity in Language, in: *Problems in General Linguistics*, Miami 1971, p. 226.
[7] Ibid., p. 225.

A further originality of Benveniste's approach is to show that the 'I' can only be understood as dialogical:

> Language is possible only because each speaker sets himself up as a *subject* by referring to himself as an *I* in his discourse. Because of this, *I* posits another person, the one who, being, as he is, completely exterior to "me", becomes my echo to whom I say *you* and who says *you* to me. This polarity of persons is the fundamental condition in language.[8]

For Benveniste, subjectivity and consciousness both have their source in this original reciprocity of language, always already caught between the 'I' and the 'you'. Any conception that would posit the 'I' in some form of precedence is thus completely erroneous – monologues themselves are necessarily dialogues.

In another article, bearing the title "Relationships of person in the verb", Benveniste opposes the 'I-you' correlation – which he names the "correlation of personality" – to the third person (he/she), which is defined as the "non-person".[9] In fact, it must be understood as absent or exterior to the situation of discursivity.

If we return to the text of Walter Benjamin, one could understand the Adamic language of the essay "On Language…" as an attempt to think such a non-discursive, depersonalized linguisticity. The paradisiacal word, taken out of all structures of address, would be 'pronounced' by a 'he', a non-person. Through the withdrawal of the 'I-you' correlation, there would be no more "content of communication"[10] – on the contrary, language would just communicate itself. Instead of speaking, assuming the role of the instance of enunciation, man would be 'spoken' by language.

In Benjamin's writings, such non-discursive language – a linguistic event that takes place paradoxically in its non-taking place – corresponds to "pure language" (*die reine Sprache*). It is in fact not without perplexity that one discovers that, in Benjamin's linguistic writings, the summit of linguisticity, the point where language appears in its purest form, is also where it is the most 'inhuman', where the 'I' must erase itself to become a bare medium or repository through which the language of creation resonates.

One might find some references to such a desubjectivized 'use' of language in Benveniste's writings – however, the linguistic events he describes are far from being the rule, as seems to be the case in Benjamin's description of paradisiacal language. They

---

[8] Benveniste, Subjectivity (see note 6), p. 225.
[9] Ibid., p. 200: "Relationships of person in the verb".
[10] Benjamin, Writings (see note 1), p. 66.

appear rather as isolated linguistic accidents. Jean-Claude Coquet identifies some of these linguistic events where one must ask "whether the agent who has thus been destabilized is still capable of assuming responsibility for a linguistic act".[11] Such is the case, for example, in an insult, that is, a "word that one allows to 'slip out' under the pressure of a brusque and violent sentiment, impatience, rage, disappointment".[12] Benveniste seems here very close to Benjamin's understanding of pure language. In his "Critique of Violence", Benjamin insists on the immediateness that belongs to anger. This latter would not be taken into the logic of communication. "It is not a means but a manifestation"[13], and in the same way as paradisiacal language, it carries the subject away to erase it without remainder.

Pure language, pronounced in the third person, is this irresistible flux that drowns all subjective intentionality. Language ceases to be inhabited by any will to/for communication or *vouloir-dire*. Purely immediate, this language is not yet taken into the fundamental and unbridgeable divide between the semiotic and the semantic that, following Benveniste, is at the heart of our language. In other words, there is no distortion between the world of signs and the sense that is to be communicated. The pure language of paradise is the language of the pure sign and nothing more.

However, the perspicacious reader of Benjamin's essay notices that the author's descriptions of this 'uncorrupted' immediateness of language cannot but fail. For instance, one might read:

> The translation of the language of things into that of man is not only a translation of the mute into sonic; it is also the translation of the nameless into the name. It is therefore the translation of the imperfect language into a more perfect one, and cannot but add something to it, namely knowledge.[14]

The passage of the silent language of things to the sonorous name is thus not as fluid as one could have expected. In fact, human voice seems already taken up in the ambiguity that Derrida, in his "Grammatology"[15], has characterized as the logic of

---

[11] Jean-Claude Coquet, La syntagmation d'Aristote à Benveniste, in: *Linx*, vol. 7 (1995), http://linx.revues.org/1242 (09/07/2014). Transl. by the author.

[12] Émile Benveniste, La blasphémie et l'euphémie, in: *Problèmes de linguistique générale*, vol. 2, Paris 1972, p. 256. Transl. by the author.

[13] Benjamin, Writings (see note 1), p. 294.

[14] Ibid., p. 70.

[15] Jacques Derrida, *De la Grammatologie*, Paris 1967, p. 208.

supplementarity. In fact, voice appears partly as a substitute for the silent language of things – it serves as their representative. However, such a substitution implies necessarily a 'supplement'. Something is necessarily added to the representation: An exterior dimension ineluctably makes an intrusion into the relation of supplementation. In Benjamin's text, this is nothing less than 'knowledge'.

Peter Fenves' reading of Benjamin's essay allows us to better understand the 'contamination' in question. In fact, the American scholar shows that Adamic language is prey to signification (or 'knowledge') from its very beginnings. For the Benjamin of "On Language…", the naming of a newborn must proceed from a pure linguistic gesture and must be free from all 'inauthentic signification'. However, as Fenves highlights, this 'commandment' is not respected in the Book of Genesis:

> God, for example, names the newly-created man in the proscribed manner: 'the LORD God formed man (adam) from the earth (adamah)'. Benjamin implicitly recognizes the violation of the commandment in the case of Eve: 'this one', Adam says, 'shall be called "Woman" (Ishah), for from man (ish) was she taken. […] Nothing changes in this respect after the expulsion from paradise: Eve, for example, names her first-born, Cain, in recognition of her 'gain' (qanithi).[16]

The paradisiacal name is thus already contaminated by 'descriptions'. Inevitably, language, even in its purest form, is subject to predication and must engage in a process of knowledge and communication. From its very origins, the word can only name in a mediate way or – as Benjamin puts it – externally. The linguistic 'fall' is thus not an event that struck Adamic language at the moment of expulsion. Pure language does not precede; it has never been there in the first place. On the contrary, the fall is a condition that is inherent to language itself.

But if our linguistic condition is 'contaminated' from the very beginning, Benjamin does still retain the idea of a linguistic degradation. In fact, the treatise on language seems to stage a 'fall in the fall', the possibility, in other words, of an additional aggravation of our already more than precarious linguistic situation. Benjamin writes:

> After the Fall, which, in making language mediate, laid the foundation for its multiplicity, linguistic confusion could be only one step away. […] The enslavement of language in prattle is joined by the enslavement of things in folly almost as its inevitable consequence. In this turning away from things, which was enslavement, the plan for the Tower of Babel came into being, and linguistic confusion with it.[17]

---

[16] Peter Fenves, *The Messianic Reduction. Walter Benjamin and the Shape of Time*, Stanford 2010, pp. 144–145.

[17] Benjamin, Writings (see note 1), p. 72.

This additional confusion can be better understood with the help of Derrida's analysis in his "*Des Tours de Babel*":

> Does he punish them for having wanted to build as high as the heavens? For having wanted to accede to the highest, up to the Most High? Perhaps for that too, no doubt, but incontestably for having wanted thus to *make a name for themselves*, to give themselves the name, to construct for and by themselves their own name, to gather themselves there ("that we no longer be scattered"), as in the unity of a place which is at once a tongue and a tower, the one as well as the other. He punishes them for having thus wanted to assure themselves, by themselves, a unique and universal genealogy.[18]

Through the project of Babel, the Semites negate the plurality inherent to language. Their construction is then nothing more than the concealment of the inevitable first fall: notwithstanding the negativity inherent in our language, their intention is to pronounce a word that is unique and immediate. Humanity thus usurps a sphere of plenitude to which it could never have access and it is this act of hubris that justifies God's punishment. However, one might consider that the 'confusion' does not require divine intervention. In fact, a word that is taken in the illusion of its plenitude cannot escape confusion, as it is by definition deaf to the word of the others, to alterity. Derrida continues his analysis:

> In seeking to 'make a name for themselves', to found at the same time a universal tongue and a unique genealogy, the Semites want to bring the world to reason, and this can signify simultaneously a colonial violence (since they would thus universalize their idiom) and a peaceful transparency of the human community.[19]

The "peaceful transparency" of the newly found universal language of the Semites holds in truth a "colonial violence". Such a language does not "name" things, but imposes on the world: It wants to "bring the world to reason". In Benjamin's conception, such an illusion of transparency can be interpreted as a real 'catastrophe'. However, Babel in this sense is not an isolated event: It is a catastrophe that takes place constantly through endless repetition.

In fact, as soon as language enters the realm of 'signification' (and we have seen that this is the case even of the 'purest' language of paradise) it engages inevitably in this cycle of violence. Giorgio Agamben writes in *The Coming Community*:

---

[18] Jacques Derrida, Des Tours de Babel, in: *Psyche. Inventions of the Other*, vol. 1, Stanford 2007, p. 195.
[19] Ibid., p. 199.

The word "tree" designates indifferently, insofar as it posits the proper universal significance in place of a singular ineffable tree (*terminus supponit significatum pro re*). In other words, it transforms singularities into members of a class, whose meaning is defined by a common propriety (the condition of belonging ε). The fortune of set theory in modern logic is born from the fact that the definition of the set is simply the definition of linguistic meaning.[20]

The necessary predicative structure of language implies that singularities are subsumed under general concepts and are thus necessarily violated. Therefore, language that takes the path of 'knowledge' sacrifices the world for a general abstraction – for the sake of an illusionary transparency –, and nature thus finds itself reduced to pure silence.

We have seen that Adamic language, understood as pure and impersonal linguistic immediacy, is not accessible to man – whether before or after the expulsion from paradise. Human language is indeed by definition condemned to mediacy and is thus inevitably already representational. Benjamin shows, however, that language in this sense necessarily runs the risk of closing up on itself, or, in other words, of the illusion of transparency and, as its corollary, the negation of all alterity.

If our reading of Benjamin is correct, it is at this point where man intends to master and dominate language that this latter comes to 'resist'. In fact, as we will shortly understand in more detail, it is when man wants to put language under his full dominance, when he wishes to pronounce a full and immediate name, that linguisticity as such, independent of subjective intention, comes to break and fragment his speech.

In order to better understand the negative linguistic dimension we are dealing with, let us refer to an early fragment of Benjamin entitled "Skeleton of the Word". In this short text, the author presents the "intentional alteration" *(intentionale Umstellung)* that takes place when a word is deprived of its meaning:

> It is strange that sometimes, if we consider a word repetitively, the intention towards its meaning is lost in order to make a place for another intention, which one could reasonably call the 'word skeleton'. (For its sign, one can designate the skeleton of any given word, for example the word *tower* in the following manner: – tower –).[21]

A word that is repeated can lose its meaning. It seems reduced to a pure sign and Benjamin chooses to symbolize this abrupt isolation of the word from meaningful discourse in the following manner: – sign –. This experience is generally accompanied by an uncanny feeling: Suddenly man feels alienated from his language, his

---

[20] Giorgio Agamben, *The Coming Community*, Minneapolis 2007, p. 9.

[21] Cited in Fenves, Reduction (see note 16), p. 133. Transl. modified by the author.

communicational intention can no longer invest the signifier. The 'skeleton of the word' is, however, still invested with an intentionality. In fact, the word – tower –, liberated from inauthentic (i. e. subjective) meaning, communicates at present a pure 'communicability'.[22] It appears, in fact, as a pure intention without object, or, in other words, as pure openness to a sense that is absent, that is still to be given. The uncanny character of experience comes exactly from the sudden discovery of a void, an abyss at the heart of our language.

The experience of the "intentional alteration" in question is a moment where language seems to speak itself. However, contrary to the full and immediate language of paradise, this auto-communication of language is that of the negativity that inhabits it. It is the original and unsolvable linguistic incompleteness that thus comes to light. In other words, language comes to resist in order to remind us that the fall is its inalienable condition and Babel the ever-recurring consequence of its illusion of fullness. Language manifests itself as a 'cry' or a 'prayer' for a sense that can never be fully attained, only 'received' at the end of times.

Benjamin, throughout his work, describes a series of linguistic experiences where the resistance of language makes itself felt. We will limit our development to the case of translation and of the naming of a newborn child.

Translation, in Benjamin's thought, is not to be understood in the common sense of the term. The task in question does not aim at the transmission of a linguistic content. On the contrary, "translation is a form"[23] and aims to liberate language from inauthentic signification that weighs upon it. "This may be achieved," writes Benjamin,

> above all, by the literal rendering of the syntax which proves words rather than sentences to be the primary element of the translator. For if the sentence is the wall before the language of the original, literalness is the arcade.[24]

In order to understand this difficult passage of his essay on translation, let us recall, with the help of Paul de Man, that

> *Satz* in German means not just sentence, in the grammatical sense, it means statement – Heidegger will speak of *Der Satz des Grundes; Satz* is the statement, the most fundamental statement, meaning – the most meaningful word – whereas word is associated by Benjamin with *Aussage,* the way in which you state, as the apparent agent of the statement.[25]

---

[22] Walter Benjamin, *Gesammelte Schriften,* Frankfurt am Main 1991, p. 16.
[23] Benjamin, Writings (see note 1), p. 254.
[24] Ibid., p. 259.
[25] Paul de Man, Walter Benjamin's "The Task of the Translator", in: *The Resistance of Theory,* Minneapolis 1986, p. 88.

The translation of the original *Wörtlichkeit* as "literal rendering" or "literality" also risks to obscure what is at stake here in the 'word for word' translation of texts – reproducing meticulously their syntactic order and articulation. For Benjamin, in other terms, all that counts is the faithful reproduction of the agent of expression to the detriment of the transposition of signification – this latter is the "wall" that is to be torn down.

At the end of his essay on translation, Benjamin defines the interlinear translation of the Holy Scriptures to be the paradigm of all authentic translation. Such a translation would perfectly illustrate the "literality" *(Wörtlichkeit)* required by the author:

ערה לכ תפש הוהי ללב םש יכ לבב המש ארק ןכ לע

world whole lips JHWH confuse there because Babel its name therefore

ערה לכ ינפ לע הוהי םציפה םשמו

world whole face on JHWH dispersed from there and

In this example, translation seems to explode sense and to mortify the language of translation. The foreign syntax annihilates the communicational content of our language, and words suddenly appear uncanny, reduced to the communication of their own communicability.

The experience in question is very similar to Saint Augustine's reflections on dead languages. In an exemplary passage of "On the Trinity" (X.1.2.), Augustine studies the extinct Latin word *temetum* – originally signifying an intoxicating beverage. One could thus hear these three syllables, but not understand them at all. The word would, however, not be perceived as pure 'noise' but rather – as in the case of the "word skeleton"– as a reference to an unavailable sense, which is to be sought after. Agamben analyses this extract in the following manner:

> This passage isolates an experience of the word in which it is no longer mere sound (istas tes syllabas) and is not yet meaning, but the pure intention to signify. The experience of an unknown word (verbum incognitum) in the no-man's-land between sound and signification, is, for Augustine, the amorous experience as a will to knowledge: the intention to signify without a signified corresponds, in fact, not to logical understanding, but to the desire for knowledge ('qui scire amat incognita, non ipsa incognita, sed ipsum scire amat'). (Here it is important to note that the place of this experience that reveals the vox in its originary purity as meaning [voler-dire] is a dead word: temetum.)[26]

In translation, language appears disentangled from communication and reveals its original resistance to any attempt at closure of signification: It manifests itself as an insatiable desire for knowledge. Another example of such linguistic resistance is the

---

[26] Giorgio Agamben, *Language and Death. The Place of Negativity,* Minneapolis / Oxford 2006, pp. 33–34.

naming of a newborn. "Of all the beings," says Benjamin, "man is the only one who names his own kind, as he is the only one whom God did not name". The given name has thus a privileged role among human names and represents "the point where human language participates most intimately in the divine infinity of the pure word".[27] The proximity with the creative Word of God would be such that Benjamin even evokes the "idea that a man's name is his fate".

We have seen in our analysis of Adamic language that the purity that Benjamin attributes to the proper name is 'spoiled' from the very beginning by the inevitable representational nature of our language. Proper names in fact imply description from the very beginning and nomination inevitably violates the named being. The performative force of naming that Benjamin alleges – the fact that names 'create' one's fate – must not be understood, in our sense, as this possibility of determining in advance the destiny of one's child.

On the contrary, if our interpretation is correct, proper names become genuinely proper because, at a certain moment, the signification the chosen name carries is suspended. The name that was chosen for a number of reasons, carrying a determinate semantic content, suddenly and in an entirely unforeseeable manner becomes the 'name of the child'.

Between the name that was chosen and this 'new' name, even though they are strictly homonymous, there is a radical discontinuity. This moment of hiatus is where the name loses its familiarity and resonates as a disturbing and uncanny sound, open to a signification that is to come.

Thus, paradoxically, the gesture of naming implies a renunciation of naming. It is because the original intention, which inhabits it, is erased that the name has the possibility of becoming proper. "By giving them a name," writes Benjamin, "parents dedicate their children to God". Instead of the violent act of determination, it is a speech act where the subject retreats and allows language to open up. The performativity of the given name can be understood here as dependent on its 'afformativity', i. e. the possibility, for the speaking agent, of not doing anything.

Translation and nomination are both experiences where language suddenly manifests its inherent intentionality, which is nothing less than an infinite quest for sense and

---

[27] Benjamin, Writings (see note 1), p. 69.

signification. Benjamin persists in calling this linguistic dimension 'pure language' – an expression that we now understand to be an oxymoron. In fact, the inhuman dimension in question can only manifest itself in threshold zones, in the cracks and breaks of our languages. There is no possibility for man to dwell in this sphere: Its effect is sudden and short-lived; inauthentic signification returns to obscure it ceaselessly. Thus, in the same way as we have seen in our analysis of Benveniste, these occurrences are rather to be understood as accidents whereby language reaffirms its own potentiality.

Indeed, Benjamin's insistence on Adamic language must not be understood, following our interpretation, as a nostalgic evocation of a paradoxical pre-linguistic language, or as a will to exhaust human language and reduce it to silence. On the contrary, the interruptions of the communicational chain that the author considers as manifestations of the highest linguisticity are there to allow the continuation of language. In an attempt to avoid Babelic closure, language is drawn back to its origins, or, in other words, to its 'place of nativity', where the word is not yet signification but available for all significations.

This threshold between what is not yet language and language can be qualified as language's inhuman dimension. "The 'inhuman'," writes Paul de Man,

> however, is not some kind of mystery, or some kind of secret; the inhuman is: linguistic structures, the play of linguistic tensions, linguistic events that occur, possibilities which are inherent in language – independently of any intent or any drive or any wish or desire that we might have.[28]

Translation and nomination are paradigmatic experiences where this inhuman dimension, which can never be subsumed in any singular language, comes to light. It emerges as the condition of possibility for all linguisticity, as the silent and secret resistance that works its way through all our discourses, allowing language to remain open to the possible.

---

[28] De Man, Benjamin (see note 25), p. 96.

# Bibliography

Agamben, Giorgio, *The Coming Community*, Minneapolis 2007.

Agamben, Giorgio, *Language and Death. The Place of Negativity*, Minneapolis / Oxford 2006.

Benjamin, Walter, *Gesammelte Schriften*, Frankfurt am Main 1991.

Benjamin, Walter, *Selected Writings*, vol. 1, 1913–1926, ed. by Marcus Bullock and Michael W. Jennings, Cambridge 1997.

Benveniste, Émile, La blasphémie et l'euphémie, in: *Problèmes de linguistique générale*, vol. 2, Paris 1972.

Benveniste, Émile, Subjectivity in Language, in: *Problems in General Linguistics*, Miami 1971.

Coquet, Jean-Claude, La syntagmation d'Aristote à Benveniste, in: *Linx*, vol. 7 (1995), http://linx.revues.org/1242 (09/07/2014).

De Man, Paul, Walter Benjamin's "The Task of the Translator", in: *The Resistance of Theory*, Minneapolis 1986.

Derrida, Jacques, *De la Grammatologie*, Paris 1967.

Derrida, Jacques, Des Tours de Babel, in: *Psyche. Inventions of the Other*, vol. 1, Stanford 2007.

Fenves, Peter, *The Messianic Reduction. Walter Benjamin and the Shape of Time*, Stanford 2010.

# Inhabiting the Thick.
## The Affects of Erosive Surfacing
*Nicole De Brabandere*

Introduction

The practice of tending to surfaces activates a relational dynamic with everyday materiality and privileges the immediacy of haptic sensation and qualities of touch in movement. Surfaces describe the spatial limits of our movement in architectural space – the wall of the corridor or the edge of the table guide movement along, beside and across. But surfaces do not merely compel our movements in space as extensive continuities. The textures and frictions that are felt in movement with material surfaces charge dynamics of touch with intensive tensions and resistance. Surfaces are intensified in dynamic relation with their material permeability, porosity, absorbency, grain, compression, elasticity, thickness, thinness, fragility and precarity. In this sense, surfaces privilege an immediate sensorial relation with the qualities of the material, social, architectural or infrastructural environment. The surface thus introduces a relation that has the potential to redistribute, modulate and expressively activate bodily tendencies to movement and sensation with the most intimate and often unconscious qualities of everyday existence.

Whitehead specifies that expression becomes active in dynamic relation with "lures for feeling", which are only possible via a "witness of the body".[1] Crucially, the notion of attending to (or with) the immediate environment is never merely a registration of the temporal present, but activates the inhabited history of embodiment itself: "This is a feeling of the world in the past; it is the inheritance of the world as a complex of feeling; namely, it is the feeling of derived feelings".[2] The process of tending to surfaces, of becoming sensitive to how they compel movement, thus engages the body in a performative and affective flux with everyday materiality. Put otherwise, in the tending to surfaces, in the process of lending them a 'witness' wherein we discover new performative techniques, we potentiate the expression of an elastic surfacing between bodies, materialities and the inhabited tendencies of everyday experience.

---

[1] Alfred North Whitehead, *Process and Reality. An Essay in Cosmology*, New York 1978, p. 81.

[2] Ibid., p. 81.

Dirt activates tension between chaos and the smooth continuity of surfaces as it covers, permeates and composes them. Dirt also erodes, spreads, and accumulates. Dirt literally redistributes the volume of surfaces in visible, touchable space-time by its uncontainable, particulate material attributes. This particulate quality of dirt also puts pressure on the active task and sensitivity of tending and maintaining inhabited ecologies. The visible materiality of dirt thus resonates between the socially charged imperative to maintain the surfaces and spaces of the everyday environment, demonstrating a visible social disposition towards cleanliness. In this sense, 'thinking dirt' connects us with processes of tending that open attention to the micro-percepts and affects that activate the social milieu via the felt intensities of its material qualities.

In this paper, I explore the dynamic relation between surfaces and dirt or dust (primarily as a dry, particulate powder) as a way of activating the lived milieu towards moving thought, feeling and sensation. This research is invested in activating expressive potential and emergence between the qualities of felt experience and theoretical thought and reflection. This dynamism between theory and practice brings felt expression in everyday experience closer to the development of new ways to inhabit the world in creative, sensitive and socially pertinent ways. Specifically, this paper activates the expressive potential of dirt as an intensive volume in the way that it affectively charges lived surface ecologies in dynamics of containment and spread, compression and erosion, persistence and temporariness. The discussion begins with the theoretical examination of the contrast between intensive and extensive surfaces. Then the paper investigates the intensive qualities of dirt in domestic, urban and rural situations and the way that these all lend specific intensity to the dynamic relation between dirt and surfaces. Finally, the paper describes some artistic examples that activate surface intensity with dirt, including my own explorations in the intensive qualities of dirt.

## Inhabiting Surface Tension

Everyday material surfaces are active within inhabited tendencies to movement in the way that they activate performative 'scripts'. The notion of 'scripting' is an important concept with which to bridge the immediacy of touch or physical contact with everyday material surfaces and the performatives that gather, organize and order everyday movements. In this sense the 'script' is the dynamic relation between objects and bodies in everyday life that compel and afford particular movement tendencies. It is then useful to distinguish 'scripts' as a stable artefact, form or instruction from the scripting milieu wherein the 'script' is always remade in its performance. This conceptualization of the 'script' poses it as a movement that generates a flux between the body as form and the emergent feeling with material qualities. The 'script' then becomes a material-movement technology with which to activate everyday relations with ledges, floors, walls, cushions, windows, handles, etc. as expressive potentials. The 'script' compels a kind of staging of everyday environments, as well as of embodied tendencies to movement and sensation.

But the material surfaces of everyday environments are not merely perimeters that limit our inhabited potential for extensive movement in space. Everyday surfaces constitute a complex milieu wherein inhabited tendency, felt quality, use and spatial extensity intermingle in dynamic flux. For example, the surface of a fabric seat cushion of a chair integrates the porous materiality of fabric with the specific gesture and function of sitting while occupying specific coordinates in space. In the immediacy of touching the seat surface – the pressure of the weight of the body against the cushion as the body rests upon it – never begins with specific categories or functions. Instead, the chair is felt in flux with our inhabited relations with it, in the immediate experience of sitting, or in shifting one's weight forward on the chair.

Importantly, what we are dealing with here is a tensile distribution between what Whitehead terms 'continuous' and 'atomic' aspects of inhabited experience. The tendencies to movement that we inhabit with the environment are only consciously experienced, or felt, when the distribution on the continuum between these contrasting poles is intensified or put under pressure. The problem of negotiating and intensifying the dynamic contrast between the 'atomism' and the 'continuity' of felt experience gets to the heart of how experience is felt and thus opens the potential for modulating the potential for inhabiting everyday 'scripts'. But it is not necessary to begin with the complexity of everyday experience to exemplify the frictions that are generated by this dynamism. If we first look briefly at the dynamic relation between paper surface and mark in the drawing process we can begin to understand the way that immediate material quality and extensive space affectively inform one another in relatively simple terms.

In surface arts such as painting and drawing there is a tension between the image of a mark and the volume of the material surface that holds the mark. This tension is characterized by a felt thickening or slowing of the space of the page, in relation to the felt extensive movement and fluidity or speed of the mark.³ The smooth, straight line is an affectively fast one that gracefully flows over or cuts through the space of the page as if the space were a thick and viscous substance. Meanwhile, a mark that reveals the beady texture of a surface on or beneath the page seems to move in pace with the textured materiality of the page. The trace of the line gesture combined with the materiality of both line and page activate the virtual potential of the mark, and the impression of being fast, slow, thick, or thin as we move with it when seeing it.⁴

It is important to briefly elaborate that the emergent potential of vision is an embodied dynamism that is motivated in the movement of seeing. As an active process of tending to the micro-perceptions of everyday experience, seeing is a 'moving with' the specific qualities that give texture, gesture and dynamism to form. Susanne Langer uses the example of an undulating motif to describe visual movement as a force or compulsion that guides attention by what it seems to "do".⁵ Paul Valéry comes to a similar insight, insisting that in the process of representational drawing the marks that compel movements of seeing cannot be reduced to their parts, nor reconstructed according to a reasoned logic, but are informing marks:

> It's not that these informing things have no form, but that their forms don't have anything in themselves that allow us to replace them in their retracing or obvious recognition. In effect, informing forms don't conjure anything but possibility.⁶

Informing forms thus compel visual tendencies in the movement of seeing but are never reducible to pre-determined forms, materials and bodies. In this sense, the force of informing relations is incipient: "They are tendencies in the making".⁷ The informing force of the mark's visual movement activates the verge of the actual as it meets the virtual or an 'edging' of the body that has the expressive intensity of being in excess of

---

³ Nicole De Brabandere, Intensive Resistances. Choreographies for intensive lining in materiality, movement, space, duration and volume, under review, 2015.

⁴ De Brabandere, Resistances (see note 3).

⁵ Susanne K. Langer, *Feeling and Form. A Theory of Art Developed from Philosophy in a New Key*, New York 1953, pp. 63–66.

⁶ Paul Valéry, *Degas Danse Dessin*, Paris 1938, p. 77. Cf. also De Brabandere, Resistances (see note 3).

⁷ Erin Manning, *Always more than One. Individuation's Dance*, Durham / London 2013, p. 69.

the possible.[8] Massumi articulates the feeling of such force as "the simultaneous participation of the virtual in the actual and the actual in the virtual, as one arises from and returns to the other".[9]

Therefore, the virtual force of the mark does not merely activate directional movement in two-dimensional space. The informing force of the mark is incipient in the complex and multiple emergences with material qualities as well as the inhabited textures that make the movement of seeing, or marking, felt in particular intensive distributions. When the roughness of a surface is revealed by drawing a thick charcoal line over it, slowing the visual movement of the mark, both charcoal and page demonstrate a material dynamic that foregrounds the intensive density, volume and qualities of charcoal as much as it does the forward force of the line movement. As the density of the charcoal powder saturates the crevices of the paper fibres or, conversely, threatens to rub or fall off the paper surface, it redistributes affect away from the plane of two-dimensional movement, intensifying the jumbling multiplicity of charcoal powder.

One might not always intentionally engage the intensity of the micro-movements of a loose or messy material texture or quality. In many cases, artists aim to reduce the affective impact of such material qualities by taking great care a drawing never comes in contact with another surface that smudges it, or by applying a spray fixative to hold the drawing's particulate materiality in tact. But even when regarded as an unhappy side effect, the affective intensity of material messiness is felt, irrespective of whether it is activated towards expressive potential or not. The unstable material volume of charcoal powder, the uneven surface of waxy pastels, or ink that drips or seeps through paper fibres charge the two-dimensional extensity of surfaces with durations, rhythms, and resonances that must be negotiated, even if only when preventing or covering their tracks. The intensive depth, density and thickness of charcoal particles generate multiple intensive frictions and resonances in all directions. Manning describes this volumetric intensity as a "dimensionalizing" that is "more feeling than form" which is not a doubling of form but "an intensive multiplying of infradimensionality in the moving".[10]

---

[8]   Ibid., p. 61.
[9]   Brian Massumi, *Parables for the Virtual. Movement, Affect, Sensation*, Durham / London 2002, p. 96.
[10]  Manning, Individuation (see note 7), pp. 144–145.

Manning's elaboration of the concept of the diagram, first introduced by Bacon as a material/spatial propositional milieu for painting on canvas, emphasizes the incipience that occurs in the attentiveness of and with the milieu "to the complex landings of experience in the making".[11] In the case of painting, this is a milieu of *in*-forming dynamics, which include the visible qualities of marks such as colour, texture, and movement, which are articulated with the viscosity of paint, agility with the brush or sensitivity in applying the paint, the surface dimensions and spring of the tautly stretched canvas as it meets the moving pressure of the brush as well as the memories and inhabited tendencies to movement and sensation of the painter 'in action'. The diagram, whether in painting or other expressive milieus, activates a "dance of attention" that opens towards the event or a concern for the force of the expressive iteration: "the dance of attention has a concern for the event in its unfolding", making "felt the ethos of its very process of coming to force of form".[12]

The diagram is thus always in active flux or always activates a process of emergent attunement within the ecology of its multiple layers. The body also 'becomes' within the multiple expressive potentials of the diagram. Importantly, the diagram activates what Manning refers to as the "biogrammatic" or the intensity of a folding, sensing, volumetric body surface in incipient becoming.[13] This is a process that refuses territorialisation or at least prolongs, spreads, and stretches it, in favour of sustaining the emergent midst of expressive iteration. In the process, the material surfaces that enclose territorial boundaries as well as the body surfaces activate a "body-emergent across series".[14] Manning explains the transversal intensity of biogrammatic surfacing: "In this amodal field of experience, the becoming-body as surface is its own intensive multiple movement-across. It resists moving into a body, a personalized human body. It remains instead a biogram on the transcendental field's topological surface".[15]

The biogram thus constitutes an intensive "edging into bodyness" or a movement that operates "on the edge of the liveable".[16] Therefore, in the milieu of our movements

---

[11] Ibid., p. 139.
[12] Ibid., p. 143.
[13] Manning, Individuation (see note 7), p. 60.
[14] Ibid., p. 61.
[15] Ibid., p. 60.
[16] Ibid., p. 61.

with surfaces, even the most mundane circumstances of marking a line or wiping the dust off of a surface are potentially charged with the affective intensity of the 'body surfacing', or with what can be described as the process of inhabiting the qualities and movements of material surfaces in the midst of dynamic movement and sensation. How, then, do we activate and align with the voluminous textures of everyday surfaces? In what ways is it possible to make the active emergence of merging with everyday inhabited surfaces felt as an iterative potential?

Deleuze in *The Logic of Sense* refers to Stoic thought in order to develop a concept of the surface wherein our encounter with it becomes a "facing up" with the incorporeal limit or edge wherein qualities, quantities, and states of experience become interchangeable. In the process, the surface generates a space of becoming: *"It is by following the border, by skirting the surface, that one passes from bodies to the incorporeal"*.[17] The intensive tension in the contrast between surface extensity and intensity thus poises a fluxing body towards the incorporeal event. It is in the midst of the incorporeal event that surfaces are lifted, making clear separations between subjects and objects untenable: "The event, being itself impassive, allows the active and the passive to be interchanged more easily, since it is neither the one nor the other, but rather their common result (to cut – to be cut)".[18]

To activate the biogrammatic potential of surfaces then involves redistributing dynamics of activity and passivity, volume and trajectory, as well as the speeds, scales and distributions of anticipation and causality in a way that we 'skirt the surface'. The materiality of dirt, its loose granularity, heavy abundance, qualities of absorption, as well as the complexity of its resonances across social, sanitary and inhabited ways of tending with dirt, make it an intensive, qualitative force that can generate holes, folds and turbulences in the inhabited tendencies with surfaces. Dirt infiltrates lived ecologies of experience as a felt friction in the inhabited tendencies to feeling with surfaces. In the process, it opens to the multiple potentials with which to activate surfaces as the expressive movements of a non-subjective body-becoming.

---

[17] Gilles Deleuze, *The Logic of Sense,* London 1969, pp. 8–10.

[18] Ibid., p. 8.

Granular Attention: Thinking with Dirt

To extend the dynamics of qualities and surfaces that are so visibly modulated in the instance of marking a line on paper, it is pertinent to examine the reverse process of cleaning the dust, dirt and grime off the surfaces of the living environment. Cleaning is always temporary, always limited in scope and always incomplete. Cleaning the dirt off the surfaces of a living environment is inescapable for most of the contemporary human population. Unlike the involuntary persistence of breathing, digesting or perspiring, cleaning requires attention in heavy contrast to the lightness of movements of exploration and imagination. Cleaning is always a beginning again for which the clock of inevitable dinginess starts the moment the surface is wiped. Cleaning is a gesture towards the impossible (the dirt never stops accumulating) and is thus out-of-date as soon as it is 'complete'. What is more, cleaning never begins from a position outside but is activated by the nudging pull of the immediate environment. A wipe against a surface glides into being in a relational movement that at once activates the space of the room perimeter, cleaning technique, and the intensive social and material qualities and affects of dirt. The dynamic rituals involved in cleanliness – the tending to surfaces which makes the surface rhythms of everyday existence felt, is thus a grasping flux with the inhabited past as much as the immediacy of the present.

Unlike the expressive gesture of marking a line in drawing, the tending to surfaces of cleaning tends to lack expressive intensity or, for Whitehead, the "concern the event has for its coming to subjective form".[19] Whitehead considers this concern a feeling of "immediate self-enjoyment" in the occasion of experience.[20] Instead, cleaning movements are narrowly guided according to the pre-determined orderings of everyday spaces as well as patterns of dirt accumulation or protocols for upkeep and maintenance. Cleaning activates a different kind of intensity. The movement to remove the chaotic debris of dirt, of jumbling particles or smears of grease charges the cleaning experience with dynamic qualitative resistance – movements push, lift and gather the particles rather than laying them down. Cleaning movements also concentrate and linger in accordance with the crevices where reach is restricted and thus intensified as a space with impossible dimensions, wherein dirt escapes control and containment rather

---

[19] Manning, Individuation (see note 7), p. 215.
[20] Ibid., p. 215.

than expressive emphasis. But when cleaning gestures accelerate on open surfaces like mirrors, tabletops or hard floors, they open to expression in the way that they activate graceful and dynamic extensions of the body's reach (despite the intensive pull of the looming imperative to complete the task efficiently).

Meanwhile, the status quo of the urban environment reduces the movement of dirt as much as possible by paving, containing and engineering it. But dirt always impinges and accumulates at the seams and in the crevices of the city. Dirt blows into and lingers in the corners and curbs of streets in tandem with the air currents generated by passing footsteps, vehicles and wind. Dirt erupts from the cracks in the sidewalks in pace with irregular compression patterns, the growth of plants, and the shifting fault lines of the earth. In cities that invest a great deal into managing the cleanliness and integrity of the street, it is easy to ignore the urban rhythms of dirt containment (except when under construction). Even the approaching drone of the street cleaner activates an affective sonic ecology of the city more than it does the affects associated with dynamics of dirt and cleanliness for which it was designed.

But in the urban environment the affective material qualities of dirt and waste are intensified by the lack of technical or procedural processes for removing it or when the movement of cleaning stops. This was made particularly palpable (and olfactory) in the case of Toronto's 'garbage strike' of 2009. The severity of the strike meant that the mounting surge of waste accumulation in the urban environment made the daunting task to remove it at once visible, affective and urgent. The immediate intensity of the disruptions caused by the accumulating garbage in the city meant that it eclipsed all other labour demands and social, economic and political affiliations of the two municipal branches of the Canadian Union of Public Employees (CUPE). The unmanageable physical presence of mounting garbage sparked a level of public outrage and media attention that far overshadowed every other issue. The affective weight of garbage acquired political intensity as streets, sidewalks and alleys became buried in litter and the air thick with the putrid seepages of organic waste, thus threatening to impede even the most basic rhythms of daily existence.

It becomes clear that the work of cleaning, whether of dirt or garbage, resonates with the very immediacy with which we habitually manage and tend to the habitual movements of the everyday. When the process of cleaning must stop in order to 'stand' for or represent its social value or right to compensation, economies of cleanliness transform from being invisible preservers of social and material continuity into visible, politicized symbols of resistance. In the union's political gesture of resistance, the very physical presence of sanitation workers fuses with the affective weight that is felt to obstruct the clean, smooth and efficient flow of the city. The myopic media response to the strike as well as the high level of public outrage and accusations against the union members suggest an affective intensity that goes beyond representational politics, striking an immediate nerve that gets to the heart of the intensive affects of boundary and containment of dirt and mess.

To continue with a final example of an everyday intensive surface tension with dirt, I will describe the extensity and the intensive qualities of the surface in the milieu of ploughed fields that are prepared for industrial agriculture. The affects of the dirt of the field propose a milieu of tensions, in particular that of property and erosion. The field is territory as well as economic potential for growing crops and poses a particular set of practices for managing the surface of the earth. The field surface is at once a loose and shifting mass of grains of dirt and a vast topography to be traversed. Dirt gains intensity as a surface when it acquires dimensions of place through the felt volume of its materiality. In traversing the surface of a field, whether wet or dry, the dirt of the field turns in on itself in a folding, kneading movement. The ploughed field is opened and churned in a grotesque turning of the inward to the outside. The notion of the surface of a field as a discreet plot of land is felt in stark contrast with the folding, spreading, crumbling, and absorbing qualities of dirt. The particulate materiality of the field lifts and blows beyond the pre-determined bounds of property. Property as an absolute legal concept or entity is contained, enclosed, and sellable only when it remains an abstract line on the surface of the land. But when the dust erodes, when it flows with the rain or blows with the wind, it becomes part of an uncontainable, breathable system of air currents, lifting and lowering, moving in irregular patterns that even the most sophisticated weather algorithms cannot fully anticipate – 'surfaces go airborne'.

## Crumbling at the Seams / Eroding Surfaces

The affects that emerge in the relation between dirt, dust and everyday surfaces adhere in our inhabited tendencies to attention. Dirt and dust charge the lived thresholds of experience with intensive, affecting material qualities. Although the particulate materiality of dry dirt and dust cannot be described as a sticky substance, dirt acquires intensive tack as it infiltrates sock fibres or gets stuck under fingernails. Sanding, shedding, sanitation, and cleaning all deal simultaneously with the looseness and accumulation of dirt or dust particles and the way that they are intensively distributed. Dust flows, blows and falls into patterns. Dirt obstructs shine and never holds a precisely delineated form. When powdered dirt falls, sprays of dirt fill the air as dry mist. But unlike water, dirt never has the effect of cleaning, of clearing off the grime so that a smooth ledge, table or sidewalk is seen or felt more clearly underneath. In the following works, dirt's particulate dynamics of coverage and spread, solidity and looseness, porosity and density are activated to redistribute and *in*form new intensive and expressive dynamics with the body, territory and inhabited experience.

In Robert Smithson's "Spiral Jetty" (1970 - present, Rozel Point, US), the distribution of land effectively expresses the mark of a spiral as the surrounding dug troughs fill with water. In this instance, trace-making is not an additive process as it is in marking charcoal onto a paper surface, but a digging away to make room for the surface to enter. The water, like paper, fills the spiral-shaped trough between the mud and stone spiral ridge with a smooth, flat surface, activating a dynamic contrast between the land as a movement of a mark in extensive space and as a dense, material intensity. The spiral-shaped ridge is at once a spiral gesture and architectural container, path and barrier. We feel the tension in the complexity of inhabiting the earth in a dynamic of both spatial extensity and material intensity.

Katharina Grosse's "Wunderblock", exhibited at the *Nasher Sculpture Center* (US) in 2013, also makes a particularly intensive tension between the surface and the volume of dirt contrast by spray-painting it with brightly coloured masses and loosely gestured striations. The brightness and saturation of the colours that are applied to loose piles of dirt visually smooth the surface of the dirt and seem to contain it. Though as loose and porous as the dirt pile itself, the surface appears to contain the dirt as an impermeable coating, making the surface appear smooth and cohesive (the intensity and saturation of the colour reduces the visible contrast that articulates the form of each grain of dirt, making them indistinguishable from the volume of which they take part). The slightly absorbent dirt must hold and support the paint colour, but only in so far as it never moves – any disturbance will cause bits of dirt to move or roll down the mound into which it is composed, breaking the fragile temporariness of the visual holding or unifying force of the painted surface. As witnesses we take part in the sensory metamorphoses of particulate looseness becoming intact by the visual homogeneity of the mound surface. The formal and qualitative parity between unpainted dirt and the thin, dry matte coating of the spray-paint (water, wax, paint, powder would all integrate into the dirt on a more structural level, pressing, moving or transforming its form) intensifies the dissensus involved in making the surface of the loose dirt piles felt as stable surface continuity. In installations of Grosse's work, the surfaces that are painted with intense colour seem to lift and detach from unpainted areas in the space, effectively doubling the affective surfaces of the space.

In Jean-Luc Vilmouth's "Café Little Boy" (2002, purchased by the Centre Pompidou, Paris in 2005), the powdery, dusty qualities of chalk are also activated in dynamic tension with extensity as drawn images fall out of articulation amidst accumulating layers of drawings on the wall surface. The installation space consists of a room that is covered in chalkboard wall surfaces from floor to ceiling. The installation evolves as the public is invited to write different coloured messages in chalk (while erasing those of others if necessary). As the drawings accumulate over time, the walls become thick with chalk powder. Each consecutive layer of chalk drawing distorts the previous so that the walls are filled with a chaotic mix of clearly differentiated lines and colours amidst a muddy mix of powdery colours dissolving into one another. In fact, the very condition for the newest and most shallow drawings to be visible at all is their contrast with the inarticulate visual ground of the residual drawings underneath. The installation activates a gradual sedimentation process, which opens to an emergent dynamic of qualitative material looseness and visual clarity, thereby intensifying the tension between the movements of the powdery material qualities of accumulating chalk and the extensive visual continuity and movement of the drawn marks.

In "Violin Phase from Fase: Four Movements to the Music of Steve Reich", performed at the New York *Museum of Modern Art* (MoMA) in 2011, Anne Teresa De

Keersmaeker activates surface tension by choreographing dance on a floor that is covered with sand. De Keersmaeker carves a series of precise geometric patterns through the sand with her feet, lifting the sand in a series of subtle kicks, turns, and jumps, revealing a smooth, dark floor underneath. De Keersmaeker likens the geometric precision of the choreography to "measuring the earth".[21] Meanwhile, De Keersmaeker states that the sand creates a dancing situation wherein it is "not easy to be precise".[22] The clear contrast in the work between the precision of movements that articulate extensive space and the intensive complexity of a body inhabiting space amidst the material and qualitative thickness and resistance of sand activates intensive contrast. The entire duration of the work is also intensively charged with the minimal, rhythmic and driving score of Steve Reich. The rhythm moves the piece forward as a temporal pattern or continuity but also makes the materiality of the violin strings felt as they resonate and connect the rhythmic intervals. The contrast between the qualities of the sound and its relentless forward movement parallel the tension between extensity and intensity that is activated by the dance in perfect proportion.

Please find in the following passages an account of some expressive iterations that I designed for thinking with the tension between the particulate qualities of dirt and the extensity of surfaces:

## Dirt Hand Railing

Proposition: Lift the loose powdery mark from the page so that it can be activated as a three-dimensional linearity, resurfacing the body in the immediacy of tactility and the movement of the entire body.

> The guiding form of the railing lifts and disintegrates under my touch. In the immediate tactility with the extensive surface, I feel the absorbency of its qualities meeting the porosity of my skin, I feel its grit wedging into the space under my fingernails, I become subsumed in the vibrating textures in movement. The formal details of texture numb and blur – immediate feeling emerges in pace and in the flux of movement as a hybrid sensation. Dirt powder lifts and falls – a gradual disintegration. Meanwhile, I acquire its intensive material qualities as an inhabited dynamic. I embody the extensity of movement as thickened in the dense, powdery coatings of dirt.

---

[21] MOMA 'On Line' Series. Anne Teresa de Keersmaeker, 2011 (video file), https://vimeo.com/21823379 (09/05/2016).
[22] Ibid.

Dirt Bags (dirt volume variable)

Proposition: Put dry dirt into a plain weave cloth bag and activate the permeability of the fabric to redistribute the dirt as a fine powder.

> Like pillows that contain up to a third of their volume in dust, Dirt Bags intensify the permeability of the fabric layer that holds their content. The fine mesh size of the fabric membrane slowly releases and exhales the dirt powder, depending on the degree to which the bag is agitated, leaving a spray of residue in the air and surrounding surfaces.
> Thump! (dust eddies and spreads). In the durations and rhythms of airborne swirling particles, the surface proportions of solidity, lift, smoothness and cleanliness mingle.

Dirt Sweats

Proposition: Sieve an even coating of dirt over a damp, stretched fabric membrane with a fine plain weave. Squirt water onto it from the clean side so that the dirt erodes on the other side as if sweating the skin off a surface.

> I hold the squirt bottle to the clean back side of the dirt-coated fabric and regularly squeeze the trigger (in time with my breath). The membrane quivers with the air pressure against it (like a heaving chest). The fabric finely distributes the volume of water that lands upon it. Fabric membrane, thin, permeates wetness through dryness, reducing the contrast of differential muddiness on its two-dimensional surface. The rate of water seepage sets the pace with which I visually tend to the qualities of dirt as it transitions from being a dry, matte coating to a thick and heavy mud. Dry dirt looks cakey, rough and pale, moisture creeps onto it. In its dampness, the dirt coating acquires a warm, velvety richness. Meanwhile, wet dirt shines with hard contrast and begins to distribute into micro-peaks and valleys as it passes the water through. The wettest dirt begins to fall onto itself in dense, slow drips, gathering into streaks and folding over itself into baroque pillars that are in high relief with the surface of the fabric. The intensity shifts from the visible, two-dimensional rate of spread outwards over the fabric surface to the grotesque, three-dimensional, grinding depth of the wet dirt particles.

## Dirt Blows / Wind Rally

Proposition: Cover a ping-pong table with fine dirt powder by distributing it through the fine mesh of the dirt bags and erode it from the table surface with the air pressure generated by approaching ping-pong balls.

> *Small, light air-filled ping-pong balls generate a thrust of air pressure against surfaces as they approach the ping-pong table. The balls' approach is charged with the friction and intensity of beach volleyball players sliding into sand to save the ball from touching it or the force of breath when blowing dust off an object. The bounds of 'in' and 'out', the extensive perimeter needed to measure and determine the criteria for winning a game are redistributed in the lift and spread of the dirt particles in specific patterns and trajectories. The intensive movement of extensity is redistributed in a multiple density of vectors by the qualitative volumes of dirt particles as they lift with the movement trajectory and incoming force of the ball.*

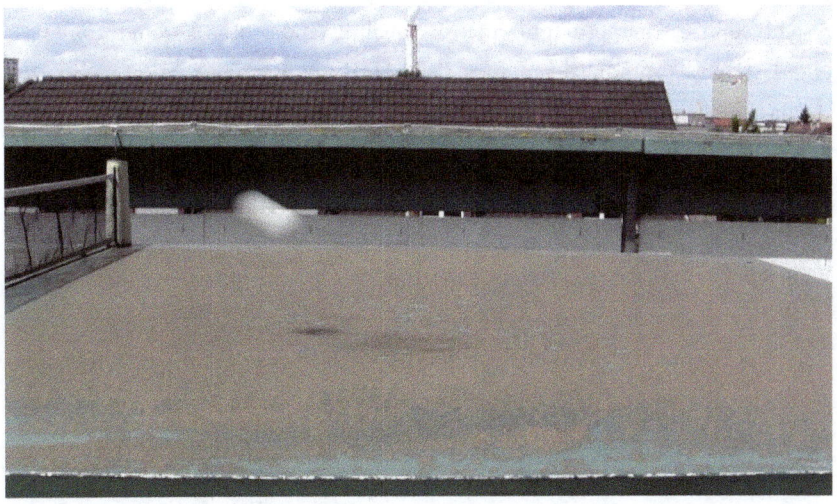

Fig. 5.1: Still from Dirt Blows / Wind Rally (2014)

## Conclusion

In a research process that activates intensity across and through multiple material, affective and conceptual vectors, form and causality are not predetermined but are *in*formed in dynamic emergence with the research process itself. Concepts, affects, and materials lift, move, and recombine in new distributions, activating the threshold wherein thought moves felt sensation and vice versa. In the case of dirt, the particulate qualities of dirt activate an intensive 'crumbling' with surfaces that lets chaos, disintegration and dispersion enter into the felt and material continuities in everyday experience. In the process of activating intensive potential with the qualities of dirt, everyday routines and materialities, thought and feeling move to meet one another, creating new expressive resonances and reiterations. Such movements emerge by modulating inhabited choreographies with the affective intensity of dirt. Movements between thought and sensation are also activated in the writing process – words are assembled and reassembled in an attempt to grip intensive qualities and contrasts from the volumes and the intensive multiplicity of immediate experience. But only some of the affective qualities of dirt and dust are activated in specific articulations with words, meaning, and experience. Others necessarily slip through, remaining ungraspable, unspeakable or inexpressible in an undifferentiated but dense multiple potential. Meanwhile, the writing process lifts and loosens words by activating them towards new compositions with significations that traverse fields and registers of experience. In the movement to articulate the specific qualities of intensive contrast from within the midst of such chaotic qualitative distributions, whether linguistic, material or otherwise, the multiple potential of expression makes itself felt. In the process, bodies as well as everyday surfaces well into newly collective hybrid and expressive distributions.

# Bibliography

De Brabandere, Nicole, Intensive Resistances. Choreographies for intensive lining in materiality, movement, space, duration and volume, under review, 2015.

Deleuze, Gilles, *The Logic of Sense,* London 1969.

Langer, Susanne K., *Feeling and Form. A Theory of Art Developed from Philosophy in a New Key,* New York 1953.

Massumi, Brian, *Parables for the Virtual. Movement, Affect, Sensation,* Durham / London 2002.

Massumi, Brian, The Thinking-Feeling of What Happens. A Semblance of Conversation, in: *Inflexions,* no. 1 (2008), http://www.senselab.ca/inflexions/n1_massumihtml.html (09/05/2016).

Manning, Erin, *Always more than One. Individuation's Dance,* Durham / London 2013.

MOMA 'On Line' Series. Anne Teresa de Keersmaeker, 2011 (video file), https://vimeo.com/21823379 (09/05/2016).

Valéry, Paul, *Degas Danse Dessin,* Paris 1938.

Whitehead, Alfred North, *Process and Reality. An Essay in Cosmology,* New York 1978.

# Image Credits

Fig. 5.1: Still from © Nicole de Brabandere, Dirt Blows / Wind Rally, video file (2014), https://www.youtube.com/watch?v=0-wu-TZURaw (09/05/2016).

# Dynamics of Medieval Production.
# The Grail Motif in the *Roman de Perceforest*

*Noémie Chardonnens*

The *Perceforest* is an anonymous French prose romance dating back to the late Middle Ages; the likeliest date for its composition is in the 14th century.[1] This puts the writing of the text well after the composition of such Arthurian prose romances as the *Lancelot-Grail* or the *Tristan* cycle; however, this vast romance could easily serve as an introduction to the Arthurian tradition on its own. It inclusively foregrounds the Arthurian epic in a description of the life of King Arthur and his knights' pre-Christian ancestors, who are all introduced as descendants of Alexander the Great. It also recounts the story of pre-Arthurian Britain, from its origins to the beginning of Christianity, which is dated to Joseph of Arimathea's voyage to England, carrying the Grail.[2] It draws on the Arthurian French tradition (in particular the *Lancelot-Grail* and the prose *Tristan*) as well as on the *Alexander* romances and medieval historiography as developed by Geoffrey of Monmouth. Along with the storytelling, the *Perceforest* author engages in a genuine poetics of external and internal repetition, multiplying references to previous texts in different branches of the tradition and importing entire parts of other texts into his own.[3] In this way, he combines fictional universes[4] that are distinct *a priori*, with the result that the *Perceforest* appears as a hybrid text presenting

---

[1] The six books of the *Perceforest* have been edited by Gilles Roussineau; cf. Gilles Roussineau, *Le Perceforest*, Geneva 1987–2014. The *Perceforest* was probably written in the 14th century and was revived at the 15th-century Burgundian court; cf. Gilles Roussineau, Réflexions sur la genèse du Perceforest, in: *Perceforest. Un roman arthurien et sa réception*, ed. by Christine Ferlampin-Acher, Rennes 2012, pp. 255–267; cf. also Christine Ferlampin-Acher, *Perceforest et Zéphir. Propositions autour d'un récit arthurien bourguignon*, Geneva 2010, where she argues for a later date of composition in the 15th century, when it was written for Philip the Bold, Duke of Burgundy.

[2] It describes itself as a "cronique d'Angleterre"; cf. Christine Ferlampin-Acher, Perceforest et le roman. "Or oyez fable, non fable mais hystoire vraye selon la cronique", in: *Études françaises*, vol. 41 (2006), pp. 39–61.

[3] With respect to this poetic of borrowings and repetitions, both at the internal and the external levels, cf. Noémie Chardonnens, *L'autre du même. Emprunts et répétitions dans le Roman de Perceforest*, Geneva 2015.

[4] The concept of a 'fictional universe' denotes an imaginary world as it is constructed by the story; cf. Thomas Pavel, *Univers de la fiction*, Paris 1988.

interfering narrative materials.⁵ By applying our analytic tools to these borrowings, we can nearer approach the dynamics of text production. In spite of the fact that the sources used by the author are not explicitly identified, it is possible to trace them more or less precisely.⁶ Pursuing these traces in order to explore the work's offstage context will give us useful insight into what the *Perceforest* author was doing with the tradition he consciously aligned himself with, hopefully enriching our reading of this massive text. In this article, we intend to highlight the relevance of specific narrative details to the process of text construction.

The concept of 'detail' has been discussed at length in the field of literary studies. Roland Barthes defined a detail as a non-significant item, of which the lone function is to denote, by its very insignificance, an external reality.⁷ Michel Charles has objected to the grounds of Barthes' theory, since whether or not something qualifies as a detail in the Barthesian sense is a relative notion, depending on the subjective interpretation of a given reader. While some readers might consider a given item a detail, others might see it as filled with significance. As a result, Charles argues that the very notion of detail is "simply impractical"⁸ and should therefore be discarded. While this argument shows that there is no rigid criterion for identifying the details for all readers in all texts, it does not logically implode the category of detail – it merely consigns to it a formal status that will impinge differently on different readers and, even more, within certain institutionalized reading regimes. In other words, that some or even all readers pick out a different set of details simply points to the fact that details and signifying elements are mixed in different ways according to dif-

---

⁵  This hybrid character is typical of late medieval storybook production and reflects the need for both the renewal of the tradition and a strong desire for narrative closure; cf. Richard Trachsler, *Disjointures – Conjointures*. Étude *sur l'interférence des matières narratives dans la littérature du Moyen* Âge, Tübingen / Basel 2000, especially pp. 239–281, which focus on the *Perceforest*.

⁶  Given the transmission conditions of medieval literary works, it is obviously difficult to isolate a precise text and even more a precise manuscript; cf. Patrick Moran, Le texte médiéval existe-t-il? Mouvance et identité textuelle dans les fictions du XIIIᵉ siècle, in: *Le Texte médiéval*. De la *variante à la recréation,* ed. by Anne Salamon, Anne Rouchebouet and Cécile Le Cornec Rochelois, Paris 2012. In this article we are not claiming to identify a precise source with which the *Perceforest* author worked, but rather aim at identifying the reworking of certain narrative sequences on the basis of salient stylistic and semantic elements, even if this leads us to multiple possible sources.

⁷  Roland Barthes, L'Effet de réel, in: *Communications*, vol. 11 (1968), pp. 84–89.

⁸  Michel Charles, Le Sens du détail, in: *Poétique*, vol. 116 (1998), pp. 387–424. Transl. by the author.

ferent ways of reading. Accordingly, then, the detail bears a very strong evidentiary witness to the tracing of different patterns of reading across a tradition as a sort of 'fingerprint'. From that perspective, the concept of a detail constitutes a fruitful tool for medievalists, who are dealing with a literary corpus that turns rewriting practices into a genuine aesthetic[9], enabling them to define an adaptation technique[10], to grasp a description[11], or, more broadly, to provide insight with respect to the reception of a given text by another author.[12]

Indeed, to the extent that a detail is defined as a minor part of a whole[13], a careful examination of the selection of the respectively retained and non-retained items in a borrowing (which can quote literally from another text or rewrite the sequence it is appropriating) yields substantial information with regards to the way an author understands and appreciates the original texts. The retained items were most likely assessed as relevant, whereas the non-retained items were regarded as details that are non-constitutive of the narrative framework. Hence, depending on the rewriting convention, an item may be demoted to the status of a minor part of a whole, or, on the contrary, be promoted to the rank of constitutive element, which may in turn introduce discrepancies or contradictions within the original sequence. The observed gaps in the repetition or omission of details need therefore be regarded as purposeful and productive reinterpretations.[14] This observation agrees with Daniel Arasse, who, in his exposition of the 'detail' in art history, goes back to the distinction made in Italian between two types of detail:

---

[9]  Emmanuèle Baumgartner, *La Harpe et l'épée. Tradition et renouvellement dans le Tristan en prose*, Paris 1990, p. 25.

[10] Astrid Guillaume, Ponthus et la belle Sidoyne et les rédactions A et B de Pontus und Sidonia. Importance du détail/ détails d'importance pour l'étude comparée médiévale, in: Études romanesques, vol. 7 (2002), p. 49–62.

[11] See the notion of the 'détail gothique' developed by Delphine Burghgraeve relative to Pasiphaé's portraits: Delphine Burghgraeve, De l'accident poétique à l'essence allégorique. Le détail gothique dans les portraits de Pasiphaé (De l'Ovide moralisé à la Bouquechardière de Jean de Courcy), in: *CRMH*, 2015.

[12] Ibid.; cf. also the other contributions about the concept of 'detail' in this issue.

[13] Études *romanesques*, Vol. 7: *Le parti pris du détail. Enjeux narratifs et descriptifs*, Caen 2002.

[14] Pierre-Olivier Dittmar, Lapsus figurae. Notes sur l'erreur iconographique, in: *Quand l'image relit le texte. Regards croisés sur les manuscrits médiévaux*, ed. by Sandrine Hériché-Pradeau and Maud Pérez-Simon, Paris 2013, pp. 319–335.

The detail *particolare* is a small part of a figure, object or set [...]. Everything would be simple – and this book would have no point – if the detail was not also, inevitably, *dettaglio*, meaning that it is the result or the trace of the action of the person who 'does the detailing' – whether this be the painter or the spectator [...]. The detail *dettaglio* can only be defined and grasped in as much as the 'program of action' eventually leaves its trace in the tableau.[15]

With respect to the literary area and the medieval practices of rewriting, the treatment of the detail within a reworking, whether it turns out to be demoted or promoted, as regards the degree of prominence it held in its source, provides us with a way of illuminating the interpretation grid, which the author or authors follow and project, in as much as they are also readers of the original text.

This paper will track the trajectory of specific retained details that are taken from several source texts within the *Perceforest*. I will determine which ones are nothing but minor parts of a whole (i. e. *particolari*) and which are important elements of a whole (i. e. *dettagli*), thus revealing the way the author conceives his project and the intentions that are encoded in the artwork. I shall focus on borrowings involving the Grail, in order to spot indications of the author's intentions regarding this particular object. As we shall see, the *Perceforest* author endows this object with an unexpected role in a text dealing with the Christianization process in Great Britain, revealing a clear tension in the text between variously discordant motives: respect for tradition, desire for completeness, and a need for originality.

## The Grail in the *Perceforest*: Minimal Presence

Since it ends with an account of the Christianization of Great Britain, the *Perceforest* cannot ignore the Grail. It recounts the early history of the object, focusing especially on its voyage across Great Britain in the hands of Joseph of Arimathea and of his companions. The Grail appears in several of the borrowings from another text, namely

---

[15] Daniel Arrasse, *Le Détail. Pour une histoire rapprochée de la peinture,* Paris 1992, p. 11. Transl. by the author. Cf. also Georges Didi-Huberman, *Devant l'image,* Paris 1990, especially pp. 296–314, where he opposes the 'detail' to the *'pan'* (for an English version, cf. Georges Didi-Huberman, *Confronting Images,* Philadelphia 2005, pp. 229–271); Georges Didi-Huberman, L'art de ne pas décrire. Une aporie du détail chez Vermeer, in: *La part de l'oeil,* vol. 2 (1986), p. 102–119. Note that the importation in the field of text analysis of a notion initially framed for the study of the image does not aim to at reducing one language to another, but rather at exploiting a theoretical similarity that has already been highlighted by several scholars. Cf., for instance, Sandrine Hériché-Pradeau / Maud Pérez-Simon (eds.), *Quand l'image relit le texte. Regards croisés sur les manuscrits médiévaux,* Paris 2013, pp. 11–38.

the *Estoire del Saint Graal*[16], under the name of "Sainct Greal"[17], "Sainct Vaissel"[18] and, above all, "vaissel".[19] These choices emphasize the *Perceforest* author's interest in the object's materiality. In the *Perceforest*, the Grail fulfils a nurturing function in the first place: it allows for the feeding of genuine faithful in the episode of the miraculous catch[20], it ensures Joseph's survival in his prison[21], it holds Mordrain alive in Corbenic[22], and it supplies the newly converted of Terre Forreine with a meal.[23] But the materiality is not important in itself: It is rather the divine character with which the object is endowed that gives it its narrative importance. Its nurturing powers are always related to God, while the term "vaissel" frequently occurs in combination with the adjective "holy". This choice is not trivial: The Grail is thus presented above all as a vehicle of divine grace and not as a marvellous object per se. The *Perceforest* author clearly has more interest in the British Christianization process than in the marvels surrounding the Grail. As noted by Christine Ferlampin-Acher, the *Perceforest* "got away from the Grail, not by excluding it, which would have been, given its project, inconceivable, but rather by avoiding integrating it directly".[24]

This characteristic is nicely illustrated by the treatment of the sequences originally featured in the *Estoire del Saint Graal*, since the Grail's importance is greatly minimized in these reprises, especially by the summary of the miraculous catch by Alain le Gros.[25] The passage allows us to draw a clear link between the *Perceforest* and the *Estoire*, since the pond where Alain le Gros makes his miraculous catch in the *Estoire* is said, in the *Perceforest*, to be the result of the overflow of the Fontaine Venimeuse. Indeed, the *Perceforest* narrator explains that the pond will later be the location of a

---

[16] Jean-Paul Ponceau (ed.), *Estoire del Saint Graal*, Paris 1997. This text also contains an account of Britain's Christianization, focusing on Joseph of Arimathea and his companions.

[17] Roussineau, Perceforest (see note 1), IV.II.896–897; VI.II.904.

[18] Ibid., IV.II.897.

[19] Ibid., IV.II.898; VI.II.819–820.

[20] Ibid., IV.II.897–898.

[21] Ibid., VI.II.1014.

[22] Ibid., VI.II.1095.

[23] Ibid., VI.II.1019.

[24] Ferlampin-Acher, Roman (see note 2), p. 49. Transl. by the author.

[25] Mireille Séguy, La tentation du pastiche dans l'Estoire del saint Graal. Retraire, refaire, défaire la Bible, in: Études françaises, vol. 46 (2010), pp. 68–71.

miracle, which is what motivates, in the *Perceforest* book IV[26], a blatant borrowing from the *Estoire*.[27] The general pattern of the passage, its main parts and the ordering of the original sequence are preserved. Nonetheless, a couple of referential elements are missing: The *Perceforest* does not mention some characters and does not describe some locations; further, the *Perceforest* author replaces most of the dialogs with indirect discourse. These elements are demoted to the rank, then, of the kind of useless detail that can be disposed of without bothering the reader. Yet, the scope of the passage is not thereby diminished. The *Perceforest* author chooses to selectively borrow from the sequence that he is embedding in his own work, which allows him to get back quickly to the intrigue that interests him by focusing on nothing but the elements that he thought to be indispensable.

However, one specific omission does more than just edit the text from which it borrows: namely the omission of the role played by the Grail itself.[28] The miraculous catch is, in the *Perceforest,* a gift from God exclusively.[29] This omission constitutes more than a decision about a dispensable detail: It is a positive production trace, clearly the result of an authorial decision. This shows how complex the intertextual dimension of borrowing really is. When a specific element that was clearly of central significance in the source material is deleted or radically modified, we have to look at the borrowing as a selective transfer of meaning to the new text, re-structuring the borrowing to better align it with the author's purposes (which, in this case, consist of the focus on the Christianization of Britain and on God's direct powers rather than on the powers of the Grail). Here we can see what qualifies as a 'detail' is a relative notion, based on a subjective interpretation of the original text; the way we interpret its use helps us to see what the author is up to in his subsequent treatment of the passage. For the *Perceforest* author, the Holy Grail and its role in the miraculous catch are treated as a contingent detail, while for the *Estoire* author, it is a central part of the story.

---

[26] Roussineau, Perceforest (see note 1), IV.II.896–898.

[27] Ponceau, Estoire (see note 16), 774–779.

[28] Ibid., 779.

[29] Roussineau, Perceforest (see note 1), IV.II.898.

Obviously, the intent of the *Perceforest* author is to minimize the Grail's importance in pre-Arthurian Britain. So we can expect that the *Perceforest* author will treat other appearances of the Grail similarly, which proves to be the case: In other borrowings from texts in which the Holy Grail plays a role, the *Perceforest* author consistently minimizes its importance at the price of having to modify pre-existing stories, as for instance in the case of the journey of Alain le Gros in Terre Foraine, an episode occurring at the end of the *Perceforest* book VI[30], which again takes its cues from a sequence in the *Estoire del Saint Graal*.[31] The standing of Gallafur II of Terre Foraine is here clearly raised. Gallafur II manifests his interest in the new religion and converts, finally, to Christianity, proposing to similarly christianize his subjects. It has to be emphasized that this conversion constitutes the end point of a slow evolution that is carefully described through the length of *Perceforest*'s six books.[32] The character is the last link in a long and carefully described chain of pre-Christian heroes who get progressively closer to Christianity.

The borrowing of Gallafur II's baptism episode is also subject to editing and reinterpretation. In the *Estoire,* Gallafur's conversion is solely motivated by the fact that he wants to be cured of leprosy.[33] The Grail plays a crucial role here, since it is emphasized that Gallafur owes his recovery directly to the power of the Grail. The *Perceforest* author's interpretation of this episode is radically different, in that, while he, too, describes Gallafur's interest in the Christian religion, he has Gallafur explicitly wonder about the possibility of resurrection and the idea of virginal conception more than about being cured of his disease. Fully convinced by Alain's answers, he asks for baptism, which is presented in this version as an act of faith. He is, however, indifferent to his own recovery: What matters to him is his new religion, which is also directly related to his previous beliefs:

---

[30] Roussineau, Perceforest (see note 1), VI.II.1011–1096.
[31] Ponceau, Estoire (see note 16), 879–884; Gallafur II is here named Galifès.
[32] About this evolution, cf. Jeanne Lods, *Le Roman de Perceforêt. Origines, composition, caractères, valeur et influence,* Geneva 1951, pp. 246–258; Jane Taylor, Reason and Faith in the Roman de Perceforest, in: *Studies in Medieval Literature and Language in Memory of Frederick Whitehead,* ed. by William Rothwell et al., Manchester 1973, pp. 303–322; Jeanne Lods, Faith and Austerity. The Ecclesiology of the Roman de Perceforest, in: *The Changing Face of Arthurian Romance. Essays on Arthurian Prose Romances in Memory of Cedric E. Pickford,* ed. by Alison Adams, Wolfeboro 1986, pp. 47–65.
[33] Ponceau, Estoire (see note 16), 559–560.

> Saint homme, dist le roy, s'il estoit ainsi que tu dis, je vouldroie croire en celluy vray Crucefié. Et desja a long temps que j'ay creu ou Dieu Incongneu que je tenoie a venir selon les secretz du ciel, si pense que ce soit celluy Dieu dont tu parles. [...] je croy fermement en lui et en sa venue sans espreuve. Or me guarisse s'il lui plaist et, s'il ne luy plaist, je n'en suis mie digne.[34]

Gallafur's full recovery is not even mentioned in the text. By reworking the borrowed text, the *Perceforest* author modifies the motivation underlying Gallafur's conversion, giving rise to a new interpretation of the episode.[35] The Holy Grail thus becomes a simply decorative item that plays no effective role. In other words, it is demoted to the status of detail *particolare,* endowed with a purely accessory role. This must have been surprising for a readership that was probably familiar with earlier versions of the story. This trace of the decisions that went into the textual production of the borrowed sequences reveals the author's intention clearly to a knowledgeable audience: He is aiming at emphasizing God's power rather than the role of the Grail.

### The Role of the Grail in Joseph of Arimathea's Imprisonment

In the *Perceforest,* the Holy Grail is given an actantial prominence in one single case only. Shortly before Gallafur's baptism, Alain le Gros tells how Joseph of Arimathea was imprisoned after Jesus' death and how he survived in prison with Christ's bowl. While the overall passage is significantly abridged in comparison to its source, the scene where Joseph receives the Grail from Christ gives rise to a detailed borrowing focusing on the Grail. In regard to the *Estoire* version, we can speak here of an 'amplification' process:

> *Estoire:*
> maintenant ke ses cors fu issus du sepulcre, vint [Jésus] a lui en la chartre ou il estoit et si li porta por compaignie et pour confort la sainte escüele que Joseph avoit ostoïe en sa maison, a tout le sanc qu'il avoit recuelli. Et quant Joseph le vit, si en fu mout liés. Et lors seut il vraiement ke ch'estoit Diex, si ne s'en repentoit mie de son service, anchois avoit tel joie ke il ne li chaloit de la prison, puis qu'il avoit le confort et la compaignie de son Signour.[36]

> *Perceforest:*
> [Jésus] meismes le [Joseph d'Arimathie] vint visiter en la prison ou les Juifz l'avoient enfermé pource que de la croix le despendy et qu'il porta tesmoing de sa resurrection. Et sachés qu'il ne fu plus de doulceur ne de pitié que d'ouir racompter a Joseph comme doulcement Jhesus le conforta la ou il estoit emprisonné sans clareté. Dont Joseph fu si famillier a Jhesus qu'il luy requist que laissier lui voulsist

---

[34] Roussineau, Perceforest (see note 1), VI.II.821–822.
[35] For a detailed analysis of Gallafur's conversion, cf. Chardonnens, Même (see note 3), chapter 5.1.
[36] Ponceau, Estoire (see note 16), 37.

aucune chose a quoy il se peust conforter en celle prison dont il ne cuidoit jamais partir. Et Jhesus lui dist lors "Joseph tu partiras d'icy plus tost que tu ne penses mais demandes ce que tu veulz avoir pour toy consoler en ceste prison. – Sire, dist Joseph, se je povoie avoir le vaissel ou l'aignel fu mis devant vous le jeudy absolut et ou vous le veistes dispenser avec voz disciples, il m'est advis que jamais n'auroie dissette ne chose qui me peust grever. Il est en ma maison car je l'achetay au seigneur de l'ostel ou vous fesistes vostre cene pour le grant desir que j'euz d'avoir aucune chose ou vous eussiez atouchié". Adont luy respondy Jhesus "Joseph, et tu l'auras". Et tantost aprés, Joseph le vey en son geron, si jetta le vaissel telle clareté par la divine voulenté que la charte en fu toute enluminee.[37]

The amplification reflects the *Perceforest* author's emphasis on the Grail in this case. The author retains the fact that the Grail provides Joseph with food in prison and how it crucially contributes to his survival. But his narrative amplification of the details that are cursory in his source is consistent with the intention of establishing a much denser and specified pre-history to the Arthurian tradition. Indeed, the text ends with the announcement of King Arthur's world. Here, the Grail serves as a transitional occasion that connects *Perceforest*'s fictional world with King Arthur's world and in the end emphasizes them to be one and the same. The Grail is here clearly a *dettaglio*, i. e. a significant detail that is not only retained but given a new affordance, in as much as the passage in which it figures reveals the direction in which the author is taking the text, with an unexpected turn at the end of the account. This is confirmed by the revelation made by Jesus to the future prisoner. While the *Estoire* emphasizes the relations between Joseph and Christ, the *Perceforest* focuses on the intervention of the saviour on the Grail:

> *Estoire:*
> et [Jésus] dist que bien fust il seürs qu'il [Joseph] ne morroit pas en la prison ains en istroit tous sains et tous saus, ne ja mal ne doleur n'i avroit; et si seroit tous jours en sa compaignie; et quant il en istroit, il tourneroit a mervelle tout le mont qui le verroit; et aprés seroit ses nons portés en estranges lieus et par lui et par ses oirs; mais encore n'estoit pas li termes ke il en issist.[38]

> *Perceforest:*
> saches qu'en brief terme tu [Joseph] partiras de ceste prison et porteras tesmoingnage de ma resurrection et te couvendra moult souffrir pour exaulcer ma foy. Et en tous lieux que tu soies garny de ce vaissel et tu le vueilles regarder en vraie foy et bonne creance, tu seras saoul de boire et de mengier de autelz boires et mengiers que ton cœur desirra sans gloutonnie ou convoitise, et autel avront ceulx qui seront en ta compaignie purs et nets de pechiés et desirans d'exaulcer ma loy. Et pareille vertu avra le vaissel en la main de celluy a qui tu le lesceras aprés, mais qu'il soit tel que je t'ay dit devant.[39]

---

[37] Roussineau, Perceforest (see note 1), Ars. 3494, fol. 369v–370r.

[38] Ponceau, Estoire (see note 16), 37.

[39] Roussineau, Perceforest (see note 1), VI.II.820.

The change from the indirect discourse of the *Estoire* to the direct speech in *Perceforest* illustrates how the perception of the detail is itself subject to textual devices that can make it more or less immediate. Besides, the parallel drawn by Jesus between Joseph of Arimathea and the Grail allows the author, who has been amplifying the role of the Grail (in as much as it has "pareille vertu"), to ultimately discard it from the central themes of the *Perceforest* history as redundant, since its place can be taken by Joseph. Thus, the Grail surfaces in a circumscribed dialogical sequence, which, by summarizing all the pertinent information the reader needs to know, also gives us the reason why this object will not be at the centre of the plot. Once Alain's account is completed, the Grail is immediately displaced in order to leave room for Christianity.

What follows in the text nicely illustrates this point. The subsequent three distinct passages that report on Joseph of Arimathea's imprisonment at the end of the *Perceforest* all omit any mention of the Grail.[40] They simply stick to the tradition represented by the Gospel of Nicodemus, which diverges from the *Estoire* in that respect.[41]

The brief emphasis on the Grail as a significant detail in the first account of Joseph's imprisonment stems from the *Perceforest* author's encyclopaedic ambition to give a complete account of the history of Arthur and his Knights. Surely, the author was aware that the audience of the work would expect some mention of the Grail, which was closely associated with his subject matter in the tradition. The same holds for the mention of the vessel in the last lines of the text, where Alain le Gros announces what follows:

---

[40] A brief mention refers to the *Gospel of Nicodemus* (account of Gallafur II to his ancestors; ibid., VI.II.1025), just before a borrowed sequence of the *Gospel of Nicodemus* that presents Joseph freed by Christ (ibid., VI.II.1047). A summary of this episode, again inspired by the *Gospel of Nicodemus*, appears in Nathanael's account to a sailor (ibid., VI.II.1069). About the presence of the apocrypha in the *Perceforest*, cf. Noémie Chardonnens, De l'apocryphe à la fiction. L'intégration de l'*Evangile de Nicodème* dans le *Roman de Perceforest*, in: *Perceforest. Un roman arthurien et sa réception*, ed. by Christine Ferlampin-Acher, Rennes 2012, pp. 87–100.

[41] In the Middle Ages, two main traditions coexist with respect to the imprisonment of Joseph of Arimathea. One is illustrated in the *Gospel of Nicodemus* and describes a very short imprisonment period without mentioning the Grail at all. Another tradition finds its way into the *Estoire del Saint Graal*, where Joseph of Arimathea is said to have spent forty years in prison and entirely owes his survival to the Grail, which he received from Christ himself.

> Et sachiés que ou temps advenir pour luy [Mordrain] trouver, sera faitte mainte queste, mainte chevallerie et mainte adventure achievee dont il sera grant renommee, car ce lieu icy est estrange et incongneu de autres paiis. Et toutefois y gist a achiever la plus haulte adventure et la plus sainte du roiaulme de la Grant Bretaigne. – Sire, dist Arfasen, eureuz sera celluy qui ce achievra. – Sire, dist Alain, vous dittes vray car il couvient qu'il soit aourné de toutes bonnes vertus.[42]

Here we have the announcement of the Grail quest, recuperating a motif that is central to the Arthurian universe. With the arrival of Galahad, the reader is now prepared to link the *Perceforest* to the *Lancelot-Graal*. Thus, the Grail goes from functioning, generally, as a contingent detail to becoming a narratively central fact in the legend that the *Perceforest* points to.

In the light of this ending, let us return to the *Perceforest* author's skill in reworking his borrowed material to make the mentions of the Grail subject to his theme. On the one hand, the Grail is put aside, omitted as we have seen from many of the borrowed passages where, in the sources, it appeared, and even where it is not omitted, demoted to the rank of *particolari*. On the other hand, the object is carefully integrated into the narrative and its mention qualifies as a *dettaglio*. The author's use of the Grail functions as a way of drawing the reader's attention to familiar incidents in the Arthurian legends in new ways, according to the author's overall intention. We can hence regard the *Perceforest* writing process as a way of conferring on a pre-existing fictional universe a new signification, which gains its effect by playing with the readership's expectations. Readers are thus put in a situation, in which their enjoyment of the text is a mixture of discovering new elements in the familiar as well as familiar items and patterns juxtaposed with the new. After carefully examining the borrowings of items retained or omitted from the original source(s), we have a much better understanding of how the *Perceforest* author was positioning himself in the tradition of these previous texts. The author seizes on the fact that the Grail in these texts is of central importance and surprises and challenges his audience by unexpectedly lowering the status of the Grail (at least in most cases) even as he fully aligns himself with his textual tradition. The reader's pleasure, then, does not only come from the familiar story, but from its treatment – from unexpected variations and the disguises thrown over expected elements. The mentions of sacred materials, such as the Grail, are used to develop a story that dynamically and constantly reshapes their signification. Thereby, the *Perceforest*

---

[42] Roussineau, Perceforest (see note 1), VI.II.906–907.

author places himself both with his content and with his style within the Arthurian tradition, where, to quote Emmanuèle Baumgartner,

> the reader's pleasure does not stem from the discovery of any *novelté* (novelty), but from the *renovelement* (renewal), more or less skillfully carried out, and from the way in which each piece of writing sorts and lays out the inherited material.[43]

The treatment of details plays a central role within the process of renewal, allowing for faithfully respecting the tradition of the initial source – and thus fulfilling the audience's expectations – or, on the contrary, introducing new elements (either positively, or by omitting old ones) and thus challenging the audience to rethink its former reception of this material. The effect of this is to lend the author a certain authority in shaping his own identity. The handling of details provides a deep insight into the machinery of this text's production and therefore cannot be ignored. It is indeed precisely because of its relative character – the elbow room allowed by the formal duality of the detail, which can be made to be significant or contingent depending on what the author is trying to convey in the text –, that the notion of detail allows us to delineate the trajectory of textual decisions that went into the production of the text and, indirectly, to access the off-stage process of text production. Of course, this is made infinitely simpler when, as is the case for most medieval literary works, we can look for borrowings from earlier sources or traditions and sift them for the editing process through which they were reworked. Hence, the study of details uncovers a process of revaluation of the tradition that might impact on the reception of both the original and of the new texts. In this sense, the treatment of detail truly constitutes an intimate mark of authorial investment[44], requiring a careful interpretation by the responsive reader and inviting the scholar to the task of source research in order to apprehend the dynamics of textual production.

---

[43] Baumgartner, Harpe (see note 9), p. 26. Transl. by the author. On that kind of reader's pleasure, cf. also Roland Barthes, *Le Plaisir du texte*, Paris 1973, pp. 55–59.

[44] Burghgraeve, Accident (see note 11).

# Bibliography

Arrasse, Daniel, *Le Détail. Pour une histoire rapprochée de la peinture*, Paris 1992.

Barthes, Roland, *Le Plaisir du texte*, Paris 1973.

Barthes, Roland, L'Effet de réel, in: *Communications*, vol. 11 (1968), pp. 84–89.

Baumgartner, Emmanuèle, *La Harpe et l'épée. Tradition et renouvellement dans le Tristan en prose*, Paris 1990.

Burghgraeve, Delphine, De l'accident poétique à l'essence allégorique. Le détail gothique dans les portraits de Pasiphaé (De l'Ovide moralisé à la Bouquechardière de Jean de Courcy), in: *CRMH*, 2015.

Chardonnens, Noémie, *L'autre du même. Emprunts et répétitions dans le Roman de Perceforest*, Geneva 2015.

Chardonnens, Noémie, De l'apocryphe à la fiction. L'intégration de l'*Evangile de Nicodème* dans le *Roman de Perceforest*, in: *Perceforest. Un roman arthurien et sa réception*, ed. by Christine Ferlampin-Acher, Rennes 2012, pp. 87–100.

Charles, Michel, Le Sens du détail, in: *Poétique*, vol. 116 (1998), pp. 387–424.

Didi-Huberman, Georges, *Confronting Images*, Philadelphia 2005.

Didi-Huberman, Georges, *Devant l'image*, Paris 1990.

Didi-Huberman, Georges, L'art de ne pas décrire. Une aporie du détail chez Vermeer, in: *La part de l'oeil*, vol. 2 (1986), pp. 102–119.

Dittmar, Pierre-Olivier, Lapsus figurae. Notes sur l'erreur iconographique, in: *Quand l'image relit le texte. Regards croisés sur les manuscrits médiévaux*, ed. by Sandrine Hériché-Pradeau and Maud Pérez-Simon, Paris 2013, pp. 319–335.

*Études romanesques, Vol. 7: Le parti pris du détail. Enjeux narratifs et descriptifs*, Caen 2002.

Ferlampin-Acher, Christine, *Perceforest et Zéphir. Propositions autour d'un récit arthurien bourguignon*, Geneva 2010.

Ferlampin-Acher, Christine (ed.), *Perceforest. Un roman arthurien et sa réception*, Rennes 2012.

Ferlampin-Acher, Christine, Perceforest et le roman. "Or oyez fable, non fable mais hystoire vraye selon la cronique", in: *Études françaises*, vol. 41 (2006), pp. 39–61.

Guillaume, Astrid, Ponthus et la belle Sidoyne et les rédactions A et B de Pontus und Sidonia. Importance du détail/détails d'importance pour l'étude comparée médiévale, in: *Études romanesques*, vol. 7 (2002), pp. 49–62.

Lods, Jeanne, *Le Roman de Perceforêt. Origines, composition, caractères, valeur et influence*, Geneva 1951.

Lods, Jeanne, Faith and Austerity. The Ecclesiology of the Roman de Perceforest, in: *The Changing Face of Arthurian Romance. Essays on Arthurian Prose Romances in Memory of Cedric E. Pickford*, ed. by Alison Adams, Wolfeboro 1986, pp. 47–65.

Moran, Patrick, Le texte médiéval existe-t-il? Mouvance et identité textuelle dans les fictions du XIIIe siècle, in: *Le Texte medieval. De la variante à la recréation*, ed. by Anne Salamon, Anne Rouchebouet and Cécile Le Cornec Rochelois, Paris 2012.

Pavel, Thomas, *Univers de la fiction*, Paris 1988.

Ponceau, Jean-Paul (ed.), *Estoire del Saint Graal*, Paris 1997.

Roussineau, Gilles, *Le Perceforest*, Geneva 1987–2014.

Roussineau, Gilles, Réflexions sur la genèse du Perceforest, in: *Perceforest. Un roman arthurien et sa réception*, ed. by Christine Ferlampin-Acher, Rennes 2012, pp. 255–267.

Séguy, Mireille, La tentation du pastiche dans l'Estoire del saint Graal. Retraire, refaire, défaire la Bible, in: *Études françaises*, vol. 46 (2010), pp. 68–71.

Taylor, Jane, Reason and Faith in the Roman de Perceforest, in: *Studies in Medieval Literature and Language in Memory of Frederick Whitehead*, ed. by William Rothwell et al., Manchester 1973, pp. 303–322.

Trachsler, Richard, *Disjointures – Conjointures. Étude sur l'interférence des matières narratives dans la littérature du Moyen Âge*, Tübingen / Basel 2000.

# The 'Unexpected' in the Context of Philosophy and the Arts as Taught at 16th- and 17th-Century Academic Institutions[1]

*Joseph S. Freedman*

During the 16th- and 17th centuries, instruction in philosophy and the arts served as a basic component of school and university curricula in Western, Northern, Southern, and Central Europe.[2] During these two centuries, European universities offered instruction within up to four faculties: the Arts Faculty and the three higher faculties (jurisprudence, medicine, and theology). The Arts faculties – which gradually (on an individual basis) began to be renamed as Philosophy Faculties during this same period – generally served to prepare students for further study in the three higher faculties.[3]

While the subject-matters taught within the parameters of philosophy instruction (which can be considered to be roughly synonymous with arts instruction) did not remain completely regionally or chronologically uniform during these two centuries, one can generally state that this instruction in philosophy and the arts at individual academic institutions consisted of some, most, or all of the following basic subject-matters: metaphysics, physics, mathematics, ethics, family life (*oeconomica*), politics,

---

[1] Library and archive locations and call numbers (shelf marks) are utilized to identify the individual copies of all of the pre-1800 published writings utilized in this article. The following abbreviations are utilized for this purpose: BSB: Bayerische Staatsbibliothek (München) / Bavarian State Library (Munich), HAB: Herzog August Bibliothek (Wolfenbüttel), LB = Landesbibliothek / Province Library, SA: Staatsarchiv / State Archives, StA: Stadtarchiv / Municipal Archives, StB: Stadtbibliothek / Municipal Library, SUB: Staats- und Universitätsbibliothek / State and University Library, UB: Universitätsbibliothek / University Library, ULB: Universitäts- und Landesbibliothek (Halle).

[2] Central Europe serves as the primary geographical focus for the purpose of this article.

[3] This change of name occurred at different times – and sometimes over a longer or shorter period of time – at individual European universities; with regard to this change of name at the University of Vienna, see Richard Meister (1958). *Geschichte des Doktorates der Philosophie an der Universität Wien*, Österreichische Akademie der Wissenschaften, Philosophisch-historische Klasse, Sitzungsberichte 232, vol. 2, Abhandlung, Veröffentlichungen der Kommission für Geschichte der Erziehung und des Unterrichts, no. 3, Beiträge zur Geschichte der Universität Wien, Vienna 1958, pp. 32–34. For the case of the University of Heidelberg, refer to Joseph S. Freedman, The Godfather of Ontology? Clemens Timpler, "All that is Intelligible", Academic Disciplines during the Late 16th and Early 17th Centuries, and Some Possible Ramifications for the Use of Ontology in Our Time, in: *Quaestio. Yearbook on the History of Metaphysics*, vol. 9 (2009), p. 5, note 10.

logic, rhetoric, grammar, poetics, and history.[4] Mathematics instruction consisted of individual mathematical subject-matters or disciplines.[5] The 'liberal arts' (*artes liberales*) also fell within the parameters of this philosophy instruction.[6]

Philosophical texts were both handwritten (for example: lecture notes) and published. The genres for these texts include textbooks, dictionaries, collections of axioms, academic disputations (dissertations) and orations as well as curriculum announcements, outlines, and summaries. Much of the 'unexpected' production pertaining to philosophical texts also occurs within writings – in the genres mentioned above – on theology, jurisprudence, and medicine. In this article, however, discussion of the 'unexpected' will be facilitated by examples falling within the subject-areas of philosophy and the arts.

With regard to neatly copied manuscript 'lecture notes', one could pose the following question: If 16th- and 17th-century students took these notes, did they do so using very good handwriting with little or no text crossed out? No answer to this question will be ventured in this context; the focus here is on published writings. Some attention, however, is given here to manuscript annotations and manuscript additions found within these published writings.

In discussing the unexpected in published 16th- and 17th-century writings on philosophy and the arts, one can distinguish between technical and intellectual producers. In the technical realm, the 'unexpected' usually involves mistakes pertaining to the production of published (and manuscript) works. A few examples of such mistakes can be mentioned here. In published writings containing page numbering,

---

[4] Here it can be noted that metaphysics was not taught for much of the 16th century in Central European schools and universities; concerning the teaching of metaphysics and other arts/philosophy subject-matters in Central Europe during the 16th and 17th centuries refer to literature cited in Freedman, Godfather (see note 3), pp. 4–6, 25–26. Concerning the classification of philosophy, the sciences, and the arts during the 16th and 17th centuries see Joseph S. Freedman, Classifications of Philosophy, the Sciences, and the Arts in Sixteenth- and Seventeenth-Century Europe, in: *The Modern Schoolman*, vol. 72, no. 1 (1994), pp. 37–65; reprinted in: Joseph S. Freedman, *Philosophy and the Arts in Central Europe, 1500–1700. Teaching and Texts at European Schools and Universities*, Variorum Collected Studies Series, CS626, Aldershot / Brookfield 1999, VII.

[5] Freedman, Classifications (see note 4), pp. 42–43.

[6] While many authors during this period considered the liberal arts to be seven in number, this was not universally the case. The number of liberal arts could range from as few as three to as many as over a dozen. Cf. ibid., pp. 44–45.

incorrect pagination occasionally did occur; some page numbers might be missing in the sequence and/or be repeated more than once.[7]

Sometimes published works contained oversized charts that needed to be folded so that they would not exceed the dimensions of the printed pages contained therein. In some copies of a given published work, such oversized charts might be incorrectly inserted – or omitted entirely – prior to the binding of the work. In other cases, prefaces and/or appendices / appended works might be missing in some copies of a given published work, possibly because they were forgotten, misplaced, or missing when it was bound. On the other hand, one published work might be bound together with a second published work where it is not clear why these works were bound together.[8]

Turning to the intellectual realm, publishers could make 'unexpected' changes to published writings. To give one example, a textbook on logic authored by Bartholomaeus Keckermann was apparently in such demand during the year 1606 that it was apparently reprinted at least three times during that same year. This can be surmised due to the fact that three variant title pages can be found in individual extant copies of that textbook published in 1606.[9]

Other 'unexpected' changes could be made by the authors of such published writings. For example, a textbook on metaphysics authored by Clemens Timpler was printed at least nine times between 1604 and 1616.[10] Authorized versions appeared in print in Steinfurt in 1604 and Hanau in the years 1606, 1608, 1612, and 1616.

---

[7] For example, one case of a published work in which some pages are missing in the pagination while other pages appear twice therein is given in Joseph S. Freedman, *European Academic Philosophy in the Late Sixteenth and Early Seventeenth Centuries: The Life, Significance, and Philosophy of Clemens Timpler, 1563/64–1624*, Studien und Materialien zur Geschichte der Philosophie 27, 2 vols, Hildesheim / Zürich / New York 1988, p. 752, no. 27.

[8] One example of this is discussed in some detail in Joseph S. Freedman, Published academic disputations in the context of other information formats used primarily in Central Europe (c. 1550–c.1700), in: *Disputatio 1200–1800. Form, Funktion und Wirkung eines Leitmediums universitärer Wissenskultur. Trends in Medieval Philology*, vol. 20, ed. by Marion Gindhart and Ursula Kundert, Berlin / New York 2010, pp. 101, 124 (table 13, D.).

[9] Bartholomaeus Keckermann, *Systema logicae tribus libris adornatum* (Hanoviae: Apud Guililelmum Antonium, 1606) [variant no. 1: Lübeck StB: Philos. 8° 1919 (1a=2) – variant no. 2: Wolfenbüttel HAB: H: 06a. 8° Helmst. – variant no. 3: Basel UB: K. fl. III 24 (nr. 1)].

[10] Refer to the annotated bibliographical citations of these nine imprints of Timpler's textbook on metaphysics in Freedman, Philosophy (see note 7), pp. 745–746 (no. 18), 746–747 (no. 19), 748–749 (no. 20), 750–751 (no. 26), 751–752 (p. 27), 754 (no. 30), 760–761 (no. 40), 761–762 (no. 41), 764–765 (no. 45).

Unauthorized versions appeared in Lich in 1604, in Frankfurt am Main in 1607, in Marburg in 1607, and in Frankfurt am Main in the year 1612. There were apparently no (or: only very minor) changes to the actual text in any of these printed versions (authorized and not authorized).[11]

While there were apparently no (or: only very minor) changes to the actual text of this work, there were a number of other changes, three of which will be highlighted here. First, in the Hanau 1606 imprint, Timpler's short treatise on the liberal arts (*Technologia*) was included prior to the text of his (textbook on) metaphysics.[12] That same treatise was included in all subsequent imprints – authorized and unauthorized – of Timpler's textbook on metaphysics.

Second, the Steinfurt 1604 imprint contains a chart (with the title *Sciagraphia totius operis*) that outlines the content of Timpler's textbook on metaphysics; his same chart appears in the Hanau 1606 edition.[13] In the Frankfurt am Main 1607 and 1612 imprint, this chart appears with the same content as previously, but with a new title: *Sciagraphia totius metaphysices*.[14] The chart does not appear in the Hanau 1608, 1612, or 1616 imprints.

---

[11] Timpler's criticisms of the unauthorized Frankfurt am Main 1607 and Marburg 1607 imprints are to be found in his preface (dated February 1, 1608) to the Hanau 1608 imprint of his textbook on metaphysics and also appears in the Hanau 1612 and 1616 imprints. This preface (and its content) is mentioned on the title page of all three of these imprints. Cf. ibid., pp. 754 (no. 30), 761–762 (no. 41), 764–765 (no. 45). The preface by Timpler referred to in no. 30 (p. 754) is erroneously dated "s.l. ; s.d." and should instead read "Steinfurt; February 1, 1608." Timpler also criticized the Lich 1604 imprint of his own textbook on metaphysics in a preface to the Hanau 1605 imprint of his textbook on general physics; this preface was reprinted in the Hanau 1607 and Hanau 1613 imprints of his textbook on general physics. Cf. ibid., pp. 747 (no. 20), 752–753 (no. 28) 763–764 (no. 44).

[12] This includes the text of the *Technologia*, the table of contents thereto, and a dichotomous chart that serves to outline the contents thereof. For Timpler, there are 18 liberal arts: theology, metaphysics, physics, geometry, arithmetic, ethics, family life (*oeconomica*), politics, medicine, jurisprudence, physiognomy, optics, grammar, rhetoric, poetics, music, logic, and history; cf. ibid., pp. 199–200, 597.

[13] Freedman, Philosophy (see note 7), pp.745–746 (no. 18), 748–749 (no. 22).

[14] In the Steinfurt 1604 imprint of Timpler's metaphysics, the label *sciagraphia totius operis* was appropriate, because Timpler's *Technologia* had not been added to it yet. But his *Technologia* did appear in the Hanau 1606 imprint. The label *sciagraphia totius metaphysices* – as used in the Frankfurt 1607 and 1612 imprints – was more appropriate once the *Technologia* had been included (in addition to the text of Timpler's textbook on metaphysics. Cf. ibid., pp. 745–746 (no. 18), 748–749 (no. 22), 750–751 (no. 26), 760–761 (no. 45).

And third, a preface by Rudolph Goclenius the Elder appears in the Steinfurt 1604 imprint and appears thereafter in all of the extent imprints of Timpler's textbook on metaphysics.[15] Commentary (*scholia*) by Goclenius to the text of Timpler's metaphysics first appears in the Hanau 1606 imprint; this same commentary also appears in the Marburg 1607, Frankfurt am Main 1607, and Frankfurt am Main 1612 imprints.[16] Expanded commentary (*notae et scholia*) by Goclenius is included within the Hanau 1608, 1612, and 1616 imprints.[17] Commentary by Goclenius on Timpler's treatise on the liberal arts (*Technologia*) only appears in the (unauthorized) Marburg 1607 imprint.[18]

The genre of disputations offered a large range of possibilities for the appearance of that which was not expected during the 16th and 17th centuries.[19] Here one can broadly distinguish between oral disputations and published disputations.[20] Oral disputations were normally a part of school and university curricula during these two centuries. They normally appear to have required at least two participants: 1. a respondent (defendant) who presented and defended a given thesis, theses, or other position(s) and 2. an opponent who presented contrary arguments to those presented by the respondent.[21]

---

[15] Concerning Rudolph Goclenius the Elder (1547–1628), his relationship with Timpler, and his relationship with some of Timpler's students refer to the discussion and documentation given in ibid., pp. 92–93, 524–525.

[16] Ibid., pp. 748–740 (no. 22), 750–752 (nos. 26–27), 760–761 (no. 40).

[17] Ibid., pp. 754 (no. 30), 761–762 (no. 41), 764–765 (no. 45).

[18] Ibid., pp. 751–752 (no. 27). It is possible that there is a link between the fact that Goclenius taught at the University of Marburg and the fact that this commentary by Goclenius on Timpler's *Technologia* was only published in the Marburg 1607 imprint.

[19] In this article, disputations are not distinguished from dissertations. Refer to the brief discussion of 'disputation' and 'dissertation' given in Freedman, Disputations (see note 8), pp. 98–99 (note 30).

[20] Refer here to the brief discussion of this distinction given in ibid., pp. 110–111.

[21] According to Augustinus Hunnaeus in the year 1552, a respondent and an opponent were the two required participants of a disputation; these two participants are referred to by him as "authors" *(auctores)*; cf. ibid., pp. 94–95, 110–111.

There also could be more than one respondent as well as more than one opponent.[22] And in the case of publicly held disputations, the audience could also play a role.[23]

Orally presented disputations were – generally speaking – a part of school and university instruction during the 16th and 17th centuries. However, it is published disputations that provide us with the bulk of that extant information concerning this genre. Disputations apparently only began to be published from about the year 1550.[24] During the second half of the 16th century they were primarily published in Central Europe.[25] From about 1600, they were published in substantially larger numbers in Central Europe, but also in the Netherlands, in Scandinavia, and in Scotland.[26] In the 1550s and 1560s disputations were frequently published as broadsheets but thereafter many were substantially longer, especially during the course of the 17th century.[27]

---

[22] As one example of a disputation with two respondents, see Rupertus Reindelius SJ *(praeses)* / Nicolaus Moritschius *(respondens)* / Jacobus Hatmiller *(respondens)*, Assertiones ex variis philosophiae partibus depromptae (Ingolstadii: Ex officina typographia Davidis Sartorii, 1593), BSB: 4 Diss. 1305, Beibd. 1, Munich. Three examples of published disputations where more than one opponent is named are given in Freedman, Disputations (see note 8), pp. 95–96 (note 20), 125 (table 13, E.).

[23] The role of persons in the audience is mentioned in Johannes-Henricus Alstedius, *Philosophia digne restituta* (Herbornae Nassoviorum), UB: XIV C 136, Marburg 1612, p. 455; this work by Alsted is discussed in Joseph S. Freedman, *Johann Heinrich Alsteds 'Philosophia digne restituta' (1612). Ein kurzer Überblick über Inhalt und Bedeutung des Werkes*, Nassauische Annalen 123, 2012, p. 161–181. The audience at a publicly held disputation is pictured within the illustrated title page of Johannes Stierus, *Praecepta doctrinae sphaerae ex probatis auctoribus collecta, et adjuvandae memoriae causa tabulis synopticis inclusa* ([s.l.]: Impensis Johannis Brickneri, 1642) [Darmstadt Landes- und Universitätsbibliothek: 33/7545]; in the Darmstadt copy of this imprint, a manuscript addition to the published texts identifies the location of the auditorium (where a disputation was then being held) pictured on the title page to be in Jena. This title page is pictured in Joseph S. Freedman, Philosophy Instruction within the Institutional Framework of Central European Schools and Universities during the Reformation Era, in: *History of Universities*, vol. 5, Oxford 1985, p. 147; reprinted in Freedman, Philosophy (see note 4), II.

[24] Refer to the brief discussion in Freedman, Disputations (see note 8), pp. 99–100, 123.

[25] Refer to the disputations published during the second half of the 16th century in Central Europe that are cited in Joseph S. Freedman, Philosophy Instruction, the Philosophy Concept, and Philosophy Disputations Published at the University of Ingolstadt, c. 1550 – c. 1650, in: *Dichtung - Gelehrsamkeit - Disputationskultur. Festschrift für Hanspeter Marti zum 65. Geburtstag*, ed. by Reimund B. Sdzuj, Robert Seidel and Bernd Zegowitz, Cologne / Vienna / Weimar 2012, pp. 316–362.

[26] Academic disputations appear to have been published very rarely in England, Italy, and Spain during the 16th and 17th centuries.

[27] For example, refer to the broadsheets published in Freedman, Instruction (see note 25), pp. 318, 330 (table A), and the lengthy disputations cited in Freedman, Disputations (see note 8), pp. 126–127 (table 13 G., 13.J.). The disputation on "the pleasant rhetoric of women" cited in note 35 is 109 pages in length.

In published disputations (dissertations) a presider is usually named and one or more respondents are virtually always named.[28] Opponents are only named very rarely.[29] Occasionally the presider (usually a teacher) or the respondent (usually a student) is mentioned as the author.[30] But in those cases where an author is not mentioned, it is only very rarely possible to make such a determination.[31]

Disputations served as a highly flexible medium that could be used for a very wide array of purposes.[32] Any 'definition' thereof serves only as a rough template.[33] In published disputations, the 'unexpected' approaches 'that which you can expect'.

The 'text' of a disputation can be supplemented by prefaces, dedications, and verse (all of which can also serve as exercises in composition and literary style), as well as by appendices or other content (which sometimes has little or nothing to do with its 'text'). To give one example, the text of a disputation (published in Heidelberg in the year 1663) focuses – as indicated on its title page – on 100 theses (*centuria thesium*) drawn from the entire scope of philosophy (*ex universa philosophia*).[34] This title in fact does apply to the content of the first 99 theses. 'Thesis' 100, however, introduces a Hebrew-Latin and Arabic-Latin word list that is far longer than all of the previous 99 theses combined. This word list is not mentioned on the title page or the dedication letter of the disputation.

---

[28] Concerning the distinction between disputations and dissertations refer to the brief comments provided in note 19.

[29] The few examples – that I have been able to locate to date – of published disputations where the opponents are named are listed in Freedman, Disputations (see note 8), pp. 95–96 (note 20), 125 (table 13, E.).

[30] An example of a disputation where the respondent is also listed as the author is given in Freedman, Disputations (see note 8), p. 126 (table 13, H.).

[31] Identification of the author of a given disputation might be possible (for example) 1. through evidence contained within the text of the disputation or 2. through a manuscript addition of text, which identifies the author. I am not able to provide a specific example here.

[32] This is a central point discussed in Freedman, Disputations (see note 8).

[33] Refer here to the definitions of 'disputation' and 'dissertation' provided by Hanspeter Marti in: Gerd Uding (ed.), *Historisches Wörterbuch der Rhetorik*, Tübingen 1994, vol. 2, col. 866–884.

[34] Sebastianus Rampeck *(praeses)* / Emanuel Sustman *(respondens)*, *Centuria thesium ex universa philosophia* [...] *ad summos in philosophia honores rite capessendos* [...] (Heidelbergae: Typis Adriani Wyngaerden, 1663), UB: DISBUI Heidelberg, Leiden as cited in full in Freedman, Disputations (see note 8), p. 126 (table 13, I.).

Disputations were sometimes published on topics that are outside the realms of subject-matters that one could normally expect to see examined. For example, a disputation on "the pleasant rhetoric of women" held at the University of Leipzig in the year 1678.[35] Other published disputations were – as evidenced by their titles – functioned as jokes or mockeries (*Spottdisputationen*) or were 'semi-serious' (*joco-seria*).[36]

In the 16th and 17th centuries, most new knowledge (and most of the resulting new academic disciplines and sub-disciplines) fell within the domain of philosophy and the arts – and not within the three higher faculties (theology, jurisprudence, and medicine). These nascent disciplines and sub-disciplines in philosophy and the arts were normally given new (and – to some extent – 'unexpected') names, which often appear within the titles of published academic writings.[37] Some examples of these new 'disciplines' and 'sub-disciplines' can be given here.

Franciscus Tidicaeus used the term φυτολογία [*Phytologia*] *generalis* in the title of a disputation held on April 21, 1582 at the University of Leipzig on the study of plants.[38] Clemens Timpler published a three-volume textbook set on physics. The first volume thereof, titled *physica generalis*, was published in the year 1605.[39]

The second and third volumes were given the titles *apsychologia* ('inanimate' physics) and *empsychologia* ('animate' physics); they were published in the years 1605 and 1607, respectively.[40]

---

[35] Georgius Schultz (*praes.*) and Johann-Heinrich Stockhart (*respondens*), *Dissertatio de blanda mulierum rhetorica, occasione axiomatis Richteriani publicae eruditorum censurae & ventilationi exposita* [...] *die ___ Octobr. Anno 1678* (Lipsiae: Literis Johannis Georgii, 1678), ULB: 99 A 6930 (8), Halle.

[36] For examples of 1. disputations as mockeries/jokes and 2. semi-serious disputations refer to Freedman, Disputations (see note 8), p. 106 (note 60) and p. 128 (table 13, N.), respectively.

[37] Not all of these new 'disciplines' and 'sub-disciplines' ended up finding general acceptance (refer to the examples given in note 40).

[38] Franciscus Tidicaeus, φυτολογία *generalis capitibus aliquot complectens ea quae ad plantarum essentiam naturamque universim explicandam pertinent: scripta et in disputationem vocatum publicam in* [...] *academiae Lipsiensis, die 11. Cal. Maij, (15)82* (Lipsiae: (Georgius Defnerus), (1582)), BSB: Phyt. 702, Munich.

[39] Timpler's textbook on general physics is cited in full in Freedman, Philosophy (see note 7), p. 747 (no. 20).

[40] Clemens Timplerus, *Pars altera physicae, complectens apsychologiam* (Hanoviae: Apud Guilielmum Antonium, 1605), StA and StB: C 1488 (2), Brunswick; Clemens Timplerus, *Pars tertia & postrema physicae, complectens empsychologiam* (Hanoviae: Apud Guilielmum Antonium, 1607), StA and StB: C 1488 (3), Brunswick; also cf. Freedman, Philosophy (see note 7), pp. 748 (no. 21), 750 (no. 25). These new 'disciplines' – *Apsychologia* and *Empsychologia* – apparently proposed here by Timpler did not seem to find any general acceptance by other authors.

In 1634, Peter Lauremberg published his *Pasicompse nova*, which is the earliest known academic treatise devoted specifically to the subject-matter of aesthetics.[41] A disputation to be held at a school in Hof (Franconia) by Georg Nicolaus Langheinrich and Michael Schlee on April 14, 1680 (but apparently actually held – as corrected by hand on this copy – on April 16, 1680) is devoted to the subject-matter of *anthropophagia* (cannibalism).[42] And a moral dissertation (*dissertatio moralis*) held by Johann Christian Adam and Georg Krebs at the University of Wittenberg in October 1682 was held on the subject-matter of ουδενοσοφία [*Oydenosophia*] *socratica, sive scientia nihil sciendi* (the science of knowing nothing).[43]

Handwritten additions, annotations, and corrections within individual copies of published writings also can be said to fall within the realm of the 'unexpected'.[44] This includes owner's marks, which were frequently written onto the title pages of such individual copies. These owner's marks can help in efforts to reconstruct personal libraries that were built in earlier centuries.[45] Owner's marks indicating the presence of a given published work and a given library by or on a certain date also can have a

---

[41] Petrus Laurembergius, *Pasicompse nova, id est, accurata & curiosa delineatio pulchritudis* (Lipsiae: Ex bibliopolio Hallevordiano, typis Ritzschanis, 1634), BSB: A.gr.b. 1457#Beibd.4, Munich.

[42] Georg Nicolaus Langheinrich (*praeses*) / Michael Schlee (*respondens*), *De Anthropophagia sive Barbara quarundam gentium consvetudine qua carnibus humanis vescuntur, dissertatio prior eaque historica [...] in illustri Gymnasio Curiano d. 14 {16} April. 1680. P.P. Praeses M. Georgius Nicolaus Langheinrich Rector, Respondente Michaele. Schlee Bindlaco-Franco* ([Curiae Variscorum]: Literis Mintzelianis, 1680), HAB: Ho 305 (8), Wolfenbüttel.

[43] Joh. Christianus Adamus (*praeses*) / Georgius Krebs (*respondens*), *Dissertationem moralem de* ουδενοσοφία [*Oydenosophia*] *socratica sive scientia nihil sciendi [...] publicae [...] disquisitioni submittet [...] ad d. ___ Octob.* (Wittenbergae: Typis Matthaei Henckelii, 1682), SUB: 8 PHIL VI, 820 (52), Göttingen.

[44] In addition to the handwritten additions mentioned in the following three footnotes, also note the example given in footnote 23.

[45] Here reference can be made to owner's marks by Bartholomaeus Keckermann (d. 1609) on his own copies of 1. a bilingual (Greek-Latin) edition of Aristotle's writings on natural philosophy and 2. Nicolas Copernicus' *On the Revolutions of the Heavenly Spheres*; these two title pages are reproduced in Joseph S. Freedman, The Career and Writings of Bartholomew Keckermann (d. 1609), in: *Proceedings of the American Philosophical Society*, vol. 141, no. 3 (1997), pp. 335, 337, 363; reprinted in Freedman, Philosophy (see note 4), VIII.

broader significance.⁴⁶ Notes were also sometimes taken on pages of published textbooks and disputations.⁴⁷

Referring to the title pages of published disputations, the date on which the disputation was to be held was sometimes left blank; in most cases, this was probably due to the fact that the presentation date had not yet been set when that disputation was published.⁴⁸ In some copies, the actual (or: assumed) presentation date was then added by hand.⁴⁹ In other cases, the date of the disputation was included in the published disputation but then – on at least one copy thereof – altered by hand; in still other cases, the date, month, and even the year of the oral presentation could be altered via one or more handwritten corrections.⁵⁰

The name of an author could also deliberately be made illegible on some published copies of a given work. The following example can be given here: a copy – owned the Mainz Municipal Library – of a logic textbook by Caspar Rudolph published in Mainz in the year 1551.⁵¹ Caspar Rudolph was a professor of logic at the (Lutheran) University of Marburg from 1533 until 1561.⁵² His logic textbook was frequently published during his lifetime and appears to have been utilized at academic institutions

---

⁴⁶ For example, dated owner's marks provide evidence that writings by Petrus Ramus – published after his conversion to Protestant faith – found their way into Roman Catholic libraries during the late 16th and early 17th centuries; refer to the documentation provided in Joseph S. Freedman, Joseph S., The Diffusion of the Writings of Petrus Ramus in Central Europe, c. 1570– c.1630, in: *Renaissance Quarterly,* vol. 46, no. 1 (1993), pp. 124, 128 (note 68); reprinted in Freedman, Philosophy (see note 4), IV.

⁴⁷ Such handwritten notes can be found in the disputation cited in Freedman, Disputations (see note 8), p. 124 (table 13, E.).

⁴⁸ Such is the case in the disputations cited in notes 35 and 43 of this article.

⁴⁹ This is the case in the disputations cited in notes 42 and 50.

⁵⁰ Such is the case in the following copy of a disputation: Bernhardus Frencelius (*praeses*) / Theodorus Heidenius (*respondens*), *Inventio logica metaphysicae inter artes liberales catholicae* [...] *publico* [...] *Heidelbergensis Academiae examini offert ad diem {21} {Febr.} In magno philosophorum auditorio* (Heidelbergae: Typis Johannis Lancelloti academicae typographi, 1606 {1607}), Bibliothek der Franckeschen Stiftungen: 54 K 2 (15 an), Halle; here the following three handwritten changes have been made: [1] the date "21" has been added, [2] "Decemb:" has been crossed out and replaced by "Febr.", and [3] 1606 (MDC. VI) has been changed to 1607 (MDC. VII.) by the addition of a handwritten "I.".

⁵¹ Chasparus Rhodolphus [Caspar Rudolph], *Dialectica* [...] *ab authore diligenter recognita, et locupletata* (Moguntiae: 1551), StB (Bibliothek des Gutenbergmuseums): Ink. a. 5., Mainz.

⁵² Refer to the article on Caspar Rudolph[i] in Franz Gundlach (ed.), *Catalogus Professorum Academiae Marburgensis. Die akademischen Lehrer des Philipps-Universität Marburg von 1527 bis 1910, Veröffentlichungen der Historischen Kommission für Hessen und Waldeck* 15, Marburg 1927, p. 281 (no. 478).

that were Roman Catholic (it was published in Ingolstadt and Mainz, apparently for purposes of instruction) as well as Protestant (it was published in Strasbourg after the establishment of the Academy there).[53]

The title page of the copy of this work at the Mainz Municipal Library has the following handwritten owner's mark: *Liber Collegii Moguntiae Societatis Jesu*. At some point – possibly after the Jesuits established themselves in Mainz in 1561 – all references to Caspar Rudolph in the entire text (on the verso side of every leaf in the text) were made illegible in this copy. On the title page of this same copy, the names of Caspar Rudolph and Juan Luis Vives were also made illegible.[54]

On the other hand, manuscript changes to published writings cannot always be described as acts of censorship. The example of a copy of a curriculum outline published as a broadsheet can be given here. This broadsheet lists those lectures and exercises to be held at the Academy in Herborn (and at a school in Siegen) during the Winter Semester beginning on October 1, 1610.[55] However, numerous handwritten changes were made on this copy. Instruction was now said to begin on April 1, 1611. Some segments of the text (of this curriculum) are crossed out and replaced by handwritten text in the margins or added thereto by hand. These changes were probably made so that this broadsheet (published for the 1610–1611 Winter Semester) could be used again during the 1611 Summer Semester. From the point of view of a contemporary researcher, these manuscript additions and changes are useful insofar that they indicate that this broadsheet reflects – at least to some extent – what was actually (to be) taught at the Academy in Herborn during the 1611 Summer Semester.

---

[53]  For example, refer to the following two imprints: Rhodolphus, Chasparus, *Dialectica* [...] *ab authore diligenter recognita* [...] (Argentinae: In aedibus Jacobi Jucundi, 1545), SB: Nl 3700, Berlin; Rhodolphus, Chasparus, *Dialectica* [...] *ab authore diligenter recognita* [...] (Ingolstadii: Excudebat Alexander Weissenhorn, 1555), BSB: L.eleg.m.304#Beibd.1, Munich.

[54]  Caspar Rudolph's name is clearly legible in at least some other copies of the title page – and throughout the text – of this Mainz (Moguntiae) 1551 imprint (for example): 1. Basel UB: A.P. V 36 – 2. University of Illinois, Urbana-Champaign (Special Collections): 160/R 618d.

[55]  *Index lectionum, hac {aestate} habendarum in illustri schola Nassovica Herbornensi publica* [...] *In utroque paedagogeo, Herbornensi et Sigensensi* [...] *Inchoabuntur lectiones {Cal. Aprilis 1611}*, SA: Abt. 95 No. 1750/1, Wiesbaden; this broadsheet has been reproduced in Freedman, Alsted (see note 23), p. 177.

In the context of published writings on European academic philosophy during the 16th and 17th century, it can be postulated here that the 'unexpected' played a significant role in many diverse – and perhaps in part surprising – venues. In this vein, the following question can be asked: To what extent can one say that the 'unexpected' has played (and still plays) a greater role in human lives than we might (wish to) think? The following passages – labelled here as [A] and [B] – from a book on how to write fiction can be quoted here in this connection:

> [A] Life is chaos punctuated by short periods of order. From day to day we don't have the vaguest notion of what will happen. [...] "Expect the Unexpected" should be our motto. If there is a chain of cause-and-effect relationships in our lives, it's under constant modification to consider current circumstances. [...] Life is filled with long shots and unbelievable coincidences. [...] In life, we expect things to happen out of the blue.
>
> [B] In fiction, we won't tolerate it [i.e.: chaos]. [...] You [i. e., the fiction writer] must work under a load of restrictions. The first restriction states that you must create a world that has its own set rules. [...] those rules must be consistent from beginning to end. [...] The second restriction states that when something happens in this world, it must happen for a reason. [...] fiction leaves no room for chance. The reason something happens must always be evident at some point in the story. Readers won't tolerate the unknown in fiction.[56]

On the basis of [A] above, one might conclude that the unexpected can be said to have a much larger role in our lives that many of us might like to believe. Referring to [B], one could conclude that fiction – with its prescribed emphasis on the 'expected' in its narratives – can serve as a respite or an escape from 'unexpected' reality.

Confrontation with the 'unexpected' could lead us to confusion, despair, and feelings of hopelessness. We might be best advised to prepare ourselves to 'expect' one or more 'unexpected' (and potentially less than desirable) outcomes.[57] But we also can focus on positive aspects of the unexpected, and to integrate such positive components thereof into our professional and personal lives.[58]

---

[56] Ronald B. Tobias, *20 Master Plots and How to Build Them*, Cincinnati 1993, p. 29.

[57] The following article focuses on expecting the unexpected: Brenda J. McCarthy, Expect the Unexpected. The Need for Control to Impose Vicarious Liability in Strategic Alliances, in: *Case Western Reserve Law*, vol. 54, no. 2 (2003), pp. 649–665.

[58] A large number of publications could be mentioned in this connection. For example, refer to the following: Rita Kop, The Unexpected Connection. Serendipity and Human Mediation in Networked Learning, in: *Journal of Educational Technology & Society*, vol. 15, no. 2, pp. 2–11; Julia M. Klein, Get an edge in arts freelancing. Land assignments by being versatile, going for the unexpected, in: *Writer*, vol. 118, no. 3 (2005), pp. 48–49; Kathleen E. Mitchell / Al S. Levin / John D. Krumboltz, Planned Happenstance. Constructing Unexpected Career Opportunities, in: *Journal of Counseling & Development*, vol. 7, no. 2 (1999), pp. 115–124; June L. Bigge, Expected Learning Often Comes through Unexpected Teaching, in: *Exceptional Children*, vol. 34, no. 1 (1967), pp. 47–50.

# Bibliography

Joh. Christianus Adamus, Joh. Christianus / Georgius Krebs, *Dissertationem moralem de ουδενοσοφία [Oydenosophia] socratica sive scientia nihil sciendi* [...] *publicae* [...] *disquisitioni submittet* [...] *ad d.* ___ *Octob.* (Wittenbergae: Typis Matthaei Henckelii, 1682), SUB: 8 PHIL VI, 820 (52), Göttingen.

Alstedius, Johannes-Henricus, *Philosophia digne restituta* (Herbornae Nassoviorum), UB: XIV C 136, Marburg 1612.

Bigge, June L., Expected Learning Often Comes through Unexpected Teaching, in: *Exceptional Children*, vol. 34, no. 1 (1967).

Rudolph, Caspar, *Dialectica* [...] *ab authore diligenter recognita* [...] (Argentinae: In aedibus Jacobi Jucundi, 1545), SB: Nl 3700, Berlin.

Rudolph, Caspar, *Dialectica* [...] *ab authore diligenter recognita, et locupletata* (Moguntiae: 1551), StB (Bibliothek des Gutenbergmuseums): Ink. a. 5., Mainz.

Rudolph, Caspar, *Dialectica* [...] *ab authore diligenter recognita* [...] (Ingolstadii: Excudebat Alexander Weissenhorn, 1555), BSB: L.eleg.m.304#Beibd.1, Munich.

Freedman, Joseph S., *European Academic Philosophy in the Late Sixteenth and Early Seventeenth Centuries: The Life, Significance, and Philosophy of Clemens Timpler, 1563/64–1624,* Studien und Materialien zur Geschichte der Philosophie 27, 2 vols, Hildesheim / Zürich / New York 1988.

Freedman, Joseph S., *Johann Heinrich Alsteds 'Philosophia digne restituta' (1612). Ein kurzer Überblick über Inhalt und Bedeutung des Werkes,* Nassauische Annalen 123, 2012.

Freedman, Joseph S., *Philosophy and the Arts in Central Europe, 1500–1700. Teaching and Texts at European Schools and Universities,* Variorum Collected Studies Series, CS626, Aldershot / Brookfield 1999, VII.

Freedman, Joseph S., The Career and Writings of Bartholomew Keckermann (d. 1609), in: *Proceedings of the American Philosophical Society,* vol. 141, no. 3 (1997), pp. 305–364.

Freedman, Joseph S., Classifications of Philosophy, the Sciences, and the Arts in Sixteenth- and Seventeenth-Century Europe, in: *The Modern Schoolman,* vol. 72, no. 1 (1994), pp. 37–65.

Freedman, Joseph S., The Diffusion of the Writings of Petrus Ramus in Central Europe, c. 1570– c.1630, in: *Renaissance Quarterly,* vol. 46, no. 1 (1993), pp. 98–152.

Freedman, Joseph S., The Godfather of Ontology? Clemens Timpler, "All that is Intelligible", Academic Disciplines during the Late 16th and Early 17th Centuries, and Some Possible Ramifications for the Use of Ontology in Our Time, in: *Quaestio. Yearbook on the History of Metaphysics,* vol. 9 (2009), pp. 3–40.

Freedman, Joseph S., Philosophy Instruction, the Philosophy Concept, and Philosophy Disputations Published at the University of Ingolstadt, c. 1550 – c. 1650, in: *Dichtung - Gelehrsamkeit - Disputationskultur. Festschrift für Hanspeter Marti zum 65. Geburtstag,* ed. by Reimund B. Sdzuj, Robert Seidel and Bernd Zegowitz, Cologne / Vienna / Weimar 2012, pp. 316–362.

Freedman, Joseph S., Philosophy Instruction within the Institutional Framework of Central European Schools and Universities during the Reformation Era, in: *History of Universities,* vol. 5, Oxford 1985, pp. 177–166.

Freedman, Joseph S., Published academic disputations in the context of other information formats used primarily in Central Europe (c. 1550–c.1700), in: *Disputatio 1200–1800. Form, Funktion und Wirkung eines Leitmediums universitärer Wissenskultur. Trends in Medieval Philology,* vol. 20, ed. by Marion Gindhart and Ursula Kundert, Berlin / New York 2010, pp. 89–128.

Frencelius, Bernhardus / Heidenius, Theordorus, *Inventio logica metaphysicae inter artes liberales catholicae [...] publico [...] Heidelbergensis Academiae examini offert ad diem {21} {Febr.} In magno philosophorum auditorio* (Heidelbergae: Typis Johannis Lancelloti academicae typographi, 1606 {1607}), Bibliothek der Franckeschen Stiftungen: 54 K 2 (15 an), Halle.

Gundlach, Franz (ed.), *Catalogus Professorum Academiae Marburgensis. Die akademischen Lehrer des Philipps-Universität Marburg von 1527 bis 1910, Veröffentlichungen der Historischen Kommission für Hessen und Waldeck* 15, Marburg 1927.

Keckermann, Bartholomaeus, *Systema logicae tribus libris adornatum* (Hanoviae: Apud Guililelmum Antonium, 1606), 1919.

Klein, Julia M., Get an edge in arts freelancing. Land assignments by being versatile, going for the unexpected, in: *Writer,* vol. 118, no. 3 (2005), pp. 48–49.

Kop, Rita, The Unexpected Connection. Serendipity and Human Mediation in Networked Learning, in: *Journal of Educational Technology & Society,* vol. 15, no. 2.

Langheinrich, Georg Nicolaus / Michael Schlee, *De Anthropophagia sive Barbara quarundam gentium consvetudine qua carnibus humanis vescuntur, dissertatio prior eaque historica … in illustri Gymnasio Curiano d. 14 {16} April. 1680. P.P. Praees M. Georgius Nicolaus Langheinrich Rector, Respondente Michaele. Schlee Bindlaco-Franco* ([Curiae Variscorum]: Literis Mintzelianis, 1680), HAB: Ho 305 (8), Wolfenbüttel.

Laurembergius, Petrus, *Pasicompse nova, id est, accurata & curiosa delineatio pulchritudis* (Lipsiae: Ex bibliopolio Hallevordiano, typis Ritzschanis, 1634), BSB: A.gr.b. 1457#Beibd.4, Munich.

McCarthy, Brenda J., Expect the Unexpected. The Need for Control to Impose Vicarious Liability in Strategic Alliances, in: *Case Western Reserve Law,* vol. 54, no. 2 (2003), pp. 649–665.

Meister, Richard, *Geschichte des Doktorates der Philosophie an der Universität Wien,* Österreichische Akademie der Wissenschaften, Philosophisch-historische Klasse, Sitzungsberichte 232, vol. 2, Abhandlung, Veröffentlichungen der Kommission für Geschichte der Erziehung und des Unterrichts, no. 3, Beiträge zur Geschichte der Universität Wien, Vienna 1958.

Mitchell, Kathleen E. / Levin, Al S. / Kumboltz, John D, Planned Happenstance. Constructing Unexpected Career Opportunities, in: *Journal of Counseling & Development,* vol. 7, no. 2 (1999).

Reindelius S. J., Rupertus / Moritschius, Nicolaus / Hatmiller, Jacobus, *Assertiones ex variis philosophiae partibus depromptae* (Ingolstadii: Ex officina typographia Davidis Sartorii, 1593), BSB: 4 Diss. 1305, Beibd. 1, Munich.

Schultz, Georgius / Stockhart, Johann-Heinrich, *Dissertatio de blanda mulierum rhetorica, occasione axiomatis Richteriani publicae eruditorum censurae & ventilationi exposita* […] *die ___ Octobr. Anno 1678* (Lipsiae: Literis Johannis Georgii, 1678), ULB: 99 A 6930 (8), Halle.

Stierus, Johannes, *Praecepta doctrinae sphaerae ex probatis auctoribus collecta, et adjuvandae memoriae causa tabulis synopticis inclusa* ([s.l.]: Impensis Johannis Brickneri, 1642), Landes- und Universitätsbibliothek: 33/7545, Darmstadt.

Tidicaeus, Franciscus, φυτολογία *generalis capitibus aliquot complectens ea quae ad plantarum essentiam naturamque universim explicandam pertinent: scripta et in disputationem vocatum publicam in* [...] *academiae Lipsiensis, die 11. Cal. Maij, (15)82* (Lipsiae: (Georgius Defnerus), (1582)), BSB: Phyt. 702, Munich.

Timplerus, Clemens, *Pars altera physicae, complectens apsychologiam* (Hanoviae: Apud Guilielmum Antonium, 1605), StA and StB: C 1488 (2), Brunswick.

Timpler, Clemens, *Pars tertia & postrema physicae, complectens empsychologiam* (Hanoviae: Apud Guilielmum Antonium, 1607), StA and StB: C 1488 (3), Brunswick.

Tobias, Ronald B., *20 Master Plots and How to Build Them*, Cincinnati 1993.

Uding, Gerd (ed.), *Historisches Wörterbuch der Rhetorik*, Tübingen 1994.

# The Hidden Space of Production.
# Virtuality in Henri Bergson and Gilbert Simondon
*Dawid Kasprowicz*

> The plague takes images that are dormant, a latent disorder, and suddenly extends them into the most extreme gestures; the theater also takes gestures and pushes them as far as they will go: like the plague it reforges the chain between what is and what is not, between the virtuality of the possible and what already exists in materialized nature.[1]

## Structures of Virtuality

When confronted with the term 'virtuality', several scenarios come to mind. In the 1990s, the most prominent of these scenarios have been related to a parallel existence called 'virtual reality', which gives the impression of a porosity between the real and the artificial. In recent years, the term 'ubiquitous computing'[2] frames the argument that we already live in the midst of virtual scenarios that surround us – that we are part of a game within sensible environments, which gather and structure our traces into networks and databanks. But this does not suppose that we are controlled by the supra-natural power of a player or government. It rather concerns the issue of where physical and biological forces end, and here the question is raised: What are the constitutive elements of the present we are conceiving, and how do we conceive of it? I will not go deeper into this question here. However, it already demonstrates that the term of virtuality both "reforges the chain between what is and what is not"[3] and, concomitantly, re-focuses on the bond between the scientifically provable and the metaphysical as a necessary condition for explaining the phenomena of life or living beings. I will focus here especially on this second, ontological element with regard to the philosophy of Henri Bergson and Gilbert Simondon. Here, virtuality is a threshold between a predetermined form of being (actualizing the possible) and a reflexion of the given experiences of an individual as the result of virtual forces that have an impact on it. Hence, virtuality is constantly related to an act of production but it does not exhaust itself in this event. Instead, we are confronted with traces of the living as traces of our being in the world.

---

[1] Antonin Artaud, *The Theatre and Its Double*, transl. by Mary C. Richards, New York 1958, p. 27.

[2] Cf., for example, Ulrik Ekman (ed.), *Throughout. Art and Culture Emerging with Ubiquitous Computing*, Cambridge 2013.

[3] Artaud, Theatre (see note 1), p. 27.

I will discuss the relationship of the virtual and the individual in the work of Henri Bergson and Gilbert Simondon, since both offer an alternative approach to the concept of the virtual that tries to overcome classic constellations of the actual and the virtual in western thinking. As we will see, the virtual is no longer bound to an anthropocentric point of view of realizing ideas for an enrichment of the present through the anticipation of a creator. It is at the heart of the process of individuation – the becoming of the individual – that the virtual takes a central role in the explanation of the living individual. From there, I will point to the radicalization of the concept of virtuality in the work of Gilbert Simondon through his relation of the technical object and the psychic individual. Through this, virtuality becomes more and more a key concept in the dynamic and manifold processes of becoming. The productive and creative psychic individual is only one possible actualization that is constantly in a tense relation with his social milieus and his technical objects.

Desubstantialising Evolution –
Henri Bergson and Antagonistic Tendencies

Since the growing interest in the work of Gilbert Simondon, the question of an alternative ontology has returned to the agenda of many theorists from different fields of the humanities. In a (western) cultural setting of subject-object hybrids, which Bruno Latour has elaborated on so much[4], of medically created cyborgs or of smart objects, which transform the phenomenologically graspable object into an active and sensible participant in our environment, it is not only the need for a new ontology that has been formulated, but ontology as a philosophical agenda has itself been brought into question. Alongside figures such as Gilles Deleuze, Félix Guattari, Alfred N. Whitehead and Gilbert Simondon, who feature so often, the name of Henri Bergson only rarely appears.[5] It would take too long to explain this circumstance here, and it would only be possible with a lot of non-assured hypothesis. However, I claim that it is Bergson's

---

[4] Bruno Latour, *We have never been modern*, transl. by Catherine Porter, Cambridge 1993; Bruno Latour, *Reassembling the Social. An Introduction to Actor-Network-Theory*, New York 2005; Bruno Latour, *An Inquiry into Modes of Existence. An Anthropology of the Moderns*, transl. by Catherine Porter, Cambridge / London 2013, here in particular chapters 7–8.

[5] Two examples that draw this systematic line from Bergson to Simondon are Jean-Hugues Barthélémys, *Penser l'individuation. Simondon et la philosophie de la nature*, Paris 2007, pp. 37–55; Anne Sauvargnagues, Crystals and Membranes. Individuation and Temporality, in: *Gilbert Simondon. Being and Technology*, ed. by Arne de Boever et al., Edinburgh 2012, p. 58.

concept of the virtual as a steady force of indetermination in the becoming of the living, which makes his inclusion in this ontological discussion so important.[6] One has to distinguish between two meanings of the term virtual in the work of Bergson: The first is more established and deals with the question of perception and knowledge. Bergson elaborates on this especially in *Matter and Memory*. The second one that interests me here is that which he develops in *Creative Evolution* as a counterpart to the biological theories of Darwinism and Lamarckism.

Both concepts of the virtual circle primarily around the question of time and how it evolves. One question in *Matter and Memory* deals with the perception of matter and how it develops in time, when former perceptions become memories and are entangled with past experiences of the subject. Bergson answers that there is neither a pure perception of matter nor is perception reducible to intra-cerebral moments processing the sensual data. Instead, in Bergson's description of perceptions, it is the body which mediates between spirit and matter by selecting the next image to be processed.[7] Time evolves and images become memories, which turn out to work

> like a compass that is being moved about, the position of a certain given image, my body, in relation to the surrounding images. In the totality of representation they are very little; but they are of capital importance for that part of representation which I call my body, since they foreshadow at each successive moment its virtual acts.[8]

Concerning the question of knowledge, the body selects what I perceive of the present, but this selection is interwoven with memories, which rise up to the present and even sketch my upcoming approach towards the world. And it is crucial to emphasize the point that these "virtual acts" are not clear images that just have to be realized as possible actions.[9] Rather, it is here where the term of virtuality already alludes to a steady-dying present that transforms the past and the virtual, as Deleuze has pointed out so clearly.[10] This does not only refer to the fact that you never definitely know what is going to happen, but also addresses the problem of the changing of 'subjective

---

[6] Henri Bergson, *Matter and Memory*, transl. by Nancy M. Paul and W. Scott Palmer, London 1911, p. 3.
[7] Bergson, Matter (see note 6), p. 10.
[8] Ibid., p. 10.
[9] Gilles Deleuze, *On Bergsonism*, transl. by Hugh Tomlinson and Barbara Habberjam, New York 1988, p. 97.
[10] Ibid., p. 94.

vision' through perception.[11] We have here the core element of virtuality in Bergson's philosophy, which flips the mechanistic order of cause and effect. It is not in *a priori* knowledge or scientific laws where we can locate the virtual but through the manifold events which have an impact on our thinking and show us what can be possible in the unfolding of time. Outside of that, argues Bergson, we tend to ignore the real and follow a prescribed program.[12] What he alludes to is the determinism in scientific explanations, especially in mechanics. Aside from mechanics, however, it is in the knowledge of life sciences such as biology that Bergson elaborates his critique of scientific knowledge. His conception of time as "real duration" challenges the scientific system of knowledge, which requires the isolation of time and space for the prediction of the behaviour of matter.[13] The 'duration' of the theory of evolution and of Lamarckism, although they bring with them the important term of transformism[14], is misleading for Bergson since both approaches reduce transformism to a morphological and therefore matter-based process. Instead, Bergson first wants to conceptualize – from a human perspective – how evolution takes place and how we 'know' of something like an ongoing transformism?

The answer to this problem is given in Bergson's *Creative Evolution,* and, drawing on Simondon's concept of individuation, I will shed light on two central thoughts related to the question of knowledge of life and ontology. In both, with regard to the theory of evolution, the tension of individuality and reproduction comes into play as the problem of an absence of a substantializable individual that can be isolated as something like a materialized proof of individuality. Bergson makes this clear at the beginning when he writes:

> A perfect definition [of individuality] applies only to a *completed* reality; now, vital properties are never entirely realized, though always on the way to become so; they are not so much *states as tendencies*. And a tendency achieves all that it aims at only if it is not thwarted by another tendency. How, then, could this occur in the domain of life, where, as we shall show, the interaction of antagonistic tendencies

---

[11] The last point is everything but a statement for a psychological approach since Bergson's *Matter and Memory* is a critical argument with the research questions of psychologists in his time. Take, for example, the sentence about 'subjective vision': "As we shall endeavour to show, even the 'subjectivity' of sensible qualities consists above all else in a kind of contraction of the real, effected by our memory." Bergson, Matter (see note 6), p. 25.

[12] Henri Bergson, *Denken und Schöpferisches Werden,* Frankfurt am Main 1985, p. 124.

[13] Henri Bergson, *Creative Evolution,* transl. by Arthur Mitchell, London 2007, p. 15.

[14] Ibid., p. 15.

is always implied? In particular, it may be said of individuality that, while the tendency to individuate is everywhere present in the organized world, it is everywhere opposed by the tendency towards reproduction. For the individuality to be perfect, it would be necessary that no detached part of the organism could live separately. But then reproduction would be impossible. For what is reproduction, but the building up of a new organism with a detached fragment of the old? Individuality therefore harbours its enemy at home.[15]

To resolve both the problem of becoming individual and being able to reproduce, Bergson has to break fundamentally with the ontological thinking of substances and accidents. According to him, every individual, being the result of individuation, would contradict the presumption of an isolatable substance suitable to explore living matter.[16] Such thinking would belong to an ontology of states. But if we turn to tendencies, one has to ask how these 'antagonistic tendencies' relate to the virtual and the fact of a (re-)production of individuals. Are they the virtual living, like the seed is the virtual tendency towards the future flower? One might answer this in the affirmative, but that would not give any explanation of the process of life. Antagonistic tendencies are a metaphysical reflection on the diversification and association of living beings treating individuality as a "composition of an undefined number of potential [*virtuelle*] individualities potentially [*virtuelle*] associated."[17] Here we have Bergson's ontogenetic basis of the *élan vital*, the tension of association and disassociation as a never finished process of individuation. But how does this process work in reality? A good example would be Bergson's elaboration on the chlorophyllian function of the plant, in which the plant stops the dissipation of energy by storing it and providing energy for other living beings, such as animals and humans. It is here that the plant – through the photosynthetic process – takes a central role as the in-between of the tendencies of becoming and going, of individuality and reproduction. Through the chlorophyllian function, life evolves continually in tendencies and creates new forms. The other crucial factor for evolution is the nervous system that connects sensorial input and motoric actions as well as inner functions of the organism. In the nervous system's concentration and distribution of energy, Bergson sees "a reservoir of inde-

---

[15] Ibid., p. 8.

[16] Here, Deleuze marks out the two types of differentiation in Bergson's work. One is related to the selective perception of the world and the other to a "virtual totality" as the basis for all actualized differentiations. Deleuze, Bergsonism (see note 9), p. 95.

[17] Bergson, Evolution (see note 13), p. 167.

termination"[18], a subsisting potential for the ongoing production of individuals out of these reservoirs.

Taking this biological background of tendencies into account, Bergson's ontology turns virtuality from a container of possible states to a key term for the dynamics of a "becoming without being"[19], as American Philosopher Manuel DeLanda has stated. Through this, the relation of virtuality and production is not a question of matter anymore, but of energetically bound forces and tendencies that weaken and reinforce each other to a systematization that creates living beings as effects of an indeterminate becoming, of an indeterminate reality. Both points are crucial for Simondon's concept of individuation that – as I will outline now – can be seen as a continuation of this transformation of virtuality, as the result of a further detachment from substantialistic ontologies. However, emphasis will be laid on the question of how the term of virtuality enables Simondon to introduce the production of technical – as opposed to living – individuals.

Productive Tensions and the Individuated Being

Before we attend to the virtuality of psychic and technical individuals, we should again throw light on the consequences of ontogenetic thinking. Bergson's shift from an ontology of states of formed matter to a flux of materializations (including de- and re-materialization, which is the death and reproduction of cells) is also at the heart of Simondon's concept of individuation. Both approaches are thus essays on a metaphysic of the living resulting from contemporary scientific questions. It was Georges Canguilhem, teacher of Simondon, who wrote that the "physico-chemical" has elaborated on the living but "[e]verything remains to be done in biology. Biology must therefore first consider the living as meaningful being, and its individuality not as an object, but as a term within the order of values."[20] Hence, Simondon's ontogenetic approach to the living results in a refusal of any substantialism that "conceives the unity

---

[18] Ibid., p. 82. This idea of a *"reservoir of indetermination"* is very close to Leibniz' monades containing all the virtual relations and properties on their inside. Monades have themselves no relations or properties because they are simple substances, which are non-material. They actualize change through an inner force because no exterior forces can have an impact upon them. This last point is important for Simondon's ontogenesis as well.

[19] Manuel DeLanda, *Intensive Science and Virtual Philosophy*, London / New York 2002, p. 84.

[20] Georges Canguilhem, The Living and Its Milieu, in: *Grey Room*, vol. 3 (2001), transl. by John Savage, p. 21.

of living being as its essence"[21] as well as of the Aristotelian dualism of hylomorphic thinking. In both cases, we meet the same metaphysical issue that we find in Bergson: How do we go beyond given structures of thinking to an ongoing production of the individual as not yet predictable?

It is here as well that the relation of cause and effect has to be flipped. To avoid the "ontological privilege to the already constituted individual"[22], Simondon develops a system of virtuality, the functioning of which brings him to a philosophy of force-driven tendencies, just as it has been the case for Bergson. But here, around half a century later, the principles of thermodynamics are no longer the only centre of metaphysical reflection. Instead of a retention of energy in cells as a 'reservoir' of indeterminate creation of the living, it is quantum mechanics which become crucial for Simondon's conception of the virtual. In quantum mechanics, matter is not steadily bound to a substance or a form.[23] One can detect matter in a certain point in space, but, although one has the data, it is not possible to tell where the next point in space is going to be. Considering the unpredictability of matter and its states, of not knowing where the individual particle is as it is, but only as it appears and then vanishes again, Simondon develops his concept of the preindividual. Individuation needs first and foremost a coming into being of the pair of the individual and the milieu, which always appears together for Simondon. What happens in the virtual sphere of the preindividual is an energetic condition for individuation, an overtension of energetic fields that have been brought into "correlation", as he states.[24] Form, matter and energy are contained in the preindividual as virtualities – their coming into being depends on what Simondon calls a 'meta-stable' system. This is a setting into relations before any matter, the constellation of two extreme poles, which have to dissolve into a new relation of milieu and individual. These meta-stable systems are called "transductions" – as the condition of two following time states. Now, what the preindividual does is to set individuation in time, or, as Anne Sauvargnagues has put it, to begin the "individuation of being" as becoming.[25]

---

[21] Gilbert Simondon, The Genesis of the Individual, in: *Incorporations*, ed. by Jonathan Crary and Sanford Kwinter, New York 1992, p. 297.

[22] Ibid., p. 298.

[23] Think, for example, of the long argument on the question if there are waves or particles.

[24] Simondon, Genesis (see note 21), p. 302.

[25] Sauvagnargues, Crystals (see note 5), p. 57.

It is here where Simondon separates the individuation of the living and the non-living. While the non-living has a meta-stability and a process of becoming matter, it does not have the ability to get into new tensions with its milieu. It just reacts, as crystal does after its materialization, to the external pole of its being and does not interact with its inner pole, which means with another extremity that would create a new meta-stable system. The individuation of the living instead always participates in the preindividual pool, which does not resolve itself after the materialization of the individual. Rather, "it is fair to assume that the process of individuation does not exhaust everything that came before (the preindividual)".[26] Moreover, the living is more than a fact of indeterminate becoming and it is less a metaphysical drive than a metaphysical claim of a discontinuous struggle. "The living entity is both the agent and the theater of individuation: its becoming represents a permanent individuation or rather a series of approaches to individuation progressing from one state of meta-stability to another."[27] Thus, the "living entity" is primarily a setting of relations as the condition of successive temporal states instead of specific matter that could be discovered as the ongoing engine of life. Virtuality here is bound to living entities as beings, who produce "limited actualities"[28] out of the virtual pool of energies. Living here has – in contrast to Bergson – an inevitable discontinuity in its meta-stable states.

### The Production of the Technical Individual

For Simondon, the technical object as a process of individuation, as a becoming of a technical individual, first has to be separated from the technical object suffering the phenomenon of 'hypertelism'. Hypertelic objects are constructed for one special milieu, which they have to adapt to or that they depend on energetically. Their milieu-to-adapt-to is already given before production, and in this way the hypertelic object resembles what Jean-Paul Sartre describes as the thing in general, in which essence takes precedence over existence.[29] For Simondon, such over-adaption in the long run leads to disadaption because the existence of the object depends either on the task it

---

[26] Simondon, Genesis (see note 21), p. 306.
[27] Ibid., p. 307.
[28] Ibid., p. 304.
[29] Jean-Paul Sartre, *The Existentialism is a Humanism*, transl. by Philip Mairet, London 1973, p. 20–21.

was built for or on the material it was made from.[30] In both cases, we have an instrumentalist approach towards technical objects. To be able to speak of technical individuals, there has to be an arrangement of two diverse – one might say antagonistic with regard to Bergson – milieus. These so called 'associated milieus' are the essential condition for progress as a "leap beyond established reality and its system of actuality towards new forms which continue to be only because they exist all together as an established system."[31] To put it bluntly, the associated milieu is the virtuality of any production as the becoming of something new. Again, like in Bergson, we here have the idea of systematization when talking about individuality.

In *On the Mode of Existence of Technical Objects*, Simondon gives several examples of such established systems. One is the construction of the traction engine for railway vehicles, such as trains. This engine does not only change mechanical into electrical energy for translation (as every electromotor does, which here represents a technical milieu), it is also acting upon the environment and reacting to it in raising the conduction current and dropping the voltage in the contact wire if the train has to go uphill or if there is a lot of snow on the road. One needs neither two engines for distributing the high voltage nor fear that the engine may become overheated. The traction engine represents a 'self-generated adaption' of a technical object. As a creation of something new out of the tension of two separated milieus, the traction engine binds two antagonistic milieus as one environment of production.

> This environment, which is at the same time natural and technical, can be called the associated milieu. By means of this the technical being is conditioned in its operation. This is no fabricated milieu, or at least not wholly fabricated; it is a definite system of natural elements surrounding the technical object and it is linked to a definite system of elements which constitute the technical object. The associated milieu is the mediator of the relationship between manufactured technical elements and natural elements within which technical being functions.[32]

Although the train has an obvious goal, its technical individual, the traction engine, is open towards the exterior world to interact with it energetically. Departing from cyberneticists such as Norbert Wiener, Simondon describes this setting in relation to the concept of 'recursive causality'. Normally, a technical milieu would function

---

[30] Gilbert Simondon, *On the Mode of Existence of Technical Objects*, transl. by Ninian Mellamphy, Western Ontario 1980, p. 51. The classical example of Simondon is here a tire that is only made for cold weather.

[31] Ibid., p. 60.

[32] Ibid., p. 61.

mechanically in the simple equation of input as cause and output, which means acceleration of mass by more power, as effect. But the ability to use the natural milieu as informed energy transforms both milieus. Now, the technical milieu, as Simondon describes it, "causes a reaction in the line that powers it" by transforming geographical properties with technical structures like cold-protective rails, with the mentioned ability to control the conduct current and line voltage in the transformation of electrical to mechanical energy.[33] On the other hand, the geographical milieu works on the train with properties of cold, snow or massive wind. Here, both milieus have to be in a balanced, homeostatic relationship, which is the condition for mediation between the two. This mode of regulation of two milieus as two modes of an energetic state in an associated milieu is something different to Bergson's philosophy of thermodynamics. Simondon's concept of 'recursive causality' describes a flux of different levels of energy as a transportation of information executed by the associated milieu.[34] While for Bergson there had to be a kind of energy stock like the chlorophyllian function of the plant to guarantee the reproduction of living beings, Simondon's teleological approach aims to explain the meta-stability of individualized beings by the maintenance of an internal cohesion through the coupling of an external energy source. Bergson's idea of delivered energy for the becoming of indeterminate beings still has its setting in a hierarchical and closed system of living beings, ranging from microbes to men.[35] In contrast, although relatively simple, Simondon has the conception of an open machine, or, in general, an open system for living beings.

Simondon considers this principle as "a system of virtualities, of potentials and moving forces, whereas forms are a system of the actual."[36] Forms of matter are actualized virtualities, which, as in the case of the traction engine, can only exist when the different forces of the technical and natural structures are brought together. Bringing virtualities into forms is only possible through an anticipation of the future in the present state, which is basically a human capability and the condition of invention.

---

[33] Simondon, Existence (see note 30), p. 55.

[34] Ibid., p. 64.

[35] For more about the problem of metastability and ontogenesis in particular, cf. Gilbert Simondon, *L'individuation à la lumière des notions de forme et d'information*, Paris 1964, especially pp. 222–233.

[36] Ibid., p. 63–64. These two concepts, the virtual and the form, are synonymous with the background and the form, both central terms in the *Gestalt* psychology that Simondon criticizes in this passage.

Simondon here talks of the "creative imagination"[37] the inventor has when he brings his ideas into actual forms, "in much the same way as an actor can play a role in absence of the real person".[38]

This seems at first glance to contradict the Bergsonian conception of virtuality as an indeterminate being. For Simondon, the imagination is the possible that turns into the actual. But behind this inventive mode of thinking, two things have to be considered: First, the created technical object is a technical individual as a self-regulative artefact that adapts autonomously to the environment. Second, the actualized forms cannot be restricted to psychic and physical constraints. The principle of an individual, which is coupled to an associated milieu as the ground of all virtualities, is here the condition for something new to arrive. The coupling of an individual and a milieu is, as we have shown, a principle of the meta-stability of life in general. Standing behind man as an inventor of technical objects through the anticipation of future associated milieus is the basic principle of Simondon's concept of virtuality, the homeostatic flow of informed energy transgressing and confronting milieus to produce new individual entities. Living beings result out of a confrontation of forces and in the same time they are potentially able to produce new relationships because, as we have shown, all living entities participate in the preindividual. Therefore, the phenomenon of a thinking being is not the only explanation for associated milieus and technical individuals.

On the one hand, man is just an effect of the virtual forces of the ongoing binding of living individuals with an associated milieu. In this sense, the living entity is, just as in Bergson, unpredictable as well as unfinished. On the other hand, man is able to produce technical objects because he has an analogous "matter-form association"[39] that brings him into correlation with the technical individuals and milieus he invents. So, to sum up briefly, we have here two meanings of virtuality: There is virtuality as a driven force of the ontogenesis that relates the individual to the preindividual and takes him from one meta-stable state to another. And then there is the anti-Bergsonian concept of a creative imagination where the inventor is capable of turning the virtual into the actual with the principle of a homeostatic state. Still, let us take a closer look at the

---

[37] Ibid., p. 62.

[38] Simondon, Lumière (see note 35), p. 62.

[39] Ibid., p. 66.

relationship of the inventor and the technical object to explain this second meaning of virtuality with regards to a 'hidden space of production'.

## The Potential of Technics and the Dynamics of Production as a Dynamics of Transindividuation

As in the production of hypertelic objects, it is the same with the invention of technical objects in general. According to Simondon, if the individual – or the community – only constructs machines to fulfil his needs or the needs of the community, then the relation of humans to technical objects is comparable to that of the master to his slave.[40] Otherwise, the individual could be determined by technical productions as well when some of his modes (speaking, moving, and behaviour) have to adapt to a technical system presupposing the transformation of those modes of expression to be integrable into the symbols of the machine, which is involved in these inter-individual communications. Such adaptions – and this is crucial here – demonstrate how the technical object has an impact on the psychic individual. Thus, there is not an equivalence between the technical and the individual since these two have two different modes to 'relate' to the world. While the technical is described by Simondon as a teleological mechanism[41], which is concerned with the constant reduction of a difference between an exterior and an interior state (representing the principle of a homeostatic state), the individual – as a participator in individuation – is forced to question and confront himself 'towards the world' in his situation and with the diverse knowledge he has of the world. Although the individual can create technical individuals out of an associated milieu, there is an ongoing problematic state of a psychic individual putting himself into question (*"de se mettre en question soi-même"*).[42] This relating to the world as a questioning of being takes place not only as a condition for the production of technical objects but moreover for the discontinuous production of the individual

---

[40] Simondon, Lumière (see note 35), p. 271, 276. After Simondon, at the beginning of the relation of the psychic individual and technical object, there is the model of the slave and the master. Then comes the prolongation of human capabilities into technical objects (anthropomorphism). Both forms of an alienation of individuality do not annihilate the technical potential of the object completely because the state of an autonomous relation to the world rests in the slave as well as in the technical object or the domesticated animal as a revolutionary potential. They are still part of an individuation.

[41] Ibid., p. 272.

[42] Ibid., p. 273.

as a part of his community or his environment. For Simondon, the complementary relation of the individual and the technical object here creates a dynamic of interacting forces participating in the preindividual.[43] While, as we have shown, technical individuals have no individuation but an independence as self-regulating objects, the technical being in general is bound to the individuation of man as the correlative force of the "self-creation of the individual" in time.[44]

As becoming is always related to the preindividual pool of forces, the technical being, as Simondon calls it, does not only actualize as a materialized object but also as a value.[45] If the individual invents, then he can generate a new kind of inter-subjective relation that could overcome the tension between individual and community. It is here where Simondon sets the concept of the transindividual as the setting of a new meta-stable state. If the goal of the existence of a technical object is not predetermined and if the community does not assign every individual their approach towards the technical beings, as in terms of production strictly relating to labour, then the virtuality of the 'self-created' individual can be actualized with the potentiality of the technical. It is this part that resides as the condition for the anticipation of an associated milieu as well. Or, to put it bluntly, thinking of individuality is only possible in correlation with the technical. If the construction of technical objects is not only about their measureable effort but also about values, then virtuality – as the hidden space of production – constitutes the potential for how the individual relates to the produced object. Technical milieu and psychic individual are co-indeterminate as correlative elements throughout the process of individuation.

---

[43] This distinction is made clear by Mark Hansen, when he differentiates between the associated milieu and the preindividual where the technical object becomes a "catalyst" for transindividuation. Cf. Mark Hansen, Engineering Pre-Individual Potentiality. Technics, Transindividuation and 21st-Century Media, in: *Substance. A review of theory and literary criticism*, vol. 41, no. 3 (2012), p. 46.

[44] Gilbert Simondon, *L'individuation psychique et collective*, Paris 2007, p. 268. Transl. by the author.

[45] Simondon, Individuation (see note 44), p. 266. Here, we have the extension of Canguilhem's demand for the meaning of individuality as a value in the world of technical objects.

Conclusion

In trying to focus on the term of virtuality in this broad sense in the work of Henri Bergson and Gilbert Simondon, this essay could only outline a tentative approach. But I would like to draw the line for the concept of virtuality from Bergson to Simondon by outlining four points: 1. A reflexion on the meaning and use of the term virtuality implies the renunciation of an ontology oriented in matter and form dichotomies. The virtual takes a central role in the conception of an ontogenesis whose ongoing production of individuals is the actualized fact of differentiation out of the virtual (that is indeterminable). 2. Instead of a search for a decisive matter of life, it is the influence of contemporary scientific theories, which add a knowledge of energetic relations (or their maintenance and delivery) to the production of the new. Through them, virtuality withdraws from ready-made relations like the possible and the actual, which are so dominant in the functional meaning of production as a paradigm of labour. 3. In this conceptualization of energetic relations, Simondon breaks with the ongoing impact of Bergson's élan vital by way of a pattern of generated and dissolved meta-stable states, which actualize a virtual pool of forces into the relation of an individual and his milieu. 4. Taking this into account, Simondon reshapes virtuality as the contingence of productive forces in individuation as well as the fundament for an evolution (or better evolutionary leaps) of biological, technical or psychic individuals. Instead of a hierarchy of beings, we see here a metaphysical program containing the explanation of the genesis of being as materialized in temporary or, to use Simondon's term, 'transductive' states. Through this, the psychic individual has an ambivalent status. As an inventor, on the one hand, he is the one responsible for the usage of technical potentiality to produce a new state of being in relation to his community. On the other, he finds himself in the 'hidden space of production' as part of an ontogenetic process. Here, the recursion of actualized technical potential of human modes of thinking, reasoning and defining life is at the very heart of a concept of virtuality that Bergson has formulated as an impact of effects. It is this impact that lets us mediate (scientific) causes. And it is here where one has to distinguish the functional term of production from a state of productive, virtual forces, bringing about new relationships of the psychic individual towards his milieu.

# Bibliography

Artaud, Antonin, *The Theatre and Its Double,* transl. by Mary C. Richards, New York 1958.

Barthélémys, Jean-Hugues, *Penser l'individuation. Simondon et la philosophie de la nature,* Paris 2007.

Bergson, Henri, *Creative Evolution,* transl. by Arthur Mitchell, London 2007.

Bergson, Henri, *Denken und Schöpferisches Werden,* Frankfurt am Main 1985.

Bergson, Henri, *Matter and Memory,* transl. by Nancy M. Paul and W. Scott Palmer, London 1911.

Canguilhem, Georges, The Living and Its Milieu, in: *Grey Room,* vol. 3 (2001), transl. by John Savage, pp. 6–31.

DeLanda, Manuel, *Intensive Science and Virtual Philosophy,* London / New York 2002.

Deleuze, Gilles, *On Bergsonism,* transl. by Hugh Tomlinson and Barbara Habberjam, New York 1988.

Ekman, Ulrik (ed.), *Throughout. Art and Culture Emerging with Ubiquitous Computing,* Cambridge 2013.

Hansen, Mark, Engineering Pre-Individual Potentiality. Technics, Transindividuation and 21st-Century Media, in: *Substance. A review of theory and literary criticism,* vol. 41, no. 3 (2012), pp. 32–59.

Latour, Bruno, *An Inquiry into Modes of Existence. An Anthropology of the Moderns,* transl. by Catherine Porter, Cambridge / London 2013.

Latour, Bruno, *Reassembling the Social. An Introduction to Actor-Network-Theory,* New York 2005.

Latour, Bruno, *We have never been modern,* transl. by Catherine Porter, Cambridge 1993.

Sartre, Jean-Paul, *The Existentialism is a Humanism,* transl. by Philip Mairet, London 1973.

Sauvargnagues, Anne, Crystals and Membranes. Individuation and Temporality, in: *Gilbert Simondon. Being and Technology*, ed. by Arne de Boever et al., Edinburgh 2012, pp. 57–72.

Simondon, Gilbert, *L'individuation à la lumière des notions de forme et d'information*, Paris 1964.

Simondon, Gilbert, *L'individuation psychique et collective*, Paris 2007.

Simondon, Gilbert, *On the Mode of Existence of Technical Objects*, transl. by Ninian Mellamphy, Western Ontario 1980.

Simondon, Gilbert, The Genesis of the Individual, in: *Incorporations*, ed. by Jonathan Crary and Sanford Kwinter, New York 1992, pp. 297–319.

# Tino Sehgal's "Constructed Situations". The Tension of Immaterial Production

*Francesca Valentini*

On June 1, 2012, Tino Sehgal was awarded the Golden Lion as the best artist of the 55th International Art Exhibition "The Encyclopedic Palace" at the Venice Biennale. Holding the Lion, he stated, "the 20th century was the century of individualism and philosophies of solitude [...] I hope that in the 21st century we can adjust it a little bit."[1] *Not Yet Titled* (2013), the artwork for which Sehgal was awarded the prize, could be experienced in one of the biggest rooms of the main pavilion at Giardini and was cryptically described by curator Massimiliano Gioni as "a situation in which a pair of disparately aged interpreters, allied in an indifference to their physical surroundings, interpret a dance and a chant."[2]

Describing *Not Yet Titled* as well as three other works by Tino Sehgal entitled *This is so Contemporary* (2004), *This is Exchange* (2003) and *This Variation* (2012), I aim to stress some of the most relevant characteristics of Sehgal's work in order to investigate the dynamics of production that the artist challenges and implies. Among the various sources I use, the writings of art historian Claire Bishop as well as philosopher Paolo Virno and media theorist Franco Berardi, two exponents of what can be defined as the Italian radical thought[3], help me to underline some of the key features of these four pieces by Sehgal, shedding new light not only on Sehgal's work but also on the contemporary tensions between producers and what is being produced, between us and the world we are living in.[4]

---

[1] Biennale Arte 2013 – Tino Sehgal, 2013 (video file), https://www.youtube.com/watch?v=EUReasWFXmg#t=47 (13/05/2016).

[2] Massimiliano Gioni (ed.), *The Encyclopedic Palace,* Venice 2013, p. 412.

[3] Paolo Virno / Michael Hardt (eds.), *Radical Thought in Italy. A Potential Politics,* Minneapolis / London 1996. Sven Lütticken already associated the work of Sehgal with the analysis of post-Fordism and immaterial labour offered by Paolo Virno and Antonio Negri; cf. Sven Lütticken, Progressive Striptease, in: *Perform, Repeat, Record. Live Art History,* ed. by Amelia Jones and Adrian Heathfield, Bristol / Chicago 2012, pp. 187–198, originally published in Sven Lütticken, *Secret Publicity*, Rotterdam 2005.

[4] This essay is the final version of a draft, which, before being presented in Düsseldorf at the conference *You Were Not Expected to Do This,* was presented at the Kunsthistorisches Institut at the University of Cologne (January 26, 2012), at the a.r.t.e.s. Graduate School for the Humanities Cologne (July 12, 2012), at the Kunstverein der Gegenwart in Leipzig

The first time I remember experiencing Tino Sehgal's work I was visiting the 2005 Venice Biennale where Sehgal was one of the two artists selected by curator Julian Heynen to represent Germany. Sehgal's work was exhibited there along with Thomas Scheibitz's painted sculptures. Entering the German pavilion, the visitors met three guards dressed in black trousers and white shirts, who suddenly began to jump back and forth while repeatedly singing, "Ooh! This is so contemporary, contemporary, contemporary…" At the end of the jingle one of the three said: "Tino Sehgal", which the second followed with "*This is so Contemporary,* 2003", and the last added "courtesy of Jan Mot". In another area of the venue, people were received by a different pavilion guard, who after a couple of welcoming words presented himself or herself by name and addressed the visitor with the following words:

> [T]his is a work by Tino Sehgal entitled *This is exchange.* The work is an offer. I offer you to pay back one half of the entrance ticket price if you tell me what you think about market economy and if you are willing to discuss this with me.

When the public took part in the discussion, they got a password to redeem half of the ticket price at the counter.[5] Leaving the pavilion, the visitors felt outraged, sceptical, or quite enthusiastic, but considering what I remember of my visit and the impassionate criticism of the pavilion that art historian Benjamin Buchloh wrote within his review of the Biennale for the Summer 2005 issue of *Artforum,* the number of outraged and sceptical visitors was higher than that of the enthusiastic ones…[6]

Tino Sehgal was born in London in 1976 and studied political economics as well as dance at the Humboldt University in Berlin and at the Folkwang University of the Arts in Essen, respectively. In 2005, when he was chosen as the youngest artist to

---

(April 20, 2013), and at the Ca' Foscari University of Venice (June 13, 2013). I am indebted to all those individuals who gave me constructive feedback as well as to all of those who, in various ways, helped me in elaborating my thoughts. Special thanks go to all interpreters of Tino Sehgal's pieces, who kindly answered my questions and shared their observations, as well as to the artist himself.

[5] As recalled by art critic Michel Gautier, one of the passwords used in Venice was "toto". Michel Gautier, *Les Promesses du zero,* Geneva 2009, p. 136.

[6] Benjamin Buchloh, The Curse of Empire, in: *Artforum International,* vol. 44, no. 1 (2005), p. 255. According to Buchloh, most of the practices presented at the 2005 Venice Biennale "between the desire for a renewed validity of aesthetic convention and a fully conventionalized radicality of the anti-aesthetic. This dialectic manifests itself most painfully […] in the German pavilion's exhibition of Thomas Scheibitz and Tino Sehgal, where desperate conventionalization, on the one hand, and an almost frenetic anti-aesthetic on the other, embody this schism as thought it were a program."

represent Germany at the Venice Biennale, he had been working as an artist for five years, after having danced in various companies such as those of dancers and choreographers Jérôme Bel and Xavier Le Roy. Following his participation at the 2005 Venice Biennale, he continued to produce and present his work on an international level, taking part in many group exhibitions and being offered solo shows, such as one organized by the Trussardi Foundation in Milan in 2008 and by the Solomon R. Guggenheim Museum in 2010.[7]

In 2012, on the occasion of the 13th edition of the documenta in Kassel – henceforth dOCUMENTA (13) – Sehgal produced a new work entitled *This Variation*. Entering an unassuming and secluded door in the backyard of the Huguenot House, an abandoned building at Friedrichstraße 25, which was renovated, re-inhabited and opened on the occasion of the international art festival by Chicago-based artist Theaster Gates[8], visitors found themselves in an utterly dark room. Your eyes could see nothing as if they were suddenly but inexplicably closed, but you could still perceive the surroundings where something was moving. People were engulfed by rhythmic noises that were actually sounds, scattered fragments of hypnotic melodies among which I could recognize the chorus of *Good Vibrations* by The Beach Boys. When you had been in the space for sixty seconds, you started to perceive the shadows of about twenty men and women dancing to the music they themselves were producing. They were dancing while beatboxing, beatboxing while dancing and moving around. You could not be sure whether the light had been augmented when you entered the space or whether it was your sight, which was getting used to the darkness. The voices, music and dance enveloped the visitors, who could not resist: Some started to move their heads, some

---

[7] Tino Sehgal's first major solo show in Italy was organized by the Trussardi Foundation and curated by its artistic director Massimiliano Gioni. The exhibition took place at the Villa Reale, a late eighteenth century royal building which hosts the Galleria d'Arte Moderna Milano, the largest municipal collection of 18th century art since 1921. It was opened from November 11 to December 14, 2008 and offered the most complete overview of Sehgal's work to date; cf: Fondazione Nicola Trussardi, *Tino Sehgal. Villa Reale, Galleria d'Arte Moderna, Milan, November 11 – December 14, 2008*, http://www.fondazionenicolatrussardi.com/tino_sehgal_1.html (13/05/2016); Tino Sehgal's Guggenheim exhibition was organized as a part of the Guggenheim's 50th anniversary. Curated by Nancy Spector, it took place in the entire Frank Lloyd Wright rotunda from January 28 to March 10, 2010; cf.: Guggenheim, *Tino Sehgal*, http://www.guggenheim.org/exhibition/tino-sehgal (13/05/2016).

[8] Theaster Gates, *12 Ballads for the Huguenot House* (2012). Cf. Eva Scharrer (ed.), *dOCUMENTA (13). The Guidebook, Catalog 3/3*, Ostfildern 2012, p. 430.

joined the dance, and some left the room. *This Variation* involved interpreters that performed fourteen diverse choreographies in the darkness that consisted of spoken words, beatbox music and songs that were sung.[9]

*Not Yet Titled*, the work presented at the 55th Venice Biennale, incorporated some elements of *This Variation*. Entering the Central Pavilion at Giardini, visitors were invited to proceed through the shady Sala Chini[10], where *The Red Book* (1914–1930) by psychotherapist Carl Gustav Jung was displayed, and continue straight on. The exit of this hall coincided with the entrance to the room in question. A wall on which the white 'burial' *Mask of Breton* (ca. 1950) hung – the mask had been cast by surrealist sculptor René Iché when André Breton was still alive – functioned as a screen to block both the light and direct access to the following room. Overcoming the obstacle through passages on the left or right of the same wall, you found yourself in the main area of the pavilion, a huge, almost square space illuminated by natural light coming from above. There, on the walls, various blackboard drawings (1923) by founder of anthroposophy Rudolph Steiner were shown. Four hieratical sculptures by visionary architect and artist Walter Pichler were scattered on the basement.[11] Most of the people did not notice Tino Sehgal's piece at once since it took place in a zone to which our visual field is not often called to focus on. Especially on days when the exhibition was very crowded, it was necessary to be extremely aware of the surroundings in order to notice the artwork. One way of becoming aware of the piece was by paying attention to the other visitors who often sat on a small bench placed behind the above-mentioned screen-wall and who looked down to watch the one, two, three, four or five kneeling individuals of different ages (from 13 to 65 years old).

---

[9] Charlotte Klinger (interpreter of Tino Sehgal, *This Variation*, Kassel 2012), in discussion with the author: The spoken or sung words of the different choreographies could be sentences as "The income men derive from producing things of slight consequence is of great consequence" (in this case the interpreters had the task to repeat the sentence with their own words – they could use any word as long as they did not change the meaning of the initial clause) and parts or refrains of different songs, among which one can cite "The Way I Are" by American producer, songwriter and rapper Timbaland as an example.

[10] The Sala Chini takes its name from Italian painter Galileo Chini, who decorated its vault in 1909. On the occasion of the 55th Venice Biennale, La Biennale di Venezia completed the restoration of the decoration series (which is titled "La Civiltà nuova" – The New Civilization) bringing the art nouveau painting back to its splendour in the shades of red, blue and gold.

[11] The four sculptures by Walther Pichler were: *Stele I* (1962–76); *Stele II* (1962–76); *Bewegliche Figur* (1982); *Composite Figure* (head by Dieter Roth) (1999).

While one of them beatboxed, mumbled a melody or sung a couple of words of a song, the others were moving, following the rhythm in a sort of trance. Most of the time, the interpreters worked in pairs. Responding to the different melodies produced by one of the members of the pair, sometimes belonging to popular songs such as Marvin Gaye's *I Want You* or Psy's *Gangnam Style*[12], the other started to move, interpreting the respective choreography. Absorbed in a ritual, which took place entirely on the floor of the space, they communicated, exchanged positions, and left the room at the end of their shift, following signals such as small gestures, guttural sounds, and quasi-spoken words. In order to interpret the choreographies elaborated by Tino Sehgal, the interpreters performed "a form of emotional barter"[13] among themselves, almost never meeting the gaze of the visitors who sometimes formed a crowd around them. They were kneeling in front of the international audience of the exhibition as if they were "kneeling in front of the world"[14], but they concentrated on themselves to find and follow their personal inner rhythm, to express the given song or to dance the given choreography: "[I]n that moment we were a little egoist, everyone thought only about herself or himself."[15] Each was also somehow trying to protect the others, acting as a "policeman for the others"[16], asking people to stop taking pictures or filming the action and preserving the integrity of the atmosphere which reverberated through the entire room.

Referring to the descriptions of Sehgal's pieces I have presented, I will now focus on and discuss some of their most relevant characteristics: their position within the practice of performance art, their constitutive implementation of visitor(s), their duration, their refusal of any kind of reproduction or documentation, their aim to be immaterial products with a given exchange value, and their being presented only within the institutional frame of art. Discussion of these aspects will permit the development of some broader reflections on Sehgal's artistic practice and question the role of such practice within contemporary society.

---

[12] Barbara Pastor (mother of Edoardo, one of the interpreters of Tino Sehgal's *Not Yet Titled*, Venice 2013) in discussion with the author, October 2014. Sehgal's musical choices and ways of implementing music, songs and covers within his choreographies deserve detailed discussion, which exceeds the boundaries of this essay.

[13] Ildo (interpreter of Tino Sehgal's *Not Yet Titled*, Venice 2013), in discussion with the author, June 2013.

[14] Ibid.

[15] Silvia (interpreter of Tino Sehgal's *Not Yet Titled*, Venice 2013), in discussion with the author, June 2013.

[16] Elena (interpreter of Tino Sehgal's *Not Yet Titled*, Venice 2013), in discussion with the author, June 2013.

As underlined by art critic Michel Gauthier, more than those of performance art, the work by Tino Sehgal seems to share the constitutive features of "une œuvre d'*exécution*, en cela proche de la représentation théâtrale, du ballet, du concert ou bien d'autres activités."[17] However, "à la différence du théâtre, de la danse ou de la musique dans leur formes de manifestations les plus fréquentes, il ne se traduit pas pour le public par l'exécution d'une seule occurrence de l'œuvre."[18] Putting Sehgal's pieces under the microscope of art history, Gauthier states that a piece by Sehgal cannot be defined in terms of 'performance' nor in those of 'happening', "la première intervenant dans un lieu voué à l'art, et non le second."[19] Furthermore, a number of performances "n'ont connu qu'une seule exécution."[20]

A number of experts in the field, among which I would cite Claire Bishop as an authoritative example, have pointed out a striking difference between the historicized concept of performance and its present developments: "[C]ontemporary performance art does not necessarily privilege the live moment or the artist's own body, but instead engages in numerous strategies of mediation that include delegation and repetition."[21] According to Bishop, Tino Sehgal's oeuvre is one of the paramount examples of what she refers to with the expression 'delegated performance', that is, "the act of hiring non-professionals or specialists in other fields to undertake the job of being present and performing at a particular time and a particular place on behalf of the artist, and following his/her instructions."[22] As she underlines:

> This strategy differs from a theatrical and cinematic tradition of employing people to act on the director's behalf in the following crucial respect: the artists [...] tend to hire people to perform their own socio-economic category, be this on the basis of gender, class, ethnicity, age, disability, or (more rarely) a profession.[23]

Compared to the practice of performance in the 1960s and 1970s, when performance was the cheapest and most direct means of expression since it enabled artists to produce art everywhere using just their bodies, delegated performance "tends to be a luxury

---

[17] Gauthier, Promesses (see note 5), p. 110.
[18] Ibid.
[19] Ibid.
[20] Ibid.
[21] Claire Bishop, *Artificial Hells. Participatory Art and the Politics of Spectatorship,* London / New York 2012, p. 219.
[22] Ibid., p. 219.
[23] Bishop, *Hells* (see note 21), p. 219.

game."²⁴ It is "an artistic practice engaging with the ethics and aesthetics of contemporary labour, and not simply [...] a micro-model of reification."²⁵

Rather than refer to his work in terms of 'performance', which is bound in a way to the concept of accomplishment, Sehgal prefers to call his pieces "constructed situations".²⁶ They involve one or more people carrying out instructions conceived by Sehgal himself. He can count on a small number of loyal professional collaborators, who interpret his pieces wherever they are presented, but the majority of interpreters are ordinary people cast on-site. Bishop stresses the fact that, in contrast to the tradition of the performances of the years 1960s-1980s, where the artist was present by bringing their own body into play, within the practice of delegated performance, "this presence is no longer attached to a single performer but instead to the *collective* body of a social group."²⁷ However, looking at Tino Sehgal's pieces, it would be better to speak of 'the collective body of the people'. In fact, only very few works implement interpreters who embody specific social categories.²⁸ Instead, more than for a cohesive group, his interpreters stand 'for the multitude of the people'. Generally, as in the case of *Not Yet Titled*, the interpreters stand out neither because of their belonging to a specific social category nor because of their age or their physical characteristics, but they are a group of people which is representative of the category 'people', among which one can find children as well as adolescents, adults as well as elderly persons. Sehgal chooses them because he is fascinated by some of their very 'unspecific gifts': the way they move (their hands, for example) or keep a position, or the way they use their voice.

Expanding on the relationship between artist and interpreters, Sehgal states:

---

[24] Ibid., p. 229.

[25] Ibid., p. 220.

[26] Hans Ulrich Obrist, *Interviews*, vol. 2, Milan 2010, p. 826. Claire Bishop has pointed out that "by using this term, Sehgal does not intend any reference to the constructed situations of the Situationist International"; cf. ibid., p. 350, note 9.

[27] Bishop, Hells (see note 21), p. 219.

[28] As an example, one could cite: *This is Occupation* (2005), which is interpreted by an unemployed person who has the task of describing their life and situation.

> I speak as Tino Sehgal through someone else. But basically it is just the classical relation of interpreting somebody else's work: those who do the work are a medium, a channel for my subjectivity, but at the same time their subjectivity also plays a part in how they interpret it. In most of my works, there is always a situation […] where the interpreter is free to say what he or she wants. […] Of course, it's a relationship based on trust. There have been a few occasions where interpreters abused that by simply doing something quite different during the part defined by me. At those moments, my work was in fact no longer present.[29]

Sehgal's choreographies can be slightly changed and allow improvisation. According to him, his work greatly depends on the reaction of the visitor(s), as in the case of *This is Exchange*:

> My works […] are much more about creating a common situation between the visitor or the viewer. Of course the situation is initiated by people doing things. The ontological status of the visitor and the person doing the piece is kind of … I am not going to say the same … but it is oscillating between almost being the same and being different.[30]

Sehgal is convinced that the more his work develops and the more the visitors know about it, the more power they have over how the piece will develop; which is even more power than that of the interpreters. Sehgal's pieces are nevertheless constructed situations, which develop following precise choreographies and do not allow for shared authorship.

All his pieces can be experienced for the entire duration of the exhibition, every day, from opening to closing time. The interpreters work in shifts that last a few hours (between two hours and forty minutes and three hours in the case of *Not Yet Titled*), allowing the pieces to function in a loop.

Sehgal's constructed situations leave no material traces. Not only does the author authorize no labels, but also no photos, audio or video records as well as no catalogue: The only traces of the pieces are kept in the visitors' memory as well as in the critical reviews of his interventions. As Bishop stresses,

> although Sehgal makes a point of renouncing photographic reproduction, his work seem actively to tear apart any equation between liveness and authenticity; indeed, the very fact that his work runs continually in the space for the duration of an exhibition, performed by a number of interpreters, erodes any residual attachment to the idea of an original ideal performance.[31]

The fact that Sehgal forbids any kind of reproduction of his work involves a number of different questions that I plan to address as a separate issue in the future. For the

---

[29] Jörg Heiser (ed.), *Funky Lesson*, Frankfurt am Main 2005, p. 104.

[30] Obrist, Interviews (see note 26), p. 837.

[31] Bishop, Hells (see note 21), p. 224.

confined purpose of this essay, it is worth noting that Sehgal's detractors have often addressed his refusal of all kinds of technical reproduction as a mere strategy to assure his work's spectacularization.[32] Overturning Walter Benjamin's well-known thesis[33], sociologists Antoine Hennion and Bruno Latour argue that "if reproduction is an active re-creation, and if technique is anything but mechanical, then multiplication cannot be defined as the passive dissolution of original authenticity into a reified consumption of fetishes."[34] It seems to me that Sehgal's practice points at undermining both extremes of this dialectic: on the one hand, the "aesthetic of the total withdrawal"[35] as a strategic means to assure hype and fame; on the other, the widespread dissemination of each type of technical reproduction as a means of communicating the existence of a work of art as well as of producing its authenticity.

The artist aims to create immaterial artworks, which remain products to be bought or sold as ordinary goods.[36] He explains:

> In this respect I consider communism and capitalism as two versions of the same model of economy, which only differ in their ideas about distribution. This model would be: the transformation of [...] 'nature' into supply goods [...], to enhance the quality of life. [...] My point is that dance as well as singing – as traditional artistic media – could be a paradigm for another mode of production which stresses transformation of acts instead of transformation of material, continuous involvement of the present with the past in creating further presents instead of an orientation towards eternity, and simultaneity of production and de-production instead of economics of growth.[37]

Sehgal associates performativity with politics. Expanding on *This is so Contemporary*, he states:

> [It] is the most performative work of mine, not in the sense of performance-like but in the true sense of the word, that it can either succeed or fail; it's like putting something to the test [...] normally we tend to think of contemporary culture as informed by the latest in technology – we are contemporary

---

[32] Buchloh, Empire (see note 6), p. 157.

[33] Walter Benjamin, *Das Kunstwerk im Zeitalter seiner technischen Reproduzierbarkeit*, Frankfurt am Main ²1955 [1936].

[34] Bruno Latour / Antoine Hennion, How to Make Mistakes on So Many Things at Once – and Become Famous for It, in: *Mapping Benjamin. The Work of Art in the Digital Age*, ed. by Hans Ulrich Gumbrecht and Michael Marrinan, Stanford 2005, p. 94.

[35] Buchloh, Empire (see note 6), p. 157.

[36] They can be purchased through a verbally conducted transaction within the presence of the salesperson, the buyer, some witnesses, and a notary.

[37] Dorothea von Hantelmann / Marjorie Jongbloed (eds.) (2002). *I promise it's political*, Cologne 2002, p. 91.

because we use contemporary technology and that is how we construct contemporariness. I was interested if we can construct a contemporariness without using contemporary technology or without even making reference to it but using the oldest means possible, just people moving around.[38]

Following the Aristotelian idea brushed up by Hannah Arendt in her *Vita Activa*, he considers every act political because every act has an influence on society.[39]

His artworks are always accompanied by a spoken label. On the one hand, these labels can be considered constative sentences because they name something which already exists; on the other, they can be seen as performative sentences, which constitute the artworks. Spoken labels grant Sehgal's pieces the status of artworks. As he underlines,

> the performative defining of this 'spoken label' is more fundamental in my case because all the other objects are given the status of artworks by the institutional framework as a matter of course, for my work this status must be actively established.[40]

Another distinctive feature of Sehgal's constructed situations is that they are always presented in institutional art spaces (museums, galleries, and so on). When I asked him what were the reasons for this choice, he answered:

> There are many reasons but maybe one of the important reasons is that for me [...] today we understand ourselves as individuals and not anymore necessarily as part of a collective. You are first and foremost yourself, you are not necessarily first and foremost an Italian. Theater always makes us be like a collective – the audience –, while the museum is a much more individualized experience. I think other things are possible in a kind of human interaction when you meet one and one rather than in front of like... is a kind of exposure of yourself in front of, like, the collective, and also I think that participation of visitors/audience becomes much easier if there is not so much pressure... of, like, you know, one hundred people watching you participate. It is just like, okay, I am participating in something, but it is like I am participating in this conversation with you, the pressure is not so on, and without this pressure also other things can arise [...] Another reason is that, like, in comparison to the street, people really want to experience something – they have attention – while in the street you are supposed... you have to spend quite some effort to get this attention, so that place is a kind of privileged space where you can start, let's say at point seven and not at point zero. But I'm interested in public space, it is just that I have not had a good idea.[41]

Sehgal's aim for immaterial production is very close to the concept of cognitive capitalism described and analysed in the past decades by scholars such as Italian philosopher Paolo Virno. In his book *A Grammar of the Multitude: For an Analysis of Contemporary Forms of Life,* Virno states that in the so-called post-Fordist era, society is no longer organized in units and forces but in a 'multitude' of isolated individuals: 'Multitude'

---

[38] Obrist, Interviews (see note 26), p. 839.
[39] Hannah Arendt, *The Human Condition*, Chicago 1958.
[40] Heiser, Lesson (see note 29), p. 104.
[41] Tino Sehgal, in discussion with the author, November 2010.

literally means "being-many".⁴² While material production is increasingly automated, living labour services are increasingly intangible. This new post-Fordist immaterial labour with communication, information, symbols, languages and emotions is similar to that of the artistic work, the work of the 'virtuoso'. According to Virno, the 'virtuoso' can be a pianist or a dancer, whose job is to play well without creating a tangible end product. The presence of the audience is constitutive of his work.⁴³ "Today, wage labour is interaction"⁴⁴, Virno summarizes. Today, mutual recognition among different individuals is given through the intangible capital represented by interaction. Suppose that Virno's views could be confirmed, Sehgal's intention would be seen in a new light. The concept of performativity, which he himself ascribes to his work, would be called into question. The intangible interaction, for which he vouches, would not be a special characteristic of his work but of the contemporary production model.

In her introductory essay to dOCUMENTA (13), curator Carolin Christof-Bakargiev underlines:

> Most recent usages of the term 'choreography' (etymologically, the writing of a script for the sequences performed by a chorus of singers or dancers coming and going on stage) are connected with forms of harmony, found relations, participating together. Notions of self-choreography and improvisation became predominant in the choreographic imagination of the 1990s – dancing together to find new forms of agreement and democratic aesthetics. However, the notion of a harmonious syncing of people through a set of relations also repeats the false and stereotypical views of the harmonious syncing of bodies in productive economies during globalization – putting people in a different place to work efficiently through the apparent improvisation achieved with smartphones and other digital technologies.⁴⁵

When invited to contribute a text for *100 Notes – 100 Thoughts / 100 Notizen – 100 Gedanken* – the publishing project initiated by the artistic direction of dOCUMENTA (13) as "a space [...] to explore how thinking emerges and lies at the heart of reimagining the world"⁴⁶ –, media theorist Franco Berardi alias Bifo compared contemporary digital reality to the existential conditions of every single individual. In his short essay *Ironic Ethics*, he refers to media sovereignty in terms of the 'Infosphere', contrasting it with the notion of the 'Psychosphere':

---

⁴² Paolo Virno, *A Grammar of the Multitude. For an Analysis of Contemporary Forms of Life*, transl. by Isabella Bertoletti, James Cascaito and Andrea Casson, Semiotext(e), New York / Los Angeles 2004, p. 77.

⁴³ Ibid., p. 53

⁴⁴ Ibid., p. 108.

⁴⁵ Carolin Christov-Bakargiev, The dance was very frenetic, lively, rattling, clanging, rolling, contorted, and lasted for a long time, in: *dOCUMENTA (13). The Book of Books, Catalog 1/3*, Ostfildern 2012, p. 31.

⁴⁶ Carolin Christov-Bakargiev, *Letter to a friend*, Ostfildern 2010, p. 12.

> When the attunement of organism and environment is disturbed by the acceleration of the Infosphere, art registers and signals this dissonance, but at the same time it sets conditions for the creation of new modalities of becoming.[47]

It seems to me that the dichotomy proposed by Bifo could be made particularly productive with respect to Sehgal's latest works. To dive into the darkness of Tino Sehgal's *This Variation* means to switch off all our devices in order not to be trapped by the Infosphere. When, once in the room, after one minute, we were able to see and distinguish the shapes of the bodies, which surrounded us, we were allowed to enter a new dimension of our Psychosphere, which I would interpret as a healing dimension, in which everyone can discover the social and embodied dimension of everyone's sensibility. In contrast, *Not Yet Titled* did not offer the visitor the terribly surprising but at the end healing and reassuring dark dimension of *This Variation*. Entering the luminous space of the main pavilion at Giardini, the spectator met a small group or a pair of individuals, engaged in what I would define a private ritual of attunement. Rather than being blinded by the darkness, we were invested by the whiteness of the natural light coming from the ceiling. Only through paying attention to the interpreters and stopping in the space for a good amount of time could we understand how their intimate relationship worked, how they managed to interact together despite the confusion and noises often produced by the visitors. Observing the interpreters of *Not Yet Titled*, you sensed and were fascinated by the internal harmony they were jealously able to reach, looking for mutual rhythmical concordance and abandoning themselves in its flow. If, on the one hand, you did not want to disturb their trance because they could lose their fragile reverberating balance, on the other, you wished to be part of the hypnotic situation even if they were not trying to encourage you to join their play.

If the darkness of *This Variation* invited the integration of interpreters and visitors, we sensed the incommensurable incommunicability in the light of Venice, as well as all the power and strength and all the weakness and fragility of our human existence. *Not Yet Titled* brought us to face the human condition, telling us that the challenges of contemporariness cannot be delegated to the 'virtuoso' of the moment.

---

[47] Franco Berardi, *Ironic Ethics*, Ostfildern 2011, p. 14.

Holding the Golden Lion in his hands, Sehgal affirms, "the twentieth century was the century of individualism and philosophies of solitude [...] I hope that in the twenty-first century we can adjust it a little bit". I think that through his work he is able to express the paradigms of contemporary societies, isolating some crucial dynamics from their inner contradictions. If art, and, in this case, contemporary performance art, seems to mirror the tensions within society rather than propose alternative ways of questioning and solving them, one should take advantage of it. One should consider it as a re-enactment through which to experience, observe and glimpse the manifold ways we act, shape and are shaped by 'reality'.[48] Moreover, one should ask oneself whether the task of providing alternatives to society's most alienating collective, economical and political implications could be delegated to the artists. Despite the goals Sehgal tries to reach, a real alternative is yet to be found, has yet to find a name, and is yet to be titled.

---

[48] For a critical account of the concept of re-enactment within contemporary art practices, cf. Sven Lütticken (ed.), *Life, Once More. Forms of Reenactment in Contemporary Art*, Rotterdam 2005.

## Bibliography

Arendt, Hannah, *The Human Condition,* Chicago 1958.

Benjamin, Walter, *Das Kunstwerk im Zeitalter seiner technischen Reproduzierbarkeit,* Frankfurt am Main ²1955 [1936].

Berardi, Franco, *Ironic Ethics,* Ostfildern 2011.

Biennale Arte 2013 – Tino Sehgal, 2013 (video file), https://www.youtube.com/watch?v=EUReasWFXmg#t=47 (13/05/2016).

Bishop, Claire, *Artificial Hells. Participatory Art and the Politics of Spectatorship,* London / New York 2012.

Buchloh, Benjamin, The Curse of Empire, in: *Artforum International,* vol. 44, no. 1 (2005), pp. 254–258.

Christov-Bakargiev, Carolin, *Letter to a friend,* Ostfildern 2010.

Christov-Bakargiev, Carolin, The dance was very frenetic, lively, rattling, clanging, rolling, contorted, and lasted for a long time, in: *dOCUMENTA (13). The Book of Books, Catalog 1/3,* Ostfildern 2012.

Fondazione Nicola Trussardi, *Tino Sehgal. Villa Reale, Galleria d'Arte Moderna, Milan, November 11 – December 14, 2008,* n.d., http://www.fondazionenicolatrussardi.com/tino_sehgal_1.html (13/05/2016).

Gautier, Michel, *Les Promesses du zero,* Geneva 2009.

Gioni, Massimiliano (ed.), *The Encyclopedic Palace,* Venice 2013.

Guggenheim, *Tino Sehgal,* http://www.guggenheim.org/exhibition/tino-sehgal (13/05/2016).

Heiser, Jörg (ed.), *Funky Lesson,* Frankfurt am Main 2005.

Latour, Bruno / Hennion, Antoine, How to Make Mistakes on So Many Things at Once – and Become Famous for It, in: *Mapping Benjamin. The Work of Art in the Digital Age,* ed. by Hans Ulrich Gumbrecht and Michael Marrinan, Stanford 2005.

Lütticken, Sven (ed.), *Life, Once More. Forms of Reenactment in Contemporary Art*, Rotterdam 2005.

Lütticken, Sven, *Secret Publicity*, Rotterdam 2005.

Lütticken, Sven, Progressive Striptease, in: *Perform, Repeat, Record. Live Art History*, ed. by Amelia Jones and Adrian Heathfield, Bristol / Chicago 2012, pp. 187–198.

Obrist, Hans Ulrich, *Interviews*, vol. 2, Milan 2010.

Scharrer, Eva (ed.), *dOCUMENTA (13). The Guidebook, Catalog 3/3*, Ostfildern 2012.

Virno, Paolo, *A Grammar of the Multitude. For an Analysis of Contemporary Forms of Life*, transl. by Isabella Bertoletti, James Cascaito and Andrea Casson, Semiotext(e), New York / Los Angeles 2004.

Virno, Paolo / Hardt, Michael (eds.), *Radical Thought in Italy. A Potential Politics*, Minneapolis / London 1996.

Von Hantelmann, Dorothea / Jongbloed, Marjorie (eds.) (2002). *I promise it's political*, Cologne 2002.

# 'Organisme d'art'. Evolution and Artistic Production in the Work of Odilon Redon

*Katharina Thurmair*

As early as during the second half of the 19th century, the artistic paradigm of vitality gains increasingly in importance.[1] Writers and visual artists who feel connected to the symbolist movement in particular often refer to the impression of animation as a criterion for a successful work of art, making an interaction of artwork and beholder possible in the first place and activating a different reception process.

In order to define this vitality, the question arises which characteristics necessarily need to be found in a finished work of art and how artists are already trying to ascribe an essential role to this concept during the creative process.

Vitality had been postulated as a starting point for all artistic creation earlier than the 19th century. The attempt to establish an analogy between nature's creational activity and artistic production has long been a key objective. Yet, the coincidence of various scientific and artistic discourses – such as evolutionary biology, psychophysics and the beginning of the exploration of the human psyche as well as the emergence of idealistic and anti-rationalistic currents particularly in symbolist circles – causes a revision, refocusing but also enhancing this concept.

Vitality may already be included in the motif, or, like in Pygmalion's statue, it can be the expression of a further stage of completion of a manually already finished work. This raises the question of how the concept of vitality has been able to change from its classical meaning in art theory to something new – from the attempt of a vivid representation of something already existent in the exterior world to the reproach the artist would transform something animate into something dead by 'fixing' it in lifeless substance, all the way to the vitality and animation of the work itself transgressing its object character.[2]

---

[1] Gert Mattenklott, Sinnlich – Übersinnlich. Verklärung des Vitalen in der ersten Jahrhunderthälfte, in: *Elan vital oder Das Auge des Eros. Kandinsky, Klee, Arp, Miró, Calder,* exh. cat. Haus der Kunst, ed. by Hubertus Gaßner, Munich 1994, pp. 16–23; cf. also in general concerning the idea of vitality: Armen Avanessian / Winfried Menninghaus / Jan Völker (eds.), *Vita aesthetica. Szenarien ästhetischer Lebendigkeit,* Zürich / Berlin 2009.

[2] Cf. also Barbara Wittmann, Anti-Pygmalion. Zur Krise der Lebendigkeit in der realistischen Malerei 1860–1880, in: Avanessian, Vita (see note 1), pp. 177–192.

In the work of Odilon Redon, this concept of vitality originates from various sources. The external reality of nature, mental transformations of received impressions, which constitute an inner reality, and finally the idea of a kind of organism in which all existing realities integrate should in the following be examined more closely as sources of a dynamic process of artistic production.

In parallel, the concepts of matter and material need to be reconsidered: Not only in the biological and chemical research of the early 19th century, but also increasingly in literature and art, the boundaries between animate and inanimate forms of existence, between *matière brute* and *matière vivante* – or *matière organisée*[3], as it is also called – become blurred. Thus, the relation between creator and work and, in analogy, between artist and material needs to be revised, as it is no longer clear which one is more crucial for the beginning of the evolutionary or creational process.

Vitalist currents – mainly noticeable in philosophy and art – are on the one hand trying to incorporate the scientific substrate of a rationalistic, mechanistic view of the world, but on the other also critically question its usefulness.[4] Against this background, in which ways will the constellation of the various agents in the process of artistic creation change regarding the connection between artist, exterior and interior reality, material, finished work, and, of course, the viewer?

If we take a look at Odilon Redon's oeuvre, we notice that after a relatively inconstant and informal artistic education – from drawing and watercolour classes with Stanislas Gorin, a Bordeaux landscape painter to unambitious architectural studies in Paris to a few months at the free studio of Jean-Léon Gérôme at the École des Beaux Arts in Paris in 1864 – he seems to have found his own way of artistic practice at a relatively late point. Furthermore, his artistic production is also characterized by very strong disruptions, both in terms of motives, turning from nightmarish creatures to

---

[3] Cf., for example, Joseph Delboeuf, *La matière brute et la matière vivante. Étude sur l'origine de la vie et de la mort*, Paris 1887. The most cited example in this context is the synthesis of urea by Friedrich Wöhler in 1828, which was contradicting vitalist theories; cf. Kristian Köchy, *Perspektiven des Organischen*, Paderborn 2003, p. 261; in literature, one can think of animated objects in literary works by Charles Baudelaire and Edgar Allan Poe.

[4] The main characteristic of a scientific worldview seems to be the determination of processes; cf., for example, in psychophysical science the chapter "Définition de la vie: Les théories anciennes et la science modern" in: Claude Bernard, *La Science Expérimentale*, Paris 1875; concerning human perception and artistic production, currents of scientific scepticism are searching for processes that evolve outside of this kind of stimulus-response-mechanism; in relation to art, cf., for example, the critical position of Jean-Marie Guyau, *Les Problèmes de l'esthétique contemporaine*, Paris 1884; in philosophy Francisque Bouillier, *Du principe vital et de l'âme pensante*, Paris 1862.

flowers and butterflies, but most of all in terms of colour. It is not before the middle of the 1890s that Redon's use of colour reaches its full spectrum – mainly in the medium of pastel, but also in oil paint or even a mixture of various materials, such as pastel, oil and gouache.

Artistic Education – "On ne fait pas l'art qu'on veut"
Redon describes his training in Jean-Léon Gérôme's atelier in Paris as a blind alley, from which he was fortunately able to escape. However, the forms of perception and correspondingly those of artistic production he learned at the Academy seem to stand in his way at the beginning of his career, as he asks himself in retrospect in his short autobiographical text *Confidences d'Artiste*, published in the Belgian journal *L'Art Moderne* in 1984: "Qu'est-ce qui me rendit, au début, la production difficile et la fit si tardive? Serait-ce une optique ne concordant pas avec mes dons? Une sorte de conflit entre le cœur et la tête?"[5]

The two poles making any artistic production impossible for Redon are, on the one hand, an *optique,* i. e. a specific standardized and systematic way of perceiving, as taught in the beginning at the official academic classes, and, on the other, his individual predisposition, which this optic does not correspond with. This conflict is perceived as a contradiction between an imposed rational approach to artistic perception and production and an instinctively emotional one.

Artistic production in academic education – at least as it was experienced by Redon during the 1860s – strongly focused on forming lines during the initial drawing classes, which demands artists to particularly focus on the exterior shape of the material reality of objects with the aim of creating a representation as correct as possible. Therefore, the position of the artist is fixed from the beginning as an objective observer distanced from the exterior world, which, for Redon, in this mode of perception, seems to be only a lifeless, empty shell, contrary to his own subjective feeling: "[C]e professeur dessinait avec force une pierre, un fût de colonne, une table, une chaise, un accessoire inanimé, un roc et toute la nature inorganique. L'élève ne voyait que l'expression, que l'expansion du sentiment triomphant des formes."[6]

---

[5] Odilon Redon, Confidences d'artiste, in: *L'Art Moderne,* vol. 34 (1894). This reference taken from a reprinted version in: Odilon Redon, À *soi même. Journal 1867–1915,* Paris 1961 [1922], p. 25.

[6] Ibid., p. 22.

In classical artistic training, the line or the *dessin* still represents an intellectual and rational principle. Redon criticises the method of his teacher Gérôme as follows:

> Il me préconisait d'enfermer dans un contour une forme que je voyais, moi, palpitante. Sous prétexte de simplification, […] il me faisait fermer les yeux à la lumière et négliger la vision des substances. […] Je n'ai jamais pu m'y contraindre. Je ne sens que les ombres, les reliefs apparents; tout contour étant sans nul doute une abstraction.[7]

This analytical approach – focusing on the linear and thus creating a kind of abstraction that already takes place during the process of perception of things, in that way reducing the originality and individuality of perception to a system of alleged objectivity – is perceived by Redon as contrary to his nature and not as an adequate perceptual response to the surrounding vibrant world, of which he feels part of.

Instead, light and shade, *chiaroscuro* contrasts and the surface texture of things seem to be characteristics of a primordial, more instinctive way of perception. *Chiaroscuro* in particular is indeed just as important in classical academic training, especially since it serves not only to evoke an impression of space, but also increases expressivity.[8] However, a difference can be noticed in this point to how Redon sees the elements of artistic production: In his opinion, the design elements derive from a natural connection between artist and reality, but by no means should they be applied arbitrarily, *'avec force',* with the sole focus on the effect of the artistic result.[9]

An earlier critique of artistic practice, concerning paintings of the Salon of the *Société des Amis des Arts* in Bordeaux, reads as follows:

> Quelques-uns veulent absolument restreindre l'art du peintre à ne reproduire que ce qu'il voit. Ceux qui restent dans ces limites bornées se condamnent à un idéal inférieur. Les maîtres nous prouvent que l'artiste une fois en possession de son langage, une fois qu'il a pris dans la nature les moyens nécessaires d'expression, est libre, légitimement libre d'emprunter ses sujets à l'histoire, aux poètes, à son imagination.[10]

From restraining the creative process already at its beginning by using a pictorial language that is not original and instinctive, the artist as a *"parasite de l'objet"* has no

---

[7] Ibid., p. 22.

[8] Redon was particularly fascinated by Rembrandt's use of *chiaroscuro* contrasts, which express his emotional sensibility and his understanding of the painful human existence; cf. Redon, Même (see note 5), pp. 35, 136.

[9] Redon characterises academic education as artificial and standardised by using the terms *rhétorique, grammaire* and *formules;* cf. ibid., pp. 22, 135.

[10] Odilon Redon about the Salon Bordelais, in: *La Gironde,* May 19, 1868; cited in: André Mellerio, *Odilon Redon,* Paris 1913, p. 38.

access to imagination either and will only produce art that Redon characterizes as *"imitation"* and *"naturalisme direct"*.[11]

Already at this early point, Redon – as he explains in the *Confidences d'Artiste* thirty years later – seems to draw an analogy between the concept of rationally shaped forms and inanimateness as well as, in contrast to that, between the amorphous and vitality. The latter is less defined by lines than by material and colour. This kind of vitality, a "triomphe du mouvement et de la passion sur les formes"[12] can be perceived in all of the works of Eugène Delacroix, of whom he was an ardent admirer. Movement and passion can be seen as primordial forces that are crucial for an *'irradiation vitale'*[13] of the artwork.

Redon attributes this preference for expression and emphatic vitality at first to the romantic artworks that he got in touch with during the relatively free artistic education he received from Stanislas Gorin in Bordeaux in 1855.[14] Paintings by Gustave Moreau and Eugène Delacroix served as input for his imagination and laid the foundation of his preference in recreating an interior world: "A nous maintenant de nous livrer à notre fantaisie, à nous de créer librement"[15] seems to have been his battle cry against reproductive art.

Artistic creation is thus not something that can be taught in any way in an institutional system. These abilities are rather a natural disposition that the artist is born with – though whether these skills flourish or wither depends on proper care: "Nous naissons tous avec un autre homme en nous, en puissance, que la volonté maintient, cultive et sauve – ou ne sauve pas."[16] As in the theory of evolution, every being is born with certain qualities, but their development nevertheless depends on environmental circumstances.[17]

---

[11] Redon, Même (see note 5), p. 132; Mellerio, Redon (see note 10), p. 127.
[12] Redon, Même (see note 5), p. 173.
[13] Redon, Même (see note 5), p. 19.
[14] Ibid., p. 16.
[15] Odilon Redon about the Salon Bordelais, in: *La Gironde*, June 11, 1868; cited in: Mellerio, Redon (see note 10), p. 38.
[16] Redon, Même (see note 5), p. 24.
[17] In the debates that followed Darwin's evolutionary theory, the question about hereditary and environmentally acquired qualities has been widely discussed, initiated by Francis Galton's publications on *Hereditary Genius* (1869) and *Natural Inheritance* (1889). In France, those ideas have been accessible to a wider public e.g. in the *Revue scientifique* or the *Revue anthropologique*.

For this reason, Redon sees the requirements of academic training as obstructive to his natural artistic development and his individual creativity. It rather has to develop freely and out of inner necessity under the influence of various factors:

> [L]'artiste est, au jour le jour, le réceptacle de choses ambiantes; il reçoit du dehors des sensations qu'il transforme par voie fatale, inexorable et tenace, selon soi seul. Il n'y a vraiment production que lorsqu'on a quelque chose à dire, par nécessité d'expansion. [...] C'est la nature aussi qui nous prescrit d'obéir aux dons qu'elle nous à donnés.[18]

As an artist, Redon sees himself rather as part of a cosmic whole than as an objective observer of a world of inanimate objects.[19] Accordingly, as early as at the beginning of his artistic activity, he feels that a new work practice must be developed out of this position, a practice that corresponds with his existence as an individual subject and as a part of nature.

## Nature and Nurture – "La loi essentiel de creation"

An artistic production that is free and only directed by imagination, like Redon's hallucination- and dream-like early charcoals, does not necessarily result in disregard of nature and its logic. Natural laws as well as the perception of reality are still important as a kind of substrate of perception: "Tout en reconnaissant comme base la nécessité de la réalité vue... l'art véritable est dans la réalité sentie."[20]

The condition for this empathic mode of perception is, as mentioned above, an attitude that does no longer originate from a separation of the human subject from the world around him, but perceives the same kind of vibrancy, inner movement or vitality in all substances:

---

[18] Redon, Même (see note 5), pp. 23–26.

[19] Mellerio, Redon (see note 10), p. 98: "Redon semble profondément frappé de cette vision du Cosmos et de l'Humanité, telle que le XIX$^e$ siècle l'a évoquée." The sources of this 'vision' cannot adequately be traced, a small overview is given by Roseline Bacou, La Bibliothèque d'Odilon Redon, in: *Festschrift to Erik Fischer. European drawings from six centuries*, ed. by Villads Villadsen and Jan Garff, Copenhagen 1990; there, she mentions i.a. Schopenhauer, *Pensées et fragments*, Schuré, *Les Grands Initiés* and Hartmann, *Philosophie de l'Inconscient*; cf. also Gamboni, Dario, Des livres au livre. Les bibliothèques d'Odilon Redon, in: *Les bibliothèques d'artistes*, ed. by Françoise Levaillant, Paris 2010, pp. 171–191; furthermore, we can only guess that Redon must also have known about evolutionary and biological theories via Armand Clavaud.

[20] Redon about the Salon Bordelais, in: *La Gironde*, June 9, 1868, cited in: Mellerio, Redon (see note 10), p. 38. Redon rarely uses the term 'perception' but prefers 'vision', which refers to the 'inner' eye.

> [T]out homme, qui a l'œil ouvert sur la vie et qui la voit palpiter sous l'épiderme des choses, tout homme qui voit les substances et qui les aime, a dans le fond de son être un peintre qui sommeille."[21]

As a living being, the artist is not only obliged to conscious, objective perception. Rather, parallel to creative processes in nature, Redon points out that he as an artist has to 'organize the structures'[22] of his works – not along a scientific-like, mechanic functional process, but rather along an instinctive, organic one:

> Il y a un mode de dessin que l'imagination a libéré du souci embarrassant des particularités réelles, pour ne servir, avec liberté, qu'à la représentation des choses conçues. J'ai fait quelques fantaisies avec la tige d'une fleur, ou la face humaine, ou bien encore avec les éléments dérivés des ossatures, lesquels, je crois, sont dessinés, construits et bâtis comme il fallait qu'ils le fussent. Ils le sont parce qu'ils ont un organisme.[23]

The idea of an organism that is following certain primordial laws in order to be viable and functional is not only applicable to composite beings of humans, animals or plants, like in Redon's charcoals and lithographic albums such as, for example, *Les Origines* (1883). All forms of substantial existence are subject to the same natural laws of which the artist must always be aware:

> Tout dérive de la vie universelle: un peintre qui ne dessinerait pas verticalement une muraille, dessinerait mal, parce qu'il détournerait l'esprit de l'idée de stabilité. [...] Mais il y a dans la nature végétale, par exemple, des tendances secrètes et normales de la vie qu'un paysagiste sensitif ne saurait méconnaître: un tronc d'arbre, avec son caractère de force, lance ses rameaux selon des lois d'expansion et selon sa sève, qu'un artiste véritable doit sentir et représenter.[24]

Like the entire exterior world, the organism of the artist, too, is subjected to natural laws and environmental factors, as, for example, in the case of climate:

> Je dirai même que les saisons agissent sur lui. Elles activent ou amortissent sa sève: tel effort, tel essai tenté hors de ces influences que les tâtonnements et l'expérience lui révèlent, sont infructueux pour lui, s'il les néglige.[25]

So there can only be an artistic production in accordance with these natural forces; all arbitrary efforts must remain fruitless.

---

[21] Redon, Même (see note 5), p. 160.
[22] Ibid., p. 28.
[23] Ibid.
[24] Redon, Même (see note 5), p. 27.
[25] Ibid., p. 23; p. 128: "Et j'ai connu la subite influence qu'exerçaient sur moi divers lieux, ou le temps, la saison, ma demeure, l'orientation du jour d'atelier, pour affirmer ici avec certitude et assurance, combien il nous faut compter avec le monde invisible, mouvant et palpant qui nous entoure, et nous ploie au dedans sous les pressions encore obscures et inexpliquées du dehors."

That is why the former, quite intellectual drawing process is also becoming more and more a somatic process as well: "Il en est de même de la vie animal ou humaine. Nous ne pouvons pas bouger la main sans que tout notre être ne se déplace, par obéissance aux lois de la pesanteur. Un dessinateur sait cela."[26] The comparison between animals and human beings that is visible in most of Redon's work also makes clear why the artist has to follow the "intuitives indications de l'instinct dans la création"[27], which seem to have gotten lost in the course of the human evolution towards a rationalistic approach to the world as well as in the scientific evolution of optics and perception and their impact on art.

Anti-rationalist philosophers like Jean-Marie Guyau also demand a return to an artistic practice that only seems to follow the primordial talent of an instinct-like genius:

> [L]'art n'a pas seulement besoin que la science laisse à l'imagination poétique son légitime domaine, celui de l'idéal, du mystère et même du rêve; l'art ne peut réaliser au dehors ses conceptions sans le génie, qui n'est autre chose qu'un instinct créateur. Quoi qu'en pensent nos ‚parnassiens' modernes, le calcul, la patience, la méthode, la bonne volonté sont impuissants à produire une grande œuvre. [...] le raisonnement même, en tant qu'il précède la conception de l'œuvre, semble un signe de médiocrité: c'est l'opposé du génie.[28]

At this point, the idea of genius does not only aim at transcendent aspects, but is clearly linked to an innate disposition, as Redon puts it:

> C'est la nature aussi qui nous préscrit d'obéir aux dons qu'elle nous a donnés. Les miens m'ont induit au rêve; j'ai subi les tourments de l'imagination et les surprises qu'elle me donnait sous le crayon; mais je les ai conduites et menées, ces surprises, selon des lois d'organisme d'art que je sais, que je sens.[29]

### Vitality and Biology – "Organisme d'art"

The concept of art as 'organic', however, is also subject to a certain development, from initially only including the imagination that is free from any academic restriction regarding perception and elements of design, to a more holistic approach. From the obstructive procedure taught at the Academy, the need of a creative process arises, which goes hand in hand with one's individual creativity, both in terms of motives, as well as of their formal elaboration.

---

[26] Ibid., p. 27.
[27] Ibid., p. 27–28.
[28] Guyau, Problèmes (see note 4), p. 137.
[29] Redon, Même (see note 5), p. 26.

A form of creation that is following the paradigm of organised structures on the one hand and the instincts of imagination on the other can be observed in the hybrid creatures of animals, plants and human features as well as microbe beings, cells and plant particles of Redon's lithographic albums, such as *Dans le Rêve* (1879) or especially *Les Origines* (1883), where he creates a very idiosyncratic interpretation of the evolutionary process.

Redon stresses that these hybrid creatures, such as "La fleur du Marécage" from the album *Hommage à Goya* (1885) or even the earlier "Éclosion" from the album *Dans le Reve*, are not only derived from the experiences in microscopy he made with the help of biologist Armand Clavaud in Bordeaux in 1857.[30] Although Clavaud's own research concerning the passage between vegetative and animalistic life has had a huge impact on Redon's imagination, he also represents a major source of his literary knowledge. Clavaud is introducing him to fantastical literary texts by Charles Baudelaire and Edgar Allan Poe and also to the philosophical ideas of Arthur Schopenhauer and Spinoza.[31]

In this context, approaches to the problem of the dualism between body and mind or between the material and the spiritual – which constitute a fundamental debate that intensifies in France particularly in the last third of the 19th century, leading to the formation of opposing camps between *matérialistes* and *spiritualistes* – may have been of special interest to Clavaud and Redon.

Whereas Redon's early etchings and charcoal drawings still reveal a pessimistic view of the existential struggle of humanity, as, for example, in the etching "La peur" (1866)[32], Spinoza's monistic conception that there is only one basic substance in the world from which all material and spiritual forms of existence are developing, may have been increasingly influential for Redon.[33] However, Schopenhauer's concept of

---

[30] On the creation of his 'monsters', cf. Redon, Même (see note 5), p. 28: "Ils ne relèvent pas, comme l'a insinué Huysmans, des secours du microscope devant le monde effarant de l'infiniment petit. Non. J'avais, en les faisant, le souci plus important d'organiser leurs structures".

[31] Clavaud's research focuses on a species of algae, which transforms its vegetative state under the influence of light. On Clavaud's influence, cf. Mellerio, Redon (see note 10), p. 100: "Ainsi Clavaud ouvrait d'immenses horizons sur l'essence même de la vitalité et ses obscures origines. Il lui révélait le sens profond des lois qui régissent la matière, lui enseignant aussi ce que sont la méthode analytique et la synthèse"; cf. also Redon, Même (see note 5), p. 18.

[32] Frederick Baekeland, Depressive themes in the graphic work of Odilon Redon, in: *The Psychoanalytic Study of Society*, vol. 5 (1972), pp. 185–211.

[33] See also Nancy Davenport, Odilon Redon, Armand Clavaud, and Benedict Spinoza. Nature as God, in: *Religion and the Arts*, vol. 1 (2006), pp. 1–38.

*Wille* and *Vorstellung* also develops from pessimistic aspects towards an emphasis of a sort of vital force: In his publication *Philosophie de l'Inconscient* (1877), German philosopher Eduard von Hartmann[34] tries to resolve this dualism by establishing the term of the '*Inconscient*':

> La matière se resout au fond en volonté et en idée. Ainsi s'évanouit l'opposition radicale de l'esprit et de la matière. Ils ne diffèrent plus que parce qu'ils manifestent sous des formes inégales le même être, l'éternel Inconscient. Leur identité consiste en ce que l'Inconscient agit dans la matière aussi bien que dans l'esprit, comme un principie idéal dont la logique intuitive réalise au dehors le mouvement dont elle porte en elle-même l'idée. La notion de l'identité de l'esprit et de la matière n'est plus un postulat incompréhensible et indémontrable, ou le produit d'une inspiration mystique: elle est élevée à la dignité de notion scientifique. Ce n'est pas en tuant l'esprit, mais en animant la matière.[35]

These anti-rationalistic philosophical ideas can be seen as the substrate of all scientific knowledge that Redon might have learned from Armand Clavaud – such as probably also Charles Darwin's theory of evolution –, and this influenced his artistic production too, particularly in terms of the idea of an animated material.

Moreover, in the 1860s, as, for example, in the physiological research of Claude Bernard, the structure of the cell is getting more and more important as the origin of all organisms. Unlike in scientific models, however, Redon is always merging the pre-conscious, only functional existence of the cell with attributes of a higher consciousness – as, for example, in his album *La tentation de Saint Antoine* (1896), and especially in the lithographs "Oannès: Moi, la première conscience du chaos j'ai surgi de l'abîme pour durcir la matière, pour régler les formes" or also "Et que des yeux sans tête flottaient comme des mollusques", where primitive cells are equipped with heads and eyes –the most advanced organs in evolution according to Darwin.[36]

Parallel to the theory of evolution, which seems to become a paradigm for every creational act, artistic production also seems to follow certain natural laws that oscillate between determined and spontaneous processes. Other conflicting theories reflecting these two paradigms result from morphologic aspects in the evolution of organisms: The theory of epigenesis is prevailing over former ideas of preformatism. The theory

---

[34] Bacou, Bibliothèque (see note 19), pp. 29–37; *Philosophie de l'Inconscient* was published in Germany in 1869, but also translated to French several years later: Eduard von Hartmann, *Philosophie de l'Inconscient,* transl. by Désiré Nolen, Paris 1877.
[35] Hartmann, Philosophie (see note 34), vol. 2, p. 147.
[36] Charles Darwin, *On the Origin of Species,* London 1859, chapter 6; Darwin is questioning how such a perfect organ can evolve only by the principle of natural selection.

of epigenesis attributes an innate capability of self-organization to the primitive organism of the cell, which already incorporates the final shape of the organism that is just not visible yet. In a sort of dynamic teleology that critically incorporates concepts of idealistic morphology, Ernst Haeckel develops certain morphological laws that become formative in the second half of the 19th century and are also intensively discussed in France.[37]

These morphological aspects also influence the use of the term 'organism'. Originally a French neologism of the 18th century, it had been used as the definition of an animated human body as a self-structured and rational wholeness.[38] In the course of scientific development of the 19th century though, the focus shifted towards physiological and mechanical aspects. When the term 'organism' was mentioned in the scientific terminology of the 19th century, it mostly referred rather to the criteria of mechanical functions and processes of single organs and their coaction that ensured the preservation of the whole organism.[39]

Yet, Redon uses the term in less of a scientific and functional perspective than the physiologists of his time, but seems to have been influenced by vitalist or even romantic philosophy that focuses more on aspects of morphogenesis. Continual growth and dynamic change, as well as – from a metaphysical point of view – the capability of reuniting the oppositions of art and nature, of functional determinism and the spontaneous development of new forms, work perfectly as a substrate for a theory of art.[40] Redon's concept of natural morphogenesis could not only have emerged under the influence of biological discoveries, but also of certain philosophical concepts of Eduard von Hartmann's *Philosophie de l'Inconscient*.[41]

---

[37] Ernst Haeckel, *Histoire de la création des êtres organisés d'après les lois naturelles. Conférences scientifiques sur la doctrine de l'évolution en général et celle de Darwin, Goethe et Lamarck en particulier*, Paris 1877.

[38] Susanne Lüdemann, Körper, Organismus, in: *Wörterbuch der philosophischen Metaphern*, ed. by Ralph Konersmann, Darmstadt 2011, pp. 171–184, here p. 171.

[39] Georg Toepfer (ed.), *Historisches Wörterbuch der Biologie*, vol. 2, Darmstadt 2011, pp. 754–776, 777–842, here p. 796.

[40] Especially in the last decade of the 19th century, morphological aspects became more and more virulent in biology and in art; cf. Toepfer, Biologie (see note 39), p. 762; Reinhard Zimmermann, Das Kunstwerk als Wirk-Organismus, in: *Animationen, Transgressionen. Das Kunstwerk als Lebewesen*, ed. by Ulrich Pfisterer and Anja Zimmermann, Berlin 2005, pp. 247–264; on the concept of self-organization, cf. Reinhard Mocek, *Die werdende Form. Eine Geschichte der kausalen Morphologie*, Marburg 1998, mainly part 1, pp. 42–102.

[41] Hartmann, Philosophie (see note 34), vol. 1, especially pp. 205–226; vol. 2, pp. 248–272.

Hartmann stated that every being is equipped with a natural instinct of building forms; even the material/matter itself has an organizing ability, which he calls *'dynamisme atomistique'*.[42]

The epigenetic and philosophical assumption that every organism has an already inherent form, which is not yet recognizable in the primordial status of a cell or the unformed material, but is already potentially existent and has the possibility to dynamically evolve out of unshaped material can also be noticed in Redon's view of the creative process. This potentiality in the pre-existing material needs to be activated or animated by the artist. In Redon's pastel and oil paintings, like "Fantaisie sous-eau" (1908; Museum of Modern Art, New York), "Oannès" (1907; Kröller-Müller Museum, Otterloo) or "Fleurs" (1903; Kunstmusem St. Gallen), we have the impression that everything is subject to this permanent process of morphogenesis and transformation.

This process of finding the right form and, often enough, leaving the final form only as a suggestion is the main characteristic regarding the formal aspects of symbolist art or *art suggestif*, as Redon calls it:

> [A]rt suggestif: formes transposées ou transformées, sans aucun rapport avec les contingences mais ayant une logique cependant. […] il ne fallait rien définir, rien comprendre, rien limiter, rien préciser, parce que tout qui est sincèrement et docilement nouveau – comme le beau d'ailleurs – porte sa signification en soi-même.[43]

Against this background, artistic activity can never be seen as an arbitrary procedure: "Rien ne se fait en art par la volonté seule."[44] The creative abilities also depend on the right nourishment, so to speak, to start the reaction of transformation – and here Redon almost uses the terminology of chemistry.

> [M]on régime le plus fécond, le plus nécessaire à mon expansion a été de copier directement le réel en reproduisant attentivement des objets de la nature extérieure en ce qu'elle a de plus menu, de plus particulier et accidentel. […] Après un effort pour copier minutieusement un caillou, un brin d'herbe, une main, un profil out toute autre chose de la vie vivante ou inorganique, je sens une ébullittion mentale venir; j'ai alors besoin de créer, de me laisser aller à la représentation de l'imaginaire. La nature extérieure ainsi reçue et dosée, devient par transformation ma source, mon ferment.[45]

---

[42] Ibid., vol. 2, pp. 118–152.
[43] Redon, Même (see note 5), p. 26.
[44] Redon, Odilon, *Lettres d'Odilon Redon*, Paris / Brussels 1923, p. 33.
[45] Redon, Même (see note 5), p. 28.

Like any other organism, the artist can be seen as a kind of transformation agent[46]: "[L]'artiste [...] sera toujours un agent spécial, isolé, seul, avec un sens inné pour organiser la matière."[47] Thus, this process is not only exposed to imagination; it must be initiated, *inter alia*, by the choice of the appropriate medium and material. The artist is confronted with the task of organizing the material in order to express his ideas and 'incorporate' them in the material world.

Materiality – "C'est par elle que l'oracle parlera"
Questioned by André Mellerio about his artistic practice, Redon explains his proceedings in front of a blank sheet of paper in the following words:

> [J]e suis obligé, dès qu'elle est sur le chevalet, de la griffonner de charbon, de crayon, ou de toute autre matière, et cette opération lui donne vie. Je crois que l'art suggestif tient beaucoup des incilations de la matière elle-même sur l'artiste. Un artiste vraiment sensible ne trouve pas la même fiction dans des matières différentes, parce qu'il est par elles différemment impressionné.[48]

As soon as the artist is confronted with empty space and the material, he feels an almost reflex-like urge to start working.

The material has some intrinsic qualities that need to be discovered by the artist; these qualities stimulate his imagination as well as they determine his formal expression during the creative process.[49] Material could be characterized in this context as an unconscious or, more precisely, pre-conscious entity that already exists before any theoretical considerations whatsoever – like the philosophical *'prima materia'* – with the potential to transform and transcend in a sort of evolution-like process. Based upon this presupposition, the advice that Redon gives an artist friend becomes comprehensible:

---

[46] François Lyotard, Materie und Zeit, in: *Materie. Grundlagentexte zur Theoriegeschichte*, ed. by Sigrid G. Köhler, Hania Siebenpfeiffer and Martina Wagner-Egelhaaf, Berlin 2013, p. 503; Lyotard's essay focuses on the function of the body in Henri Bergson's theories; certain analogies concerning central concepts like Bergson's *élan vital* and évolution *créatrice* and Redon's artistic theory cannot be denied; unfortunately, they cannot specifically be proven with concrete examples in Redon's writings.

[47] Redon, Confidences (see note 5), p. 270.

[48] Redon, Lettres (see note 44), p. 33.

[49] Redon, Même (see note 5), p. 128: "Outre les dispositions reçues sous l'influence du monde et du lieu qui l'entourent, l'artiste cède aussi, dans une certaine mesure, aux exigeants pouvoirs de la matière qu'il emploie: crayon, charbon, pastel, pâte huileuse, noirs d'estampe, marbre, bronze, terre ou bois, tous ces produits sont des agents qui l'accompagnent, collaborent avec lui, et disent aussi quelque chose dans la fiction qu'il va fournir. La matière revèle des secrets, elle a son génie, c'est par elle que l'oracle parlera."

> [Q]ue votre ami ne se cherche pas dans des formules, des doctrines; qu'il travaille: l'oracle lui parlera, comme par surprise, à la minute où il aura le pinceau à la main. Non, quand il réfléchira. Pas tant d'analyse, sauf celle des matières qu'il emploie, et qui l'attirent. Elles détiennent [...] une part du secret. Elles sont de meilleur conseil que les maîtres. Elles priment toutes les théories. Qu'il 'ausculte' avec subtilité leurs ressources. Plus il les connaîtra, plus son esprit les illuminera. L'art expressif n'irradie dans sa plénitude que par des substances.[50]

The artist appears in these sentences as a kind of prophet or seer who speaks through the material. Accordingly, any delay of using an 'obstructive' material or integrating some sort of ideology or moral implications would be a falsification of this spontaneous divination process: "Soumettre le talent et même le génie à des concepts de justice ou de morale est une grande erreur. Elle provient chez l'artiste d'une prédominance de l'intelligence spéculative sur la libre divination."[51]

During the creation process, neither the attempt of reproducing nature – as we have already heard – nor the transmission of content has priority, but only the emergence of the material or – one could almost assume through Redon's use of the term *'belle substance'* – matter in a philosophical sense: "Peindre, c'est user d'un sens spécial, d'un sens inné pour constituer une belle substance. C'est, ainsi que la nature, créer du diamant, de l'or, du saphir, de l'agate, du métal précieux, de la soie, de la chair."[52]

Seeing artistic production as a dynamic and spontaneous process, any kind of routine has to be avoided: "Le peintre qui a trouvé das technique ne m'interesse pas. Il se lève chaque matin sans passion, et, tranquille et paisiblement, il poursuit le labeur commencé la veille. [...] Il n'a pas le tourment sacré dont la source est dans l'inconscient et l'inconnu."[53] Without inner emotional participation, the production of art is being reduced to a purely mechanical activity, which does not deserve the term of art, but has to be described as craft.[54]

Special characteristics of different materials also influence the artistic process and either work in a conducive or obstructive way. This phenomenon manifests itself for

---

[50] Redon, Même (see note 5), p. 112.
[51] Ibid., p. 113.
[52] Ibid., p. 108.
[53] Ibid., p. 110.
[54] Redon keeps a critical distance towards the impressionist and neo-impressionist movements; in general, these avant-garde groups are often confronted with the reproach of being an outgrowth of rationalist currents of the time, only obliged to a purely mechanical optic and technique and not satisfying the complexity of the human sensorium; cf. Redon, Même (see note 5), pp. 116, 162–163.

example in Redon's lithographic oeuvre. He avoids drawing directly on the lithographic stone but rather prefers the technique of the *papier report*: "[L]a matière agit beaucoup sur ma sensibilité [...] ce silex grave, revêche et dur ne permet guère les aventureuses entreprises de ma fantaisie. Le papier cède, la pierre résiste."[55] A more resistant material hinders the free, instinctive flow of inspiration. However, the paper has its own character too: "Elle est revêche, elle est maussade, comme le serait une personne qui a ses caprices et ses nerfs. Elle est impressionable, elle subit les influences les plus mobiles et variées du temps."[56]

The direct link between the artists' hands and the material may also have been a reason why Redon always preferred pastel and charcoal over lithography – a technique which leaves the final product without the 'spirit' or the touch of the artist[57]; it initially served him only as a technique of reproduction of his *Noirs*.[58] In his opinion, the creation of an artwork always has to be a union of spiritual and material processes: "[Q]uand le peintre donne de son rêve, n'oubliez pas l'action de ces linéaments secrets qui le lient et le tiennent au sol, avec l'esprit lucide et bien éveillé, tout au contraire."[59]

## The Artwork as Agent – "L'art suggestif"

Direct contact with the material aspects of artistic production seems to have an appeasing influence on his mind and body:

> Combien de fois [...] ai-je pris le fusain d'une main brunie par la terre qu'en jardinant je venais de toucher! Sainte et silencieuse matière, source réparatrice et refuge, que je vous dois de doux apaisements! Quel baume eut jamais sur moi, sur mon esprit et même sur mes peines, une action plus subite, plus bienfaisante que la vue de l'herbe verte ou le contact de tout autre élément inconscient.[60]

The material as *élément inconscient* needs to be incorporated into the artistic process as a balancing element that keeps reminding the artist of the organic origin of his production and prevents art from only being a rational activity.

---

[55] Redon, Lettres (see note 44), p. 34.
[56] Redon, Même (see note 5), p. 130.
[57] For a more detailed analysis of Redon's technical approach, cf. Harriet Stratis, Beneath the surface. Redon's methods and materials, in: *Odilon Redon. Prince of Dreams*, exh. cat. Art Institute Chicago, ed. by Douglas Druick et al., Chicago 1994, pp. 354–377.
[58] Redon, Confidences (see note 5), p. 269.
[59] Redon, Même (see note 5), p. 129.
[60] Redon, Même (see note 5), p. 127.

Not only the artist himself, but also the viewer is part of the production process in terms of how his imagination is activated by the artwork: "[L]'action qui en dérivera dans l'esprit du spectateur l'incitera à des fictions selon sa sensibilité et son aptitude imaginative".[61] Due to the apparent incompleteness and indefiniteness of the artworks[62] – both in a motivic and formal sense – as well as to their seemingly incessant vital motion and indeterminacy, the participation and empathy of the viewer are highly involved.[63]

This involvement surpasses rational and instructive aspects and has an impact on the strengthening of the vitality in a way that is not consciously perceptible:

> Une œuvre conçue en vue d'enseignement sera dans sa facture conduite par de mauvais chemins. Un tableau n'enseigne rien; il attire, il suprend, il exalte, il mène insensiblement et par amour au besoin de vivre avec le beau; il lève et redresse l'esprit, voilà tout.[64]

Thus, the viewer becomes part of this *'organisme d'art'* as he is in a way actively completing the creative process.

This efficacy of an art which seems to activate via evocative and suggestive techniques primarily an emotional and inconscious, but also spiritual level; this *art suggestif*, for Redon, seems to be an essential step in the evolutionary process, as he describes it as "croissance, évolution de l'art pour le suprême essor de notre propre vie."[65]

A certain evolutionary-teleological paradigm can thus be noticed as a substrate of Odilon Redon's concepts in terms of artistic production. It refers to intrinsic components, such as those of the material, which have a certain influence on the productivity of an artist due to its specific qualities. However, transcendent aspects seem to hold an important position too: Redon assumes that spiritual art, or *l'art suggestif*, in the end, is an art form that is consistent with the highly developed human consciousness of his time during the *fin de siècle*, as it addresses not only exteriorly-oriented, mechanical perception, but also inner 'vision'.

---

[61] Ibid., p. 27.

[62] Ibid., p. 27: "Mes dessins inspirent et ne définissent pas. Ils ne déterminent rien. Il nous placent [...] dans le monde ambigu de l'indéterminé. Ils sont une sorte de métaphore, loin de tout art géométrique."

[63] For the viewer-artwork relation in Redon's works, cf. Matthias Schatz, *Der Betrachter im Werk von Odilon Redon. Eine rezeptionsästhetische Studie*, Hamburg 1988.

[64] Redon, Même (see note 5), p. 113.

[65] Ibid., p. 26.

Philosophical ideas that tend towards a vitalist direction as well as scientific ideas of evolution formed a relatively eclectic conglomerate that sometimes risked to slip into a theosophical, esoteric world view, a *'mysticisme moderne'*, as several symbolist art critics were noticing.[66] Redon's use of the term 'organism' has clearly vitalist-metaphysical, holistic and natural philosophical implications. It also includes several 'organs' or agents: the artist's mind and body, environmental influences and experiences, different materials, and, in the end, the artwork itself and the viewer. This organism is less dominated by functionality than by a dynamic processuality, which leaves space for 'spontaneous mutations', transformation and indeterminacy.

A major concern seems to be the compatibility of a 'material' and a 'spiritual' form of art, the "idées intermediaries qui lient les sensations avec les pensées."[67] At this point, the artist represents the interface between a material and a spiritual world and thus links them in a fruitful way in the *'organisme d'art'*, enabling both of them to become animated. In doing so, he avoids a too intellectual, analytic and lifeless form of art, but also the risk of the other extreme, which is to create a purely mechanical, inanimate reproduction of the external world.

---

[66] Roland Scotti, *Kunstkritik in Frankreich zwischen 1886 und 1905. Zwischen Sichtbarkeit und literarischer Spekulation*, Mannheim 1994, mainly chapter 6; cf. also Fred Leeman, Redon's spiritualism and the rise of mysticism, in: *Odilon Redon. Prince of Dreams*, exh. cat. Art Institute Chicago, ed. by Douglas Druick et al., Chicago 1994, pp. 215–236.

[67] Redon, Même (see note 5), p. 115.

## Bibliography

Avanessian, Armen / Menninghaus, Winfried / Völker, Jan (eds.), *Vita aesthetica. Szenarien ästhetischer Lebendigkeit*, Zürich / Berlin 2009.

Bacou, Roseline, La Bibliothèque d'Odilon Redon, in: *Festschrift to Erik Fischer. European drawings from six centuries*, ed. by Villads Villadsen and Jan Garff, Copenhagen 1990.

Baekeland, Frederick, Depressive themes in the graphic work of Odilon Redon, in: *The Psychoanalytic Study of Society*, vol. 5 (1972), pp. 185–211.

Bernard, Claude, *La Science Expérimentale*, Paris 1875.

Bouillier, Francisque, *Du principe vital et de l'âme pensante*, Paris 1862.

Darwin, Charles, *On the Origin of Species*, London 1859.

Davenport, Nancy, Odilon Redon, Armand Clavaud, and Benedict Spinoza. Nature as God, in: *Religion and the Arts*, vol. 1 (2006), pp. 1–38.

Delboeuf, Joseph, *La matière brute et la matière vivante. Étude sur l'origine de la vie et de la mort*, Paris 1887.

Gamboni, Dario, Des livres au livre. Les bibliothèques d'Odilon Redon, in: *Les bibliothèques d'artistes*, ed. by Françoise Levaillant, Paris 2010, pp. 171–191.

Guyau, Jean-Marie, *Les Problèmes de l'esthétique contemporaine*, Paris 1884.

Haeckel, Ernst, *Histoire de la création des êtres organisés d'après les lois naturelles. Conférences scientifiques sur la doctrine de l'évolution en général et celle de Darwin, Goethe et Lamarck en particulier*, Paris 1877.

Köchy, Kristian, *Perspektiven des Organischen*, Paderborn 2003.

Leeman, Fred, Redon's spiritualism and the rise of mysticism, in: *Odilon Redon. Prince of Dreams*, exh. cat. Art Institute Chicago, ed. by Douglas Druick et al., Chicago 1994, pp. 215–236.

Lüdemann, Susanne, Körper, Organismus, in: *Wörterbuch der philosophischen Metaphern*, ed. by Ralph Konersmann, Darmstadt 2011, pp. 171–184.

Lyotard, François, Materie und Zeit, in: *Materie. Grundlagentexte zur Theoriegeschichte*, ed. by Sigrid G. Köhler, Hania Siebenpfeiffer and Martina Wagner-Egelhaaf, Berlin 2013, pp. 498–508.

Mattenklott, Gert, Sinnlich – Übersinnlich. Verklärung des Vitalen in der ersten Jahrhunderthälfte, in: *Elan vital oder Das Auge des Eros. Kandinsky, Klee, Arp, Miró, Calder*, exh. cat. Haus der Kunst, ed. by Hubertus Gaßner, Munich 1994.

Mellerio, André, *Odilon Redon*, Paris 1913.

Mocek, Reinhard, *Die werdende Form. Eine Geschichte der kausalen Morphologie*, Marburg 1998.

Redon, Odilon, Confidences d'artiste, in: *L'Art Moderne*, vol. 34 (1894), pp. 268–270.

Redon, Odilon, *Lettres d'Odilon Redon*, Paris / Brussels 1923.

Redon, Odilon, À *soi même. Journal 1867–1915*, Paris 1961 [1922].

Schatz, Matthias, *Der Betrachter im Werk von Odilon Redon. Eine rezeptionsästhetische Studie*, Hamburg 1988.

Scotti, Roland, *Kunstkritik in Frankreich zwischen 1886 und 1905. Zwischen Sichtbarkeit und literarischer Spekulation*, Mannheim 1994.

Stratis, Harriet, Beneath the surface. Redon's methods and materials, in: *Odilon Redon. Prince of Dreams*, exh. cat. Art Institute Chicago, ed. by Douglas Druick et al., Chicago 1994, pp. 354–377.

Toepfer, Georg (ed.), *Historisches Wörterbuch der Biologie*, vol. 2, Darmstadt 2011.

Von Hartmann, Eduard, *Philosophie de l'Inconscient*, transl. by Désiré Nolen, Paris 1877.

Zimmermann, Reinhard, Das Kunstwerk als Wirk-Organismus, in: *Animationen, Transgressionen. Das Kunstwerk als Lebewesen*, ed. by Ulrich Pfisterer and Anja Zimmermann, Berlin 2005, p. 247–264.

# Aesthetic Mechanisms of Bio-Production
*Claudia Mongini*

> The interest united with the beautiful does not therefore bear on the beautiful form as such, but on the *content* used by nature to produce objects capable of being reflected formally.[1]

## Between Microphysics and Aesthetics

In a conversation held in 1985 with Michel Butel, which was published in *Les Années d'hiver*[2], Félix Guattari gives an interesting definition of territory. Territory is understood as

> the ensemble of the projects or the representations on which a whole series of behaviors and commitments will pragmatically unfold both within time and within social, cultural, aesthetic and cognitive spaces.[3]

It is thus extended from its purely geographical definition towards the inclusion of mechanisms investing features of bodily production, intervening in the production of subjectivity and leading to the organization of a field in its political, ethical and aesthetic facets.

In recent years, sociologist Franco Berardi and mathematician Alessandro Sarti have attempted to examine contemporary behaviours through their microphysical conditions. With the intention of grasping the roots of current technical, social and subjective mutations, they coined the concept of bio-info sensibility.[4] In "the age of planetary computerization"[5], they argue, imaginary, technological, psychic and aesthetic states are currently deeply interrelated.[6] Bio-info sensibility aims to understand (some of) the knots determining these connections and to express the entanglement between material and abstract strata. It delineates the core of a morphogenetic operation; that is, it connects the mathematico-physical conditions of emergence – i.e. the 'material aspects of formation' from the perspective of self-organizing microscopic features – to the paradigmatic composition of an ethico-aesthetic dimension.

---

[1] Gilles Deleuze, *Kant's Critical Philosophy. The Doctrine of the Faculties*, Minneapolis 1985, p. 53.
[2] Guattari, Félix, *Les Années d'hiver, 1980–1985*, Paris 2009.
[3] Ibid., pp.133–134. Transl. by the author.
[4] Berardi, Franco / Sarti, Alessandro, *Run. Forma, vita, ricombinazione*, Milan / Udine 2008, p. 69.
[5] Guattari, Félix, *Schizoanalytic Cartographies*, New York 2012, p. 12.
[6] Berardi / Sarti, Run (see note 4), p. 117.

Matter is expressed from the point of view of its intensive condition, located in-between the state of biological substrate and its physical operation of constitution. It is not understood in terms of an object occupying a pre-constituted space, but, by itself, configures a space up "to a given degree – to the degree corresponding to the intensities produced".[7]

Sensibility develops within organic (human and nonhuman) matter, but also becomes specified and thus determined through the interplay of a more abstract relation. This level is addressed by the concept of information, which is not understood as a stable factor but in terms of its ability to alter, connect as well as disconnect heterogeneous domains in current capitalist society.[8]

Seen from this perspective, bio-info sensibility comes to register the problematic interplay between the material (bio) and the abstract (info) level, inasmuch as it grasps minimal operative constraints of diverging entities, and reconfigures them into a wider collective dimension.

In this paper, I envisage addressing this topic philosophically; that is, I will relate the question of the physico-aesthetic conditions described above to an ontological inquiry concerning the transition between the liminal levels of microphysics and the wider constitution of an aesthetic realm.

"What is the being *of* the sensible?" Deleuze asks in *Difference and Repetition*.

> Given the conditions of this question, the answer must designate the paradoxical existence of a 'something' which simultaneously cannot be sensed (from the point of view of the empirical exercise) and can only be sensed (from the point of view of the transcendent exercise).[9]

In the following I will delineate this paradox by some of its possible contours.

---

[7] Deleuze, Gilles / Guattari, Félix, *A Thousand Plateaus. Capitalism and Schizophrenia*, Minneapolis / London 1987, p. 278.

[8] In *Chaosophy. Soft Subversions*, Guattari states: "All of […] the 'mystery' [of capital], lies in the fact that it is thus able to connect, within the same general system of equivalency, entities which at first seem radically heterogeneous: material and economic *goods,* individual and collective human *activities*, and technical industrial and scientific *processes*" (Félix Guattari, *Chaosophy. Soft Subversions*, New York 1996, p. 268). This, Guattari states, is a sort of "minimal model" of how it works, "necessary" but "barely sufficient" (ibid., p. 271). Strategies of counter-actualization of this degree zero rule – like the concept of bio-info sensibility described here – do not aim to reduce capitalism to a single dimension, but rather to address this bare level of production in order to allow complexities and contradictions carried along by the singularity of each single case to emerge.

[9] Deleuze, Gilles, *Difference and Repetition*, Columbia 1995, p. 236.

Dynamics: Heterogenesis

In the fifth chapter of *Difference and Repetition*, Gilles Deleuze introduces the concept of 'disparation'. He defines it as the unequal as such, "the condition of that which appears".[10] Disparation is conceived as the intensity of difference, a motor enacting a process of individuation. Throughout the pages of the chapter, the philosopher explains that the condition of disparation is enacted when disparate factors have found modalities of relation 'in-depth', that is, modalities of intensive communication out of which qualified modalities of extension unfold to emergence. This is the onset of a process, which is both individuating and dramatizing: The intensity of the original disparity emerges into the formation of physical and sensual extensive qualities. Heterogeneous elements unfold into their actual space-time conditions and acquire a performative character, as their very modalities of constitution account at the same time for the creation of new relations and of the materiality of new deep communicative channels. In other terms, the resonance between different entities does not only open up new levels of communication, but lies at the very onset of their conditions of creation. The term dramatization, before being fully developed in *Difference and Repetition*, constituted the title of a lecture Deleuze gave at the French Society of Philosophy in 1967.[11]

In this text, Deleuze re-elaborates Gilbert Simondon's idea of disparation within the concept of the obscure precursor. The obscure precursor is, in his own terms, an abstract 'difference operator', which relates difference to difference. With the notion of the difference operator, Deleuze transposes the concept of disparation from a physical level onto a more abstract, mathematical one. In this way, Deleuze sets the conditions for breaking up Simondon's topology, still characterized by a sort of general uniformity due to its straightforward analogy with physical fields of potential energy. In reference to differential calculus, Deleuze poses the problem at the level of infinity. It is in the infinitesimal condition that the intensive condition becomes tangible, that the 'intensity' of disparity becomes indistinguishable from its 'extensity', i.e. from its more proper physical and sensuous qualities.

---

[10] Ibid., p. 222.

[11] Deleuze, Gilles, *Desert Islands and Other Texts, 1953–1974,* Cambridge 2004, p. 94.

The uniform field of energy becomes the theatre of "spatiotemporal dynamisms".[12] The field splits up into a coupling between different series of singularities, multiple phenomena of internal resonance, and an inevitable movement in the form of an amplitude, which give rise to a series of states of intensity. This micro-level of dynamic communication becomes generatively individuated in the Signal Sign Systems, accounting for the 'flashing' in-between disparate orders of singularities. As Alberto Toscano depicts it, "a complex interpenetration of formation and functioning"[13] is at stake, which fully unfolds in the theatre of 'indi-drama-different/ciation' proposed in *Difference and Repetition*. Individuation becomes thus the moment of intensity that dramatizes the differential potential of the virtual and accounts for the creation of divergent lines of actualization.

The border between the individual and the collective that Simondon already questioned on the level of the oversaturated preindividual, the generative condition of both individuality and collectivity becomes further disintegrated in the Deleuzian move: We witness here a complete break with the dialectical opposition between the one and the many and the consequent opening towards the dynamics of a theatre of multiplicity.

This ontological or, more properly, ontogenetic move acquires a level of pragmatic consistency in *A Thousand Plateaus*, a book which Deleuze wrote together with Félix Guattari.[14] There, the complex topology of spatiotemporal dynamisms becomes materialized in the dynamics of the 'haecceity' of libidinal fluxes, and the preindividual field acquires the contours of real speed and slowness:

> The plane of consistency knows nothing of substance and form: haecceities, which are inscribed on this plane, are precisely modes of individuation proceeding neither by form nor by the subject. The plane consists abstractly, but really, in relations of speed and slowness between unformed elements, and in compositions of corresponding intensive affects.[15]

Under which conditions does this complex ontological topology account for a relation between a microphysical operator and a wider dimension of aesthetic production?

---

[12] Ibid., p. 96.

[13] Toscano, Alberto, *The Theatre of Production. Philosophy and Individuation between Kant and Deleuze*, Basingstroke 2006, p. 181.

[14] Deleuze / Guattari, Plateaus (see note 7).

[15] Ibid., p. 507.

## Aesthetics as *sensus communis*

In his essay "The Idea of Genesis in Kant's Aesthetics", Deleuze asks: "How does this genesis of the sense of the beautiful shape up?"[16] This problem is developed along a fundamental topic characterizing the Kantian critical period: the agreement between faculties, between natural harmony and discordant exercises. The answer is given by way of a process of composition; that is, it is not a question of postulating an agreement, but of the genetic production of a dimension of concordance.

In the 1968 work, *Difference and Repetition*, Deleuze expresses his criticism of the idea of common sense in terms of a static correspondence between outside and inside. The internal unitarian idea of a 'self', understood as a basis of all subjective faculties, is reflected externally in the unity of the object as well as in the construction of the relation between fixed outside and inside poles, which results in the constitution of common sense *qua* habit. The philosophical (and epistemological) condition for breaking this pattern is entailed in the paradox:

> Subjectively, paradox breaks up the common exercise of the faculties and places each before its own limit, before its incomparable: thought before the unthinkable which it alone is nevertheless capable of thinking; memory before the forgotten which is also its immemorial; sensibility before the imperceptible which is indistinguishable from its intensive. [...] Objectively, paradox displays the element which cannot be totalized within a common element, along with the difference which cannot be equalized or cancelled at the direction of a good sense.[17]

And the problem, Deleuze continues, lies in the fact that difference tends towards explication. It is exactly this tendency, however, that drives the intensity of difference towards annulment. The node of the question lies precisely in the constitution of the relation between surface and depth, between what is already developed and what constitutes the onset of its individuating potential. While, in the remainder of the fifth chapter, Deleuze opens the schism between pure intensity and extensity in terms of the development of the process of 'different/ciation', in the antecedent 1963 texts on Kant – the book on critical philosophy and the article published in *Revue d'esthétique* –, he delineates the problem of the genesis of the faculties. He identifies aesthetic common sense as "the ground, the condition of every other common sense".[18]

---

[16] Deleuze, Islands (see note 11), p. 64.
[17] Deleuze, Difference (see note 9), p. 227.
[18] Deleuze, Kant (see note 1), p. 60.

It is by tracing the genesis of common sense that the agreement between faculties can develop.[19] Aesthetic common sense cannot be postulated, as this would result in a logical affirmation, but only presumed as a condition.[20] But this idea is per se paradoxical, as it cannot be analytically resolved; instead it results from a deduction: the "meta-aesthetic"[21] level of "the deduction of aesthetic judgements".[22] It is at the level of this supersensible point of concentration[23], that "the objective reference to a nature capable of producing beautiful things, and the subjective reference to a principle capable of engendering the agreement of faculties"[24], that is, the subjective condition of all modalities of communication, intersect in a juncture protracted upon its very limits.

What sets the limits of this juncture? It is exactly the intensity produced by the differentiating 'motor' of disparation, introduced above. It constitutes on the one hand a physical concept – the energetic difference between different levels of potential – and on the other a philosophical paradox:

> [I]t is the imperceptible, that which cannot be sensed because it is always covered by a quality which alienates or contradicts it, always distributed within an extensity which inverts or cancels it. In another sense, it is that which can only be sensed or that which defines the transcendent exercise of sensibility, because it gives to be sensed, thereby awakening memory and forcing thought. [...] [T]he harrowing character of intensity, however weak, restores its true meaning: not the anticipation of perception, but the proper limit of sensibility from the point of view of a transcendental exercise.[25]

How is sensibility defined in its utmost transcendental condition? This answer is made clear in Deleuze's last lecture on Kant. The problem, which this question opens up, is that of creating a correspondence between the level of sensibility as a concept and that in which sensibility gets sensed, i.e the realm of a spatio-temporal determination. In order to create the conditions for this passage, Deleuze continues, Kant provides two operations: synthesis, which provides a rule of recognition, leading from a cer-

---

[19] And therefore, the agreement between faculties is not posed categorically, but becomes the product of an aesthetic development.

[20] It is this condition of deduction that clarifies why "common sense" or *doxa* precludes the concept of "aesthetic common sense". In the moment in which the relation between existing faculties is already legislatively determined, the very problem of its genetic unfolding has no reason to be posed and studied as such; cf. Deleuze, Islands (see note 11), p. 61.

[21] Ibid., p. 65.

[22] Ibid., p. 61.

[23] Ibid., p. 95.

[24] Ibid.

[25] Deleuze, Difference (see note 9), p. 236–237.

tain (spatio-temporal) 'here and now' to a concept, and the schema which generates the conditions of the sensible out of a particular conceptual determination. Because of these features, the schema expresses a rule of production; it creates the conditions for what is to 'become' in space and time.

What operates as a schema? In the *Critique of Pure Reason,* the schema was the synthetic product of "time determinations"[26] concurring towards a "unity in the determination of sensibility".[27] Deleuze, however, points out the problem, which characterizes this modality of reasoning: "[S]pace and time are not presented as they are represented".[28] In other words, space and time are the entities in which external relations and forms of 'extensive magnitude' unfold. Can those same entities be the operators of 'internal difference'?

I will extend this line of inquiry by addressing Kant's last work, the *Opus Postumum.*

## A Paradoxical Schema

The *Opus Postumum* constitutes Kant's unedited work, which the philosopher had written between 1796 and 1804. This work is of interest because it expresses a sort of criticism of Kant himself, inasmuch as it transposes the question of the metaphysics of the subject to that of an ontology of force. The idea of force constitutes a *leitmotiv* in Kant's work. Since his first writings on the true estimation of forces, Kant emphasized an inherent principle of construction in the concept of force. "It is easy to demonstrate, that there would be no space and no extension *(Ausdehnung),* if substances were not entailed with any force to act outside themselves".[29]

The Italian translation by Vittorio Mathieu in particular emphasizes that in this work the German philosopher came to delineate the contours of a "'new' schematism", bound to the existence of a "system of a priori forces, inasmuch as it can be thought aprioristically".[30] This means that the notion of force acquires the 'cosmological' status of an entity which precedes the emergence of physical bodies and thus the relation

---

[26] Kant, Immanuel, *Critique of Pure Reason,* New York 2009, p. 217.
[27] Ibid., p. 212.
[28] Deleuze, Difference (see note 9), p. 231.
[29] Kant, Immanuel, *Opus Postumum, erste Hälfte,* Bonn 2008, p. 23. Transl. by the author.
[30] Ibid., 265; cf. Mathieu, Vittorio, *La filosofia trascendentale e l'"Opus postumum" di Kant,* 1958, p. 137–138.

between subjects and objects. Force here becomes deeply interrelated with an original, all-pervading material: 'Ether'.

It is by departing from an inquiry into the notion of force, examined both from its metaphysical grounding and its operative features of transition, that I intend to address the problem of the investigation of the *sensus communis aestheticus* in its genetic development. This way of proceeding is admittedly problematic, as the *Opus Postumum* is posterior to Kant's critical investigation into the genesis of common sense.[31] Nevertheless, it is here that force is considered in terms of a proto-entity, a sort of degree zero motor of production. It is thus inferable that force, in its intrinsic features of construction, might come to adequately express "the supersensible point of concentration", the meta-aesthetic level which is generative of the *sensus communis aestheticus*.

Moreover, this problematic level of reasoning is intrinsic to the text itself:

> There is something strange about this method of proving the existence of a *special world material* which penetrates all the bodies and constantly agitates them internally, by attraction and repulsion.[32]

'Strangeness' expresses the difficult condition of the task performed by Kant. It concerns the question of an empirical proof[33], which nonetheless aims to grasp features of matter before they can be experienced.[34]

In other terms, the ontological question of determining the material essence at the basis of the constitution of singular bodies is closely bound to an epistemological concern: the establishment of a 'transition' between the results and the problems of empirical science and the *a priori* conditions of metaphysics. The very beginning of one of the main sections of the *Opus Postumum* is reflective of the perplexity stated by Kant: The "possibility" of a "transition to physics"[35], i.e. the operation which is understood as "an empirical science of the moving forces of matter", depends upon the *a priori* "[d]*ivision* of the doctrine of nature". This division is reflective of the fundamental heterogeneity at the basis of the 'special world material', which entails both the ontological problem of material composition and the epistemic (or meta-epistemic) one of a transdisciplinary transition between philosophy and physics.

---

[31] Deleuze, Kant (see note 1), p. 35.
[32] Kant, Immanuel, *Opus Postumum*, Cambridge / New York 1993, p. 70, emphasis by the author.
[33] Kant, Opus a (see note 29), p. 181; ibid., p. 62.
[34] Kant, Opus a (see note 29), p. 477.
[35] In this paper, physics is strictly understood as an empirical science.

It is from an analysis of the mechanisms of production of this 'new' schema that I intend to approach the 'strangeness of the world material'. The delineation of this issue will lead back to the initial questions regarding sensibility and the creation of a territory.

## The Materiality of Force

Both the concept of force and its interactions with matter derive from the intensive study Kant dedicated to Newtonian science and to the general scientific development of his time.

My argumentative line departs from the logical operations at stake in the *Metaphysical Foundations of Natural Science*. In his preface to the 1786 work, Kant defines his intention to consider nature in its "material meaning", that is, to restrict the area of general metaphysics to the special realm of physics. This operation entails that the transcendental principles developed in the idea of pure reason are 'applied' to "objects of our senses".[36] What is the meaning of the term 'application' here? It means that physics cannot assess itself as an autonomous science, but needs the existence of another discipline, which Kant identifies in mathematics.[37] Through the synthetic action of mathematics, Kant solves the dilemma between *a priori* and experimental knowledge: an *a priori* foundation can be assigned to forms of knowledge, which are derived from our senses.

The task of establishing a philosophical relation between the abstract laws of mathematics and the investigation of the material composition of objects means to "provide an analysis of the concept of matter".[38] This analysis involves conceiving matter from the point of view of its physical ground: Forces, in concomitance with Newtonian theory, are conceived as being the very "conditions of existence" of matter itself.[39] It is through force that it is possible to define matter from the point of view of its 'action upon' space: "Matter fills a space, not through its mere *existence*, but through a *particular moving force*".[40] The extended property of matter is grasped from the point of

---

[36] Kant, Immanuel, *Metaphysical foundations of Natural Science,* Cambridge / New York 2004, p. 6.

[37] For an extensive explanation of the role of mathematics in terms of the condition of the relation between metaphysical and transcendental principles, cf. Paolo Pecere, *La Filosofia della Natura in Kant,* Bari 2009, pp. 329–333.

[38] Kant, Foundations (see note 36), p. 8.

[39] Ibid., p. 22.

[40] Kant, Foundations (see note 36), p. 34.

view of its modality of production; this is the reason why Kant prefers the dynamical notion of 'filling' to the more phenomenological one of 'occupying'. What kinds of forces are at stake? Precisely those which on the one hand account for its expansion in space and those which on the other provide for its containment, the restrictions which are caused by other antagonistic material actions. This specific argumentative logic is part of a more general idea permeating the whole work: It is the concept of movement which accounts for an explication of all the properties defining matter.

This idea is already contained in the very first sentence of the *Metaphysical Foundations:* "*Matter* is the *movable space*".[41] Why does Kant depart from this assertion? It is through movement that he can relate matter to mathematics, the medium allowing him to synthesize experience with *a priori* conditions.

While in the *Metaphysical Foundations of Natural Science* the system of forces was conceived as being in tension with sensible matter, in the *Opus Postumum* the dynamic interplay refers to a transcendental matter: 'Ether'[42]; matter becomes the constitutive basis of Nature itself. The shift from matter *qua* experience to matter *qua* construction has the effect of inverting the subsisting relation between matter and forces. While in the *Metaphysical Foundations* forces constitute the *causa prima* of movability and thus of experience, in the latter work it is matter which grounds the actions of forces.

After this digression, let us now come back to the core problem determining the problem of 'matter *qua* constitution', which is central to the current inquiry regarding the aesthetic mechanism of bio-production. How does Matter become a transcendental condition? What are the effects of this proposition upon the genesis of sensible experience?

Kant provided the Ether proofs in the "Übergänge 1–14", a series of drafts written in 1798. Significantly, the Ether 'proofs' appeared only two years after the thinker had 'declared' Ether to be the grounding material. Pecere understands this delay by claiming that the operation of proof constituted a problem conceived and developed after that of inventing Ether. The proof had to be meticulously constructed by means of the extraction of philosophical conditions from scientific results of the time.[43]

---

[41] Ibid., p. 15.
[42] Mathieu, Vittorio, *Kants Opus Postumum*. Frankfurt am Main 1989, p. 54.
[43] Pecere, Filosofia (see note 37), pp. 679–683.

While the question of the *Metaphysical Foundations* consisted of examining the transition from metaphysics to physics, the *Opus Postumum* entailed the task to create "a whole of nature of still greater extent": to transcend the laws of physics and to create a wider dimension of "hyperphysics".[44] The introduction of a universal material had produced the necessity of a 'logical change' of transcendental conditions and as such had set the ground for a new problem, which Kant started to actively address only in the years between 1798 and 1799.[45]

In order to examine this issue, I would like to approach the *Opus Postumum* from its beginning, i. e. from the *Oktavenentwurf,* the series of 9 drafts written in 1796. In these writings, Kant summarizes the problem of the relation between matter and forces, but approaches the topic from a different perspective than that provided in the *Metaphysical Foundations*.

In the previous work, matter was considered in terms of a sensible concept, i. e. it was thought of in relation to a definite portion of space, which it filled with determinate content.[46] The forces under consideration were thus merely targeted to enlarge or to shrink the "physical division(s)"[47] provided by the organization of space.

By taking the assumption of matter as a whole – the hypothesis of the *Opus Postumum* –, a third force has to accomplish the task previously performed by an operation of geometrical abstraction (i. e. the division of physical space). It is the force of cohesion, an intrinsic force of matter[48], which accounts for its quantitative organization. It entails a different nature: If attraction and repulsion in the *Metaphysical Foundations* were derived from a question of motion, i. e. if they were dynamic forces, cohesion would be a chemical force. It separates different kinds of matter by creating the possibility of fluid and continuous transitions.

Because of the hypothesis of cosmic filling, cohesion becomes "the first thing which requires an explanation", as it produces an "original difference of density".[49] And because its action is limited to the contact between parts of matter and not to

---

[44] Kant, Opus b (see note 32), p. 12.
[45] Kant, Reason (see note 26), p. 683.
[46] Kant, Foundations (see note 36), p. 64.
[47] Ibid., p. 39.
[48] Kant, Opus b (see note 32), p. 4.
[49] Ibid., p. 10; Kant, Opus a (see note 29), p. 374.

their motion, cohesion plays the role of a primordial surface force[50], a force operating at the heart of self-organization before matter is moved and subsequently structured into the physical entity of a body. The primordial and static features of this force already anticipate a transcendental mutation which Kant resumes summarizes as such: "Space is not an external object of our senses, time not an internal one by which we perceive things and their effects, but both are forms of our active forces".

What kind of aesthetic mutation does this consideration entail? If the section on transcendental aesthetics in the *Critique of Pure Reason* considered *'reine Anschauungen'*[51] as being the conditions for the sensible[52], how then is the sensible to be grasped if it is generated not from the abstract conditions provided by a static geometry, but out of the emergence of a 'general physiology' of active forces?

I will adumbrate this question by reconnecting the open issue of the 'logical change' provided by the ether proofs to the aesthetic conditions of the first *Critique*. The reason for this assertion is that the *'Anschauungen'* in space and time are only forms, and, without something which would make them even only a little acquainted to the senses, they would not provide any real objects to touch, objects nobilitating both existence and spatial extension, and would leave both space and time completely emptied of experience. This material, which lies *a priori* at the bottom of general possible experience, can be assumed to be not only hypothetical, but to be a given "world material" at the origin of movement. It cannot be seen as problematic, because it characterizes the *'Anschauung'*, which would otherwise be empty and left without (the possibility of) perception.

In order to come to approach the "Object as such"[53] through its own means of production, it is not possible to depart from the formal *'Anschauung'* of the first *Critique*, but access may be gained from the basis of a real action of matter upon the senses:

---

[50] Förster, Eckart, Kant's final synthesis. An essay on the Opus postumum, Cambridge 2000, p. 70.

[51] The term "Anschauung" is currently translated as ‚intuition'. However, this translation is currently debated among Kantians; cf. Julian Rohrhuber, Intuitions / Anschauungen (2007), wertlos.org/faits_divers/files/faits_divers_01.pdf (14/05/2016). The choice to leave the concept in German derives from the perception of the problems which this translation brings up.

[52] Kant, Reason (see note 26), p. 99.

[53] Ibid., p. 119. The necessity to approach the "empirical as such" already constituted a vivid problem at the very onset of the critical period, as demonstrated by the position taken by Kant with regard to the philosophy of Leibniz and Wolff; cf. ibid., A44–A46, B62–B63.

empiricism requires the condition of a full material ground. And it is through the action of forces that matter both organizes into objects and constitutes the grounding for sensibility.[54] Matter establishes a plane of organization for forces.

This kind of omnipresent matter also sets epistemic conditions. It allows for "[t]he transition from one science that already exists to another that is only in the idea".[55] This sort of transition demarcates the passage between an *a priori* concept and a system of forces. It consists of the determination of a middle level. Forces no longer act upon matter (which would be the case in physics) nor are they set as an aprioristic dimension (in correspondence with metaphysics). They are located in the intermediate 'physiological' state. This state, Kant argues, corresponds epistemologically to "a doctrine of the investigation of nature"[56], which is philosophical in its totality, as it provides a basis for the fragmentary points of view adopted in the exact sciences. That is, unlike physics, the task of which is to establish how matter moves in space and which forces are at stake (the 'why'), the problem for physiological thought consists of exploring the 'topic' of forces, their location within the general (common) interplay of forces. This is the level on which a 'new' synthesis between the intellectual and the sensible is produced.

A series of open questions will lead to the conclusion of this paper:

Given the change in the *a priori* conditions produced by the *Opus Postumum*, the schema of which no longer corresponds to the pure condition of a subjective *"Vorstellung"*[57], but demarcates instead what Pecere has called "the collective condition of external empirical intuition"[58], the current question regards the philosophical shape of *sensus communis aestheticus*. What are its conceptual modalities of expression if its meta-aesthetic condition is provided by the cosmological concept of force and no longer by the limits of a relation between subject and object? What are its bio-technological implications?

---

[54] Pecere stresses the originality of the Kantian move in terms of the position of an idea of matter which conditions the onset of a dynamic; cf. Pecere, Filosofia (see note 37), p. 745.

[55] Kant, Opus b (see note 32), p. 4.

[56] Kant, Opus b (see note 32), p. 42.

[57] Ibid., p. 98.

[58] Pecere, Filosofia (see note 37), p. 763.

If, as Deleuze has observed, the 'paradox of sensibility' has confronted us with an idea of *sensus communis aestheticus,* which is engendered by the differential limit of intensity, what would its mechanisms of production be if sensual experience is no longer located on the subjective level of *"Vorstellung"* (as is the case in the first *Critique*), but is built upon the physiological interplay of dynamic forces?

What kind of 'beauty' emerges out of this cosmologic of material production?

In the third *Critique*, Kant still presupposes the organizational principle of reason as being constitutive for matter in its forms of self-organization.[59] Can the material dynamic of moving forces mutate the relation between cognitive reflection and material organization and thus the bio-political constitution of a territory as conceived by Guattari?

And, finally, what are the effects of this 'new' common sense on the contemporary question of the (re-)singularization of aesthetic experience?

---

[59] Kant, Immanuel, *Kritik der Urteilskraft,* Stuttgart 1981, p. 347.

# Bibliography

Berardi, Franco / Sarti, Alessandro, *Run. Forma, vita, ricombinazione,* Milan / Udine 2008.

Deleuze, Gilles, *Desert Islands and Other Texts, 1953–1974,* Cambridge 2004.

Deleuze, Gilles, *Difference and Repetition,* Columbia 1995.

Deleuze, Gilles, *Kant's Critical Philosophy. The Doctrine of the Faculties,* Minneapolis 1985.

Deleuze, Gilles / Guattari, Félix, *A Thousand Plateaus. Capitalism and Schizophrenia,* Minneapolis / London 1987.

Förster, Eckart, *Kant's final synthesis. An essay on the Opus postumum,* Cambridge 2000.

Guattari, Félix, *Les Années d'hiver, 1980–1985,* Paris 2009.

Guattari, Félix, *Chaosophy. Soft Subversions,* New York 1996.

Guattari, Félix, *Schizoanalytic Cartographies,* New York 2012.

Kant, Immanuel, *Critique of Pure Reason,* New York 2009.

Kant, Immanuel, *Kritik der Urteilskraft,* Stuttgart 1981.

Kant, Immanuel, *Metaphysical foundations of Natural Science,* Cambridge / New York 2004.

Kant, Immanuel, *Opus Postumum,* Cambridge / New York 1993.

Kant, Immanuel, *Opus Postumum, erste Hälfte,* Bonn 2008.

Mathieu, Vittorio, *La filosofia trascendentale e l'"Opus postumum" di Kant,* 1958.

Mathieu, Vittorio, *Kants Opus Postumum.* Frankfurt am Main 1989.

Pecere, Paolo, *La Filosofia della Natura in Kant,* Bari 2009.

Rohrhuber, Julian, Intuitions / Anschauungen (2007), wertlos.org/faits_divers/files/faits_divers_01.pdf (14/05/2016).

Toscano, Alberto, *The Theatre of Production. Philosophy and Individuation between Kant and Deleuze,* Basingstroke 2006.

# Empty Time. The Temporality of Self-Affection in Kant's Analytic of the Sublime
*Louis Schreel*

## Introduction

For Kant, time is the structure of the processes through which we engage with things and the world around us. But outside of these relations, time is nothing. There is no deeper reality of time 'in itself', in which all of our past experiences would be stored, so to speak. Less than reality itself, time is what makes our engagement with reality possible. We are not 'in time' as we are 'in reality', but time rather makes the structured appearance and engagement with reality possible. Without this structure, there would be no unity of consciousness throughout our perceptions, and our experience would be "nothing but a blind play of representations, i. e., less than a dream".[1] Time is thus not an object that can be observed. At most, we can try to observe and describe the structure of our dynamic engagements with reality. We can deduce the necessary conditions that make it possible for those engagements to lead to, for example, knowledge of the world. And having obtained those *a priori* conditions, it would be possible to think time as a pure form of intuition in general, with all *de facto* phenomenal givens stripped away. "In regard to appearances in general," Kant writes, "one cannot remove time, though one can very well take the appearances away from time. […] The latter could all disappear, but time itself (as the universal condition of their possibility) cannot be removed".[2] If we perform such an abstraction, we must conclude that time "has only one dimension: different times are not simultaneous, but successive".[3] Space would then, on the contrary, be the *a priori* condition for givens to be intuited "outside and next to one another".[4] Time alone is the "*a priori* formal condition of all appearances in general".[5] Whereas inner givens are not subject to the spatial form of juxtaposition (which, temporally speaking, means simultaneity), all givens, both inner

---

[1] Kant, Immanuel, *Critique of Pure Reason*, transl. by Paul Guyer and Allen W. Wood, Cambridge 1998, A112.
[2] Ibid., A31, B46.
[3] Ibid., B47.
[4] Ibid., B38.
[5] Ibid., A34.

and outer, are subject to time's form: succession. From this, it follows that time, as the succession imposed on "givens" for them to be given, "is nothing other than the form of inner sense, i. e., of the intuition of our self and our inner state".[6]

In the *Critique of Pure Reason*, Kant introduces the imagination as the synthetic faculty that constitutes time as the form of inner sense. Relative to the cognitive interests of the understanding, the imagination synthesizes the progressive sequence of representations in time, thereby 'preparing' them for conceptual grasp. In the Analytic of the Sublime of the *Critique of Judgment*, however, the imagination is related to reason and is said to institute a 'regression' which annihilates the condition of time. Introducing the possibility of an aesthetic mode of comprehension, Kant proposes a function of the imagination that contrasts with its previously assigned functions: The imaginative regression allows the spectator of sublime states of affairs or events to comprehend as a simultaneous whole what is normally apprehended as temporally discrete. Instead of progressively constituting time as the form of inner sense through synthesis, the regression is said to be "a subjective movement of the imagination by which it does violence to inner sense."[7] Nonetheless, the spectator does not lose all phenomenal stability; she does not sink away in "a blind play of representations, i. e., less than a dream".[8] The suspension of time in sublime feeling does not annihilate time as such but produces what Jean-François Lyotard calls an "exit from inner sense".[9] In sublime feeling, both our imagination and our power of reasoning experience a form of "empty time" (*"rien de temps"*) that creates a feeling of non-coincidence with ourselves. Lyotard specifies that this exit from inner sense consists, in fact, of two moments: On the one hand, he discerns a "weakening" of time (*"extenuation"*) due to the regress of the imagination and, on the other hand, an "extemporalization" (*"extemporalisation"*) due to the presence of an idea of reason. Given the complexity of both accounts, and the limited space at our disposal here, we will focus only on the first moment, that of the regress of the imagination. We will examine (1) how Kant's

---

[6] Ibid., B49.

[7] Immanuel Kant, *Critique of the Power of Judgment*, transl. by Paul Guyer and Eric Matthews, Cambridge 2000, AA259.

[8] Kant, Reason (see note 1), A112.

[9] Lyotard, Jean-François, *Leçons sur l'Analytique du sublime*, Paris 1991, p. 179; Lyotard, Jean-François, *Lessons on the Analytic of the Sublime*, transl. by Elizabeth Rottenberg, Stanford 1994, p. 145.

account of the imaginative regression in sublime feeling relates to his earlier theory of the imagination given in the first *Critique* and (2) how Lyotard interprets the former as an exit from inner sense.

Time as Self-Affection

In the Transcendental Aesthetic of the *Critique of Pure Reason*, Kant uses the term 'aesthetic' to designate the sensory reception of matter, which is structured by the forms of intuition in space and time. As noted, Kant determines the latter, space and time, as the *a priori* forms of intuition, which are to be distinguished from empirical presentations or from *a posteriori* contents (for example, the colour black). In themselves, space and time are but the "empty" forms through which phenomena can be apperceived. In the Transcendental Deduction, this complex understanding of time and space as the pure, *a priori* forms of experience is further elaborated. Kant explains that for the manifold of sensations that arrives to us through our receptive faculty of sensibility to have any order or unity, it is required that we apply determinations to it. For example, when viewing a dog, Febo, we might see a sweet gaze, hear a soft groan, and feel a wet tongue; but in Kant's view, there is nothing about these sensations 'in themselves' that suggests we should associate them in a meaningful sort of way. In Kant's words, "the combination (*conjunctio*) of a manifold"[10] can never come to us 'directly' through the senses. Rather, the experience is dependent upon the faculty of the understanding and the way in which its concepts – for example 'dog' – are applied to the manifold of sensations. To account for this construction of the spatiotemporal, integrative flux of phenomenal experience, Kant distinguishes three basic synthetic operations that transform sensory data into a meaningful, coherent experience: apprehension, reproduction, and recognition.[11] Together, these time syntheses enable the subject to integrate and represent sensible diversity so as to form a properly spatiotemporal object capable of being subsumed under concepts of the understanding and thereby of being cognized as experience. The empirical exercise of sensibility (1) apprehends representations given in intuition one instant to the next. The reproductive imagination (2) gathers the passing apprehensions and the productive imagination

---

[10] Kant, Reason (see note 1), B129.
[11] Ibid., A98–110, B141, B150–152.

synthesizes them together in such a way that the given flux of data is prepared for the conceptual grasp (3) of the understanding. For the model of recognition – the understanding recognizing the synthesized intuitive manifold by means of its concepts – to function properly, all the faculties must envision the 'same' object and the exercise of the faculties must remain 'limited' to its contribution to the process of recognition. The object of sensibility, of recollection, of the imagination, and eventually of thought is, for the representation, identical.

When encountering Febo, for example, we first apprehend this "manifold's parts" little by little. For the gaze, groan and tongue to possess a meaningful relationship to one another, the reproductive imagination must retain these tiny and otherwise fleeting apprehensions while the productive imagination must reproduce them as a 'combination' into an image of a dog. The imagination performs this reconstruction in accordance with the concept of 'dog', which indicates a rule (a "schematism"[12]) according to which it can delineate the figure of a four-footed animal in general. Nothing in sensibility or in imagination accounts for that operation by which we go from 'gaze-groan-tongue' to the concept of a 'dog-object,' of which we could predicate each of these qualities. It is, instead, our faculty of 'understanding' that manifests the capacity to relate a combined manifold of sensations to a single 'object' through the act of 'recognition'. For this recognition to be possible, we need an empty concept of an object, a 'placeholder' object, to which we can relate the combination of sensory data. Kant calls this the 'object=x': it is not the object that is given to us in experience, Febo, but is instead the necessary condition under which the experience of the object 'can be given'. The 'object=x' is an elementary determination of the object, as an 'any-object-whatsoever', that must be in place in order for any other conceptual determinations of the object to be applied.[13]

---

[12] Ibid., A141, B180.

[13] Kant, Reason (see note 1), A103–106.

This 'object=x' is in fact what enables a connection between the spatiotemporal operations of sensibility and imagination and the understanding's conceptual determinations, resulting in the experience of an object with both conceptual and sensible content. This mediating role of the imagination is elementary because there is a 'tension' between the temporal flux and the conceptual unification. As Corry Shores writes in an instructive article:

> The moments of apprehension, although temporally exclusive to one another, are taken together simultaneously in the reproductive imagination. There must somehow be a unified consciousness that is the same throughout the moments, for otherwise they would belong to a different consciousness and thus be unavailable for synthesis.[14]

This unified consciousness is for Kant not a 'product' of the syntheses of the imagination, but a precondition for these syntheses themselves to be possible. Indeed, for Kant, the very possibility of synthesizing different moments of empirical consciousness requires that I am able to regard the latter as all belonging to 'me' – even if I do not always consciously do so.[15] Behind each empirical consciousness, there must therefore lie a "transcendental ground of the unity of consciousness".[16] This *a priori* unified self-consciousness is the 'transcendental apperception', or the 'I think', which accompanies all of our conceptual acts.[17] The latter must be distinguished from the 'empirical apperception' or 'inner sense', which is our self-consciousness under a stream of alterations.[18] Empirical self-consciousness is not enough to allow us to apprehend ourselves as enduring persons because it is plunged in time as a flow of succession. In this flow of inner sense, we are aware of ourselves as contingent objects in the world, as passive, receptive beings that are ever inconsistent and disunited. The means to make all our empirical variations belong together and relate to the identity of the subject

---

[14] Corry Shores, Self Shock. The Phenomenon of Personal Non-Identity in Inorganic Subjectivity, in: *The Yearbook on History and Interpretation of Phenomenology 2013*, Frankfurt 2013, p. 177.

[15] Kant, Reason (see note 1), A155, B194: "The synthesis of representations rests on the imagination, but their synthetic unity (which is requisite for judgment), on the unity of apperception." This basic claim of the *Critique of Pure Reason*, namely that no connected whole representation can have an objective unity without a concept provided by the understanding, is reinforced by the second edition of the first *Critique*, where Kant drops the Transcendental Deduction with its three syntheses and starts the new Deduction by directly affirming the fundamental role of the understanding and its categories for all synthesis.

[16] Ibid., A106, A117 (note).

[17] Ibid., B131–132.

[18] Kant, Reason (see note 1), A107.

come from the transcendental apperception, which itself somehow falls outside the flow of time and is "unchanging".[19] Yet, the latter cannot alone apprehend itself or cognize itself, because it has of itself no intuitive content. As Shores writes:

> In order to do this, it *[the transcendental apperception]* needs to synthesize itself into a manifold of the phenomenal self-appearings happening at temporally distinct moments. In other words, the consciousness of our unified non-temporal subjectivity, in order to become explicitly aware of itself, needs to manifest itself as being disunified through time.[20]

Accordingly, we must distinguish two different ways in which the imagination temporalizes: empirically and transcendentally.[21] Empirically, it connects (through the syntheses of apprehension and reproduction) a perception with all previous experiences and thereby produces a unified picture, an image. An example of such an enriched experience is the appearance of snow, which, through the filter of the imagination, 'looks' cold even when we do not come near it.[22] But the imagination also has another transcendental function by which it creates a temporal-spatial field in which a perception can appear. The process of temporalization means, here, that the imagination 'detaches' the object from live experience, from the sensory present, and that it places it under the concrete universality of time.[23] This detachment from the present moment in which I remain immersed in things is an act of interiorization, which is expressed by the 're-' of 'representation', just as the 'con-' of contemplation expresses the possibility of a survey and a simultaneity, which evokes space.

Thus, there is a clear division in the subject between two different and unbridgeable self-consciousnesses: empirical apperception, which is tied to the contingent, uncontrolled vagrancies of sense experience and empirical imagination; and transcendental apperception, which designates my self-determining abilities. Kant develops this division in the subject along the distinction between 'inner' and 'outer sense'. Whereas

---

[19] Ibid., A107.

[20] Shores, Shock (see note 14), p. 178.

[21] Kant, Reason (see note 1), A100–102.

[22] This example is taken from Louis Dupré, Aesthetic Perception and its Relation to Ordinary Perception, in: *Aisthesis and Aesthetics. The Fourth Lexington Conference on Pure and Applied Phenomenology*, ed. by Erwin W. Straus and Richard M. Griffith, Pittsburgh 1970, p. 172.

[23] Mikel Dufrenne, *Phénoménologie de l'expérience esthétique*, vol. 2, Paris 1993, p. 434. Cited in: Dupré, Perception (see note 8), p. 172.

external objects modify our outer sense, "self-affections" modify our inner sense.[24] Under the name of the transcendental synthesis of imagination, the understanding exercises an activity upon the passive subject, whose faculty it is. Inner sense is nothing but the affection of this action. It is our awareness of ourselves as not merely passive, causally determined beings or objects in the world, but as also intentional, actively determining beings, i. e. subjects, for the world. Kant gives an example of self-affection: our acts of attention.[25] When we focus our attention on our dog, Febo, we notice a modification in our awareness, as it is becoming more focused. This results not from the external object itself but from an internal influence: "In such acts the understanding always determines the inner sense, in accordance with the combination that it thinks, to the inner intuition that corresponds to the manifold in the synthesis of the understanding."[26] Thus, as Shores concludes, "It [attention] gives us a representation of our active subjectivity as a self-affecting subject, but it appears only phenomenally as a passively modified empirical self-consciousness."[27]

We can summarize by saying that in the *Critique of Pure Reason* the imagination serves to order a manifold of sense, which it cannot comprehend directly as a whole. It is bound by a progressive form of time – a linear sequence, which moves on incessantly. Concepts of the understanding are necessary to go beyond the successive and ephemeral nature of inner sense and to comprehend coexistence in space. With these distinctions we can now turn to Kant's differentiation between cognitive consciousness and aesthetic consciousness.

## The Indeterminacy of Aesthetic Temporality

In the *Critique of Judgment*, the meaning of the term 'aesthetic' changes profoundly, from the study of the pure *a priori* forms of sensibility to the analysis of judgments of the beautiful and the sublime. Now, 'aesthetic' means no longer the grasp of the givens of sensible intuition in *a priori* forms of space and time but reflective judgment, insofar as it excites the interest of the 'faculty of the soul' that is the feeling of pleasure or

---

[24] Kant, Reason (see note 1), B153–156.
[25] Ibid., B156.
[26] Ibid., B157.
[27] Shores, Shock (see note 14), p. 178.

displeasure. Thus, the term 'sensation' as the 'determination of the feeling of pleasure or displeasure' is given an entirely different meaning than in the first *Critique*, where the sensation is 'the representation of a thing'. While in the latter sense sensation is a necessary 'building' block of the conditions of possibility for objective knowledge in general, in the analytic of taste, sensation no longer has any cognitive finality. It no longer gives any information about an object but only about the 'subject' itself.

This 'subject' is no longer the transcendental apperception or 'I think' which accompanies all of our conceptual acts. The feeling accompanying our act of thinking and informing us about our state of mind, our *'Gemütszustand'*, is not the self-affection of the first *Critique*. In the third *Critique*, 'reflection' is determined as the state of the faculty of judging when "only the particular is given, for which the universal is to be found".[28] Reflective judgment concerns itself with objects only in their particularity, as they are given at this singular moment, and not as they are subjected to the *a priori* rules of the understanding. In this sense, the sensations of beauty and sublimity are tied to that which is essentially contingent, which does not let itself be anticipated and only lets itself be sensed in the process of a veritable encounter. Reflective judgment judges objects as if the rules that determined their possibility *a priori* were not sufficient to account for their particularity. As we have seen, relative to the cognitive interests of the understanding, the imagination's most important function is to produce schemata that make possible the application of universal concepts to particulars of sense. In reflective judgment, however, intuitions are related and compared without any conceptual synthesis.

Each act of thinking is always accompanied by a feeling that signals to thought its 'state'. In other words, sensation is always there every time there is an act of thought, what Kant calls 'knowledge' or 'representation'. And, as we have seen in the previous section, "as contained in one moment [*in einem Augenblick enthalten*] no representation can ever be anything other [*niemals etwas anderes*] than absolute unity [*als absolute*

---

[28] Kant, Judgment (see note 7), AA179. The first *Critique* introduces the term in the Appendix to the Analytic of Principles entitled "On the amphiboly of concepts of reflection." Here, Kant calls reflection, Überlegung *(reflexio)*, "the state of mind in which we first prepare ourselves to find out [*ausfindig zu machen*] the subjective conditions under which we can arrive at concepts"; cf. Kant, Reason (see note 1), B316.

*Einheit*]".[29] Therefore, the question is how we become conscious of the agreement of the faculties of knowledge,: whether it is by sensation or 'intellectually'. Kant addresses this question in the ninth paragraph of the third *Critique*, where he introduces sensation:

> If the given representation, which occasions the judgment of taste, were a concept, which united understanding and imagination in the judging [*Beurtheilung*] of the object into a cognition of the object, then the consciousness of this relationship would be intellectual (as in the objective schematism of the power of judgment, which was dealt with in the [first] critique). But in that case the judgment would not be made in relation to pleasure and displeasure, hence it would not be a judgment of taste. Now the judgment of taste, however, determines the object, independently of concepts, with regard to satisfaction and the predicate of beauty. Thus that subjective unity of the relation can make itself known [*kenntlich machen*] only through sensation.[30]

The *Analytic of the Beautiful* shows that in judgments of taste the imagination can apprehend "the form of an object of intuition without a relation of this to a concept for a determinate cognition".[31] This apprehension of form is subjectively purposive in producing a pure aesthetic pleasure consisting of a feeling of harmonious play between the imagination and the understanding. Just as the schema unites the two faculties, imagination and understanding, in order to make knowledge of an object possible, so sensation is the sign of their union (pleasure) or of their disunion (displeasure), on the occasion of an object and on the side of thought. Yet, whereas in the case of knowledge there is a determinate relation where a specific intuition is subsumed under a specific concept to provide knowledge, the felt harmony between imagination and understanding is an 'indeterminate' relation between two faculties in general.

The temporality inherent to the feeling of the beautiful is addressed briefly in the "Third Moment" of the Analytic of the Beautiful. The two central characteristics of cognitive time, which allowed the first *Critique* to deduce the 'I think' – succession and the affection of the self by itself – are here suspended. Essential for aesthetic pleasure is that it "lingers" (*"weilen"*) to "maintain" (*"in demselben zu erhalten"*) the state of mind.[32] The *Verweilung*, the way we "linger" – a lingering that the play of the faculties imposes on thinking that judges aesthetically – puts thought into a state 'analogous' to the passivity it feels (*"wobei das Gemüt passiv ist"*) when it is attracted to an object.[33]

---

[29] Kant, Reason (see note 1), A99.

[30] Kant, Judgment (see note 7), AA219, B30.

[31] Ibid., AA189.

[32] Ibid., AA222.

[33] Ibid.

Yet, whereas the attraction paralyzes the faculties, for example in the case of fascination, the beautiful throws them into a play. This reduction of the 'subjective' to a state of passivity makes the 'I think' forget itself as the thought of the object turned toward experience by means of the forms of coexistence (space) and succession (time). Lyotard describes the time of aesthetic lingering as a kind of "pause of diachronic time": "the sensation provided by the free play of the faculties institutes a manner of being for time that cannot involve an inner sense."[34]

The imagination enters into a "free play" with the understanding, although the rules of the latter remain in effect. The imagination, operating aesthetically, is productive, 'creative' and not only 'reproductive', as it had to be for the purposes of theoretical knowledge. It takes liberties with the postulates of empirical thought in general and in particular with the analogies of experience, which are permanence, succession, and coexistence – in short, with everything that Kant refers to as 'the law of association', which belongs to the empirical employment of the imagination. The imagination is granted its own spontaneous activity in judging and producing beautiful forms but does not have its own laws. Artistic imagination may not violate the categorical framework provided by the understanding, as that would result in metaphysical speculation or transcendental illusion. It may, however, explicate, by means of analogy, possibilities left open by that framework. Drawing on the objects of experience, the imagination remodels the latter and presents an object that is not present in it. It presents, in Kant's terms, "aesthetic Ideas", which are representations of objects such that there is no corresponding property in the 'concept' of this object.[35] The aesthetic idea is the presentation of an 'object' that escapes the concept of this object; it is an intuition (of the imagination) for which a concept can never be found adequate. It presents what Kant calls the "unnameable" (*"das Unnennbare"*)[36], which "stimulates so much thinking"[37], "though without it being possible for any determinate thought, i. e., concept, to be adequate to it, which, consequently, no language fully attains or can make in-

---

[34] Lyotard, Leçons (see note 9), p. 85; Lyotard, Lessons (see note 9), p. 64. For the temporal structure of judgments of taste, cf. pp. 34–41; pp. 19–26.
[35] Kant, Judgment (see note 7), AA342.
[36] Ibid., AA316.
[37] Ibid., AA315.

telligible."[38] As Lyotard puts it: "A storm of Ideas suspends ordinary time in order to perpetuate itself."[39] The object thus produced by the imagination escapes not only its identification by understanding but 'recognition' in the strongest sense that the Deduction of pure concepts gives to this term in the first *Critique.*"[40] "In the strongest sense," writes Lyotard, because it is a matter not of "mere" recognition, but of nothing less than the constitution of the 'inner sense', that is, of the time implicated in all knowledge. Thus, as a result of the productive imagination in taste, a proliferation of representations is grafted upon a single given such that the conceptual consciousness that is supposed to make these representations 'recognizable', that is, to situate them in one singular series of apprehensions of reproductions of the manifold, is missing.

In the Analytic of the Sublime, Kant considers the imagination in relation to reason instead of understanding. The sublime feeling results from "the effort of the imagination to treat nature as a schema" for the ideas of reason.[41] Whereas the understanding is the faculty of finite knowledge, reason strives to comprehend the infinite. In the sublime 'state', thought gets carried away: The imagination is forced by reason to do violence to itself in order to present that which it cannot present, and reason seeks, unreasonably, to violate the critical interdict it imposes on itself and to find objects corresponding to its concepts in sensible intuition. In both of these aspects, thinking defies its own finitude and is, to use Lyotard's words, "fascinated by its own excessiveness."[42] In the sublime state of mind, thinking feels a "desire for limitlessness."[43] Although it is all too obvious within the critical framework that this desire is relegated to inevitable illusion, to insanity even (the "delirium" [*"Wahnsinn"*] of enthusiasm, denying it of any moral value[44]), Kant's account of the imagination calls for a reconsideration of its relation to time.

In sublime feeling, the imagination will no longer appear as the synthetic origin of time, but a conflict (*"Widerstreit", "différend"*) will rather arise between time and

---

[38] Ibid., AA314.
[39] Lyotard, Leçons (see note 9), p. 88; Lyotard, Lessons (see note 9), p. 67.
[40] Ibid., p. 96; p. 74.
[41] Kant, Judgment (see note 7), AA265.
[42] Lyotard, Leçons (see note 9), p. 75; Lyotard, Lessons (see note 9), p. 55.
[43] Ibid.
[44] Kant, Judgment (see note 7), B126.

the imagination. In an unexpected reversal of its normal operation, the imagination institutes a 'regress', which suspends the progressive sequence of inner sense and makes possible the intuition of coexistence, an 'aesthetic' comprehension independent of the understanding. Kant describes this in the following key passage:

> The measurement of a space (as apprehension) is at the same time the description of it, thus an objective movement in the imagination and a progression; by contrast, the comprehension of multiplicity [*Vielheit*] in the unity not of thought but of intuition, hence the comprehension in one moment [*Augenblick*] of that which is successively apprehended, is a regression, which in turn cancels [*aufhebt*] the time-condition in the progression of the imagination and makes *simultaneity* intuitable. It is thus (since the temporal succession is a condition of inner sense and of an intuition) a subjective movement of the imagination, by which it does violence to the inner sense.[45]

The same synthesis that the first *Critique* designated as the origin of time seems here to be determined, nonetheless, as a violence imposed on time.[46] The idea of a conflict between the imagination and time, of a regress 'annihilating' the "time-condition" seems entirely contradictory to the idea defended in the first *Critique*. Here, as we have seen, the imagination played the crucial mediating role of producing schemata that make possible the application of universal concepts to particulars of sense – an application without which there could be no comprehension whatsoever. The productive imagination performed a transcendental synthesis by schematizing all the categories in terms of time – the form of inner sense. By translating the rules implicit in the categories into a temporally ordered set of instructions, it made possible the construction of an objectively determinate nature. Aesthetic judgment, as a form of reflective judgment, may not require the temporal determinacy in the way that it is necessary for cognitive consciousness, but this does not account for the more radical claim that the imagination violates inner sense and annihilates the condition of time. How then should we understand the violence done to time in relation to the claim of the first *Critique* that time cannot be annihilated as such? In Lyotard's reading, the regress of the imagination does not mean an annihilation of time as such, but it rather suggests the possibility of negating the mathematical or linear form of time.

---

[45] Ibid., AA258–259.

[46] In an essay on the theme of a "transcendental violence" imposed upon time, Jacob Rogozinski points to the importance of Jacques Derrida's "Violence et métaphysique", which was published in *L'écriture et la différence* (Paris 1967); cf. Jacob Rogozinski, Le don du monde, in: *Du sublime*, ed. by Michel Deguy, Paris 1988, pp. 179–210.

## The Regression of the Imagination

As noted, aesthetic judgment as a mode of reflective judgment does not require the numerical progression of time, which is based on the spatial analogy of a measurable line. This linearly ordered time required for the progressive apprehension and mathematical determination of nature as extensive magnitude is built upon the synthesis of the manifold, that is, through what Kant calls "composition (*Zusammensetzung*) of the homogeneous manifold".[47] In the latter, in the successive composition of units requisite for the representation of magnitudes, "the imagination, by itself, without anything hindering it, advances to infinity [...], the understanding, however, guides this [*leitet sie*] by numerical concepts, for which the former must provide the schema".[48] This composition is in fact nothing other than the apprehension and reproduction necessary to the constitution of the time of knowledge (and of space secondarily) but applied to the constitution of objects of knowledge according to their extensive magnitude. In this composition, the imagination lets itself be 'guided' by the concept, which is in short the 'consciousness' of the unity produced by the imagination's synthesis. However, as long as this (logical) estimation of magnitude is subordinated to the 'concept of an end', namely cognitive determination, it cannot be aesthetic. As long as the understanding provides the logical comprehension, a 'limit' experience, such as that of the sublime, remains impossible.

In the logical comprehension of quantity, the understanding measures the dimensions of the object by means of relative quantities. However, for this arithmetic calculation not to remain abstract and empty of sense, it requires the support of a "primary measure"[49], which is an aesthetic evaluation of size and distance, where we take the measure of the given "in a single glance" (*"in einem Augenblick"*). This evaluation "in mere intuition" (*"nach dem Augenmaße"*) tells us, without the need of comparison with other things, that the given is a *quantum*. But it does not yet tell us how 'great' something is, for then the question is not to apprehend it as *quantum* but to measure its quantity, its *quantitas*, which requires a "numerical formula" that works *a posteriori* on the given object. As Lyotard explains:

---

[47] Kant, Reason (see note 1), B203.
[48] Kant, Judgment (see note 7), AA253.
[49] Kant, Judgment (see note 7), AA251.

Quantity is not magnitude, but the number of times the same unit is contained in the extensive magnitude. It must be measured in relation to a unit, that is, by comparing it to another magnitude taken as a unit of measure. This unit is in turn chosen after being compared with other magnitudes. Unlike the *quantum,* the *quantitas* is thus not provided with an *a priori* synthesis in intuition.[50]

The sublime is said to be "that which is absolutely great".[51] Since it is 'absolute' without possible comparison, it is not measurable as a quantity.[52] If the evaluation of quantity or greatness were 'merely' mathematical, an experience of the sublime would, therefore, be impossible. It is only at the pre-logical, pre-objective level, "in its naïve embrace of the world"[53], that the finite, essentially limited comprehension of the imagination can encounter its maximum, the sublime limit on which it breaks.

The aesthetic comprehension instantiated by the regression of the imagination is a comprehension 'in one moment' not of a 'manifold' (*Mannigfaltigheit*), but of a 'multiplicity' (*Vielheit*). Although Kant does not elaborate on this distinction in the passage on the imaginative regress, it provides an important tool for understanding this specific mode of intuition. It indicates, as Rudolf Makkreel has shown in an instructive reading of the "Imagination and temporality in Kant's theory of the sublime"[54], that "the plurality-unity relation in aesthetic comprehension differs from that in logical comprehension."[55] Makkreel notes that the distinction between *Vielheit* and *Mannigfaltigheit* is lost in the standard English Bernard and Meredith translations of the third *Critique* where both terms have been rendered as 'manifold', thereby giving the misleading impression that the imaginative regression is dealing with the 'comprehension

---

[50] Lyotard, Leçons (see note 9), pp. 104–105; Lyotard, Lessons (see note 9), p. 80. Lyotard also points to an important conceptual confusion due to a wrong correction of Erdmann in Kant's original German text. In Kant, Reason (see note 1), A252 we read: "For when apprehension has gone so far that the partial representations of the intuition of the senses that were apprehended first already begin to fade in the imagination as the latter proceeds on to the apprehension of further ones, then it loses on one side as much as it gains on the other, and there is in the comprehension a greatest point beyond which it cannot go." The latter, "comprehension" ("*Zusammenfassung*") is not the concept used by Kant in the original German text, but a correction made by Erdmann. Kant had written "*Zusammensetzung*", "composition". On this confusion and its consequences, cf. Lyotard, Leçons (see note 9), p. 130–137; Lyotard, Lessons (see note 9), p. 102–109.

[51] Kant, Judgment (see note 7), AA248.

[52] Kant introduces the term "*magnitudo*" in opposition to "quantity", which cannot be absolute; cf. ibid.

[53] Rogozinski, Don (see note 46), p. 202.

[54] Rudolf Makkreel, Imagination and Temporality in Kant's Theory of the Sublime, in: *The Journal of Aesthetics and Art Criticism,* vol. 42, no. 3 (1984), pp. 303–315.

[55] Makkreel, Imagination (see note 54), p. 308.

of the manifold' reserved for the conceptual synthesis of the understanding. However, the imaginative regression is dealing with the comprehension of a multiplicity as a unity, not with the successive composition of units. Whereas, for the logical comprehension, the content of sense is regarded as a manifold, i. e. a complex of temporally determined parts, "in aesthetic comprehension, by contrast, the content of sense is regarded as a multiplicity of indeterminate parts of a whole."[56] While the unity of the former must be inferred through a concept and involves an objective progress of the imagination, the unity of the latter can be instantaneously comprehended in the subjective regress of the imagination.

The distinction between *Vielheit* and *Mannigfaltigkeit* goes back to the distinction between extensive and intensive magnitudes, made in the Anticipations of Perception of the first *Critique*.[57] An extensive magnitude involves a manifold generated by a successive synthesis proceeding from parts to a whole. By contrast, an intensive magnitude is not apprehended successively but in an instant. The intensive magnitude, which Kant calls a degree (*"Grad"*), represents the multiplicity in the content of sense. It is the *quantum* corresponding to "the matter of sensation" or "the real of the sensation [...] by which one can *only* be conscious *that* the subject is affected".[58] Kant writes: "Now I call that magnitude which can only be apprehended as unity, and in which multiplicity (*Vielheit*) can only be represented through approximation to negation=0, *intensive* magnitude."[59] Makkreel refers to H. J. Paton's interpretation of this obscure passage:

---

[56] Ibid.

[57] The Anticipations of Perception are one of the four Synthetic Principles of Pure Understanding. These principles are the *a priori* rules that understanding observes in constituting not experience in general but the objects of experience or in experience. The principles regulate the relation of understanding to inner sense, which, as we have seen, is time, or the universal form of intuition; cf. Lyotard, Leçons (see note 9), pp. 116–118; Lyotard, Lessons (see note 9), pp. 90–92.

[58] Kant, Reason (see note 1), B207, emphasis by the author.

[59] Ibid., B210.

The multiplicity in an intensive magnitude is not represented by parts outside one another. Instead, "every degree contains a plurality, because it contains all lesser degrees down to zero."⁶⁰ The multiplicity involved is not of discriminated parts of a manifold, but of degrees of intensity. This multiplicity in unity is given in an instant: yet, apparently, it can be represented *as* a multiplicity only when we imagine a possible diminution of the sensation. Such an imaginative act would require a process in time, and is not easily squared with Kant's assertion that apprehension of intensive magnitude is instantaneous. This difficulty is part of a more general one posed by the Anticipations of Perception. […] Certainly in the context of the first *Critique,* the idea of an instantaneous *synthesis* through which we intuit multiplicity remains problematic at best.⁶¹

Without further pursuing the intrinsic difficulties of the Anticipations here, we will only indicate how Makkreel sees in the imaginative regress of the third *Critique* a 'more readily conceivable' intuition of multiplicity that will help us to grasp in what sense the sublime involves an 'exit from inner sense', as Lyotard puts it in the *Lessons*. From the point of view of the first *Critique*, an instant is never sufficient to allow us to apprehend the manifold contained in a given intuition, for it requires temporal discrimination. The manifold contained in an intuition can only be represented by the mind as a manifold if it has the time to do so, that is, if it can distinguish time in the sequence of one impression upon another. Since, in the aesthetic comprehension, unlike in the logical one, the content of sense is regarded as a multiplicity of 'indeterminate' parts of a whole, the unity of the comprehension does not have to be inferred through a concept and does therefore not require an objective progress of the imagination. Much rather, from the point of view of the third *Critique,* "the intuition of multiplicity is more readily conceivable through the idea of a imagination annulling the linear form of time."⁶² "Thus," Makkreel concludes, "aesthetic comprehension intuits multiplicity as an indeterminate unity, which is to be conceived as a totality or continuum without discrete parts."⁶³

In this sense, as Lyotard remarks, "the sublime thing [*la chose sublime*] is not exactly a phenomenon."⁶⁴ The sublime, for Kant, is not a quality of the object. Rather, it is an experience, which is not yet 'covered', one might say, with extensiveness and

---

⁶⁰ H. J. Paton, *Kant's Metaphysics of Experience* II, London 1965, p. 136, note 1. Cited in: Makkreel, Imagination (see note 21), p. 309.

⁶¹ Makkreel, Imagination (see note 54), p. 309.

⁶² Ibid.

⁶³ Ibid.

⁶⁴ Lyotard, Leçons (see note 9), p. 106; Lyotard, Lessons (see note 9), p. 81.

qualities, as in the empirical exercise of the imagination. The state of mind that experiences sublimity is provoked by an intensive sensory impression that does not serve here as an anticipation of perception, but that 'directs' it at the 'supersensible', determined by Kant as the 'idea' that 'transcends' all sensibility and even as the sensibility transformed by the imagination. Imagination's regression to reason, annihilating time as produced by the transcendental imagination of the first *Critique* and transcending all empirical sensibility, is, however, as such not so much transcendent, but can be seen to have a transcendental character itself.[65] That is to say, instead of extending the imagination beyond its limits, it provides the occasion to recognize them.

## Conclusion

Whereas the first *Critique* presupposes the possibility of knowledge and, accordingly, the transcendental ground of the unity of consciousness, the third *Critique* raises the question of this possibility. In the *Analytic of the Sublime,* Kant meditates on the possibility of an involuntary spasm that breaks the solid assemblage of representations in their temporal sequence and results in a kind of incapacity to maintain the unity of the consciousness of these representations in the change of their succession. The convulsion in which the before and after lose their maintenance does, however, not lead to a total abolishment of phenomenal stability. The sublime is not, to use the terms of the first *Critique,* "nothing but a blind play of representations, i. e., less than a dream".[66] The unchained ocean and distorted storms of nature awaken this threat, which is the insistence of chaos, without leading to absolute formlessness and paralysis of our faculties. As Kant writes: "The mind feels itself *moved* in the representation of the sublime in nature".[67] This sublime movement "may be compared to a vibration, i. e., to a rapidly alternating repulsion from and attraction to one and the same object."[68] The imagination, driven in apprehension to what is 'repellent' for sensibility (imagination's "abyss"[69]), is however still attracted by reason. Through the very

---

[65] Lyotard illustrates this by comparing the imaginative regress to the cosmological regress of traditional metaphysics, which Kant discusses in the Antinomy of Pure Reason of the first *Critique;* cf. ibid., pp. 162–169; pp. 131–137.

[66] Kant, Reason (see note 1), A112.

[67] Kant, Judgment (see note 7), AA158.

[68] Ibid., AA258.

[69] Ibid., AA265.

impotency of the imagination, the destination of the mind, namely its receptivity to ideas (which is superior to each exemplification) is signalled. In this way, the sublime is said to be an indirect pleasure, a delight generated by "a momentary inhibition [*Hemmung*] of the vital powers and the immediately following and all the more powerful outpouring [*Ergießung*] of them".[70]

Sublime feeling, as a form of self-affection, designates from the perspective of the first *Critique* a disturbance of the transcendental level, which threatens the subject in its most minimal power, namely thought's ability of synthesizing givens (its own included). The aesthetic comprehension in 'one glance' of what is successive does 'violence' not only to the *a priori* condition of the intuition of any given or succession, but to the eminent and unique condition that such a grasp imposes on the intuition of ourselves and of our state. The subject, for a moment at least – namely, at least for the duration of the *Zugleich* of the regression –, is deprived of the means of constituting its subjectivity. The sublime, in Lyotard's words, "for a moment threatens the subject to make him disappear."[71] The spectator, for a moment, is thrown back into the uncontrolled nature of her receptivity. The synthesis of the given becomes impossible, and the quality of the state, in which the thought that imagines finds itself, is reversed: It is afraid of this *Überschwengliche*, of this transcendent, this movable and confused (*schwingen*) beyond (*über*), "like an abyss [*Abgrund*] in which it fears to lose itself"."[72] This affection does not primarily concern the empirical individual, but must be seen as a transcendental affection. What happens is more serious than an obstacle to the *Zusammenfassung* of a magnitude, the presentation of an object in intuition. It is the destruction of the very condition of self-affection, namely the temporality proper to all presentation. We encounter a moment of temporal simultaneity emptied of all phenomenal determinability, which is the first condition of the possibility for the human experience of the sublime:

> In Kant, possibility does not disappear with the sublime but becomes a possibility *to lack* [une possibilité au manque]. It is precisely the beautiful forms with their destination, our own destiny, which are missing, and the sublime includes this sort of pain due to the finitude of 'flesh', this ontological melancholy.[73]

---

[70] Ibid., AA245.

[71] Lyotard, Leçons (see note 9), p. 177; Lyotard, Lessons (see note 9), p. 144.

[72] Ibid., p. 139 ; p. 110.

[73] Jean-François Lyotard, *L'inhumain. Causeries sur le temps*, Paris 1988, p. 129; Jean-François Lyotard, *The Inhuman. Reflections on Time*, transl. by G. Bennington and R. Bowlby, Cambridge 1991, p. 118.

## Bibliography

Dupré, Louis, Aesthetic Perception and its Relation to Ordinary Perception, in: *Aisthesis and Aesthetics. The Fourth Lexington Conference on Pure and Applied Phenomenology*, ed. by Erwin W. Straus and Richard M. Griffith, Pittsburgh 1970, pp. 171–177.

Kant, Immanuel, *Critique of Pure Reason*, transl. by Paul Guyer and Allen W. Wood, Cambridge 1998.

Kant, Immanuel, *Critique of the Power of Judgment*, transl. by Paul Guyer and Eric Matthews, Cambridge 2000.

Lyotard, Jean-François, *L'inhumain. Causeries sur le temps*, Paris 1988.

Lyotard, Jean-François, *The Inhuman. Reflections on Time*, transl. by G. Bennington and R. Bowlby, Cambridge 1991.

Lyotard, Jean-François, *Leçons sur l'Analytique du sublime*, Paris 1991.

Lyotard, Jean-François, *Lessons on the Analytic of the Sublime*, transl. by Elizabeth Rottenberg, Stanford 1994.

Makkreel, Rudolf, Imagination and Temporality in Kant's Theory of the Sublime, in: *The Journal of Aesthetics and Art Criticism*, vol. 42, no. 3 (1984), pp. 303–315.

Rogozinski, Jacob, Le don du monde, in: *Du sublime*, ed. by Michel Deguy, Paris 1988, pp. 179–210.

Shores, Corry, Self Shock. The Phenomenon of Personal Non-Identity in Inorganic Subjectivity, in: *The Yearbook on History and Interpretation of Phenomenology 2013*, Frankfurt am Main 2013, pp. 157–183.

# Working Traces in the History of Art
*Ralph-Miklas Dobler*

The definition and meaning of the term 'trace' is manifold.[1] Generally speaking, traces can be either mental, that is, psychological, or material, which means that traces can be visible and perceivable or they can be invisible to the human eye and lost to the sense of touch. This distinction can already be found in Plato, and Socrates declared in Georgias:

> Again, if anyone had been a sturdy rogue, and bore traces of his stripes in scars on his body, either from the whip or from other wounds, while yet alive, then after death too his body has these marks visible upon it.[2]

Traces are thus phenomena interpreted as signs of a passing presence. However, the trace is not the matter – in this case the corpse of the deceased –, but the form given to it through the act of touch. Furthermore, Socrates explains to Theaitetos:

> [W]hen, for example, knowing you and Theodorus, and having on that block of wax the imprint of both of you, as if you were signet-rings, but seeing you both at a distance and indistinctly, I hasten to assign the proper imprint of each of you to the proper vision, and to make it fit, as it were, its own footprint, with the purpose of causing recognition.[3]

Thus, according to Socrates, a block of wax preserves the imprints of perception in the soul of human beings. As the philosopher points out, these traces are empty forms that enable the identification of things, at least if they are not too far away. Indeed, it is a matter of fact that experiences are inscribed onto the mind as traces and that traumatic events leave traces on the psyche.

In the history of art, this first definition of traces – and there are many more than the two by Plato – is well-known, for artistic production can leave various working traces on the material chosen for a work of art. However, there are also invisible working traces to be found in paintings and sculptures. Saint Augustine reframed the platonic idea of traces in a Christian context. According to him, the trace of God, the Creator, is visible in every creature, a principle that was taken over for the following

---

[1] Hans-Jürgen Gawoll, Spur, in: *Historisches Wörterbuch der Philosophie*, ed. by Joachim Ritter and Karlfried Gründer, Basel 1995, pp. 1550–1558.

[2] Plato, *Lysis Symposion Georgias*, ed. by W. R. M. Lamb, Cambridge 1961, p. 523.

[3] Plato, *Theaetetus Sophist*, ed. by Harold North Fowler, Cambridge 1961, p. 193.

centuries.[4] Pico della Mirandola acknowledges the existence of Trinitarian traces in all creatures: "Est trinitatis divinae in creatura multiplex vestigium." Accordingly, Giordano Bruno confirms divine traces in everything: "non possiamo conoscer nulla, se non per modo di verstigio".[5] Following Thomas Aquinas, intelligent creatures have an image resembling that of the Creator – a "similitudo per modum imaginis" –, whereas all other creatures only have a trace of similarity – "per modum vestigii."[6] Johannes Scotus Eriugena uses an imagery of light to explain divine traces in the world. For him, the divine ground shines upon the world as traces of sensual lights, while, for Bonaventure, reality reflects bright shining traces in which the power of God is visible.[7]

Similarly, art theory, especially from the Renaissance onwards, concentrated on the concept of divine perfection and ideal beauty in works of art. Particularly interesting in this context is Giorgio Vasari's use of a comparable imagery of light for such kinds of traces in *The Lives of the Artists*. Finally, painter and art theorist Federico Zuccari represents the Lord of the Arts, the *disegno*, as a god-like majesty with a nimbus surrounding his head (see fig. 13.1).[8] Two inscriptions below his feet emphasize the light: "lux intellectus et vita operationum" – *disegno* is thus the divine light of knowledge as well as the life of the work – and "una lux in tribus refulgens" – one light shines in painting, sculpture and architecture. Therefore, the three arts reflect the divine trace in the form of light. For that reason, as is written on the picture frame, *disegno* is the "scintilla divinitatis" – the "spark of divinity". In his treatise "Origine et Progresso dell'Academia del Disegno di Roma", Federico Zuccari explains this idea further.[9] The divine *disegno* is the guide of the artist – "nostra guida, nostra scorta, e nostro duce, cioè, luce all'intelleto" –, he is the light of cognition.[10] Hence, the duty of every artist

---

[4] Gawoll, Spur (see note 1), p. 1551.

[5] Ibid., p. 1552.

[6] Tommaso d'Aquino, *La somma teologica*, Bologna 1985, p. 221: "Respondeo dicendum quod, cum in omnis creaturis sit aliqualis Dei similitudo, in sola creatura rationali inventur similitudo Dei per modum imaginis, ut supra dictum est: in aliis autem creaturis per modum verstigii."

[7] Gawoll, Spur (see note 1), p. 1551.

[8] Kristina Herrmann-Fiore, Die Fresken Federico Zuccaris in einem römischen Künstlerhaus, in: *Römisches Jahrbuch für Kunstgeschichte*, vol. 29 (1979), pp. 78–81.

[9] Federico Zuccari, Origine e Progresso dell'Accademia del Disegno di Roma, in: *Scritti d'arte di Federico Zuccari*, ed. by Detlef Heikamp, Florence 1961, p. 1–99.

[10] Ibid., p. 84.

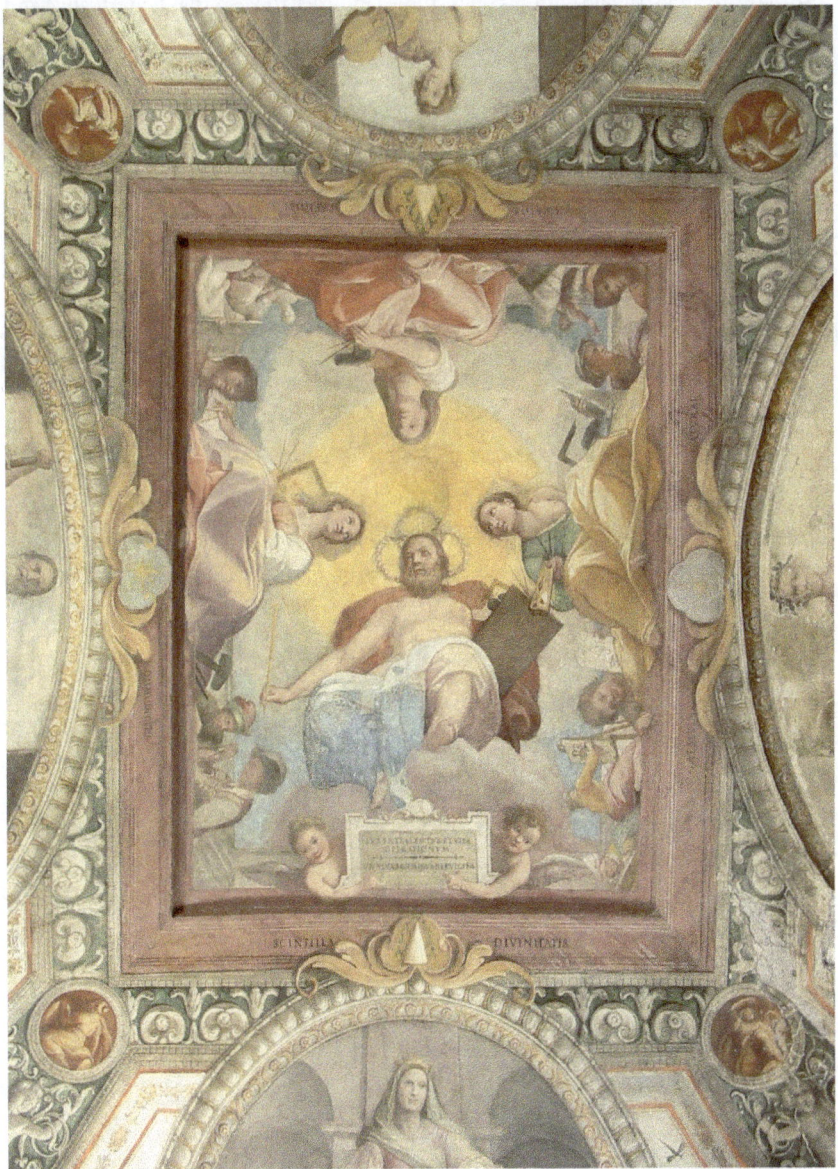

Fig. 13.1: Federico Zuccari, ceiling fresco representing the *disegno*

is to activate and struggle with his own studies in order to keep that lantern alive and burning – "così adunque ciascuno di noi si dovrà inanimare, e sforzarsi con in proprii studii e diligenza avanzandosi d'operare e mantener viva questa luminosa laterna," for the *disegno* is an invisible albeit sensible working trace of the divine in aesthetic representations.[11] Zuccari was the first art theorist who mixed the old platonic concept with an 'idea' superior to nature: The *disegno* is the idea, which is produced by the intellect as a sign of the divine.[12] The *disegno interno* – the interior design – expresses itself as a trace of the divine in the *disegno esterno* – the exterior design or drawing – of the work of art.

In the 17th century, the divine trace in painting and sculpture was called the *idea dell'bello*.[13] In accordance with Giovanni Battista Agucchi the idea must be contemplated by the artist as a divine thing outreaching nature – "come cosa divina la contempla".[14] Giovanni Pietro Bellori explains that people do not understand the idea because they are mainly focused on the visual – "il popoli riferisce tutto al senso dell'occhio" – and therefore not able to contemplate the idea as a divine thing – "come cosa divina".[15] Nonetheless, the *idea del'bello*, the divine, remains a trace of artistic production in the work of art, even though it can only be perceived by noble minds – "i spiriti elevati".[16]

Easier to notice for the common viewer are the visible working traces left behind by the artist's tools – the brush, the chisel, and so on. In this case, the trace is a material phenomenon and a sign of something older. Without emphasizing the question whether or not traces are signs, they are at least an index pointing to the referenced object by means of their physical form. At the same time, the working trace represents the past as material evidence in the absence of the force that created the trace.

---

[11] Ibid., p. 85.

[12] Luigi Grassi / Mario Pepe, *Dizionario die termini artistici*, Milan 1995, p. 396.

[13] Denis Mahon, *Studies in Seicento Art and Theory*, London 1947, pp. 109–154; Grassi / Pepe, Dizionario (see note 12), pp. 395–397; Anna Gamiccia / Federica Piantoni (eds.), *L'idea del Bello. Viaggio per Roma nel Seicento con Giovan Pietro Bellori*, 2 vols, Rome 2000.

[14] Mahon, Studies (see note 13), p. 146: "Ma l'uomo intendente sollevando il pensiero all'Idea del bello, che la natura mostra di voler fare, da quello vien rapito, e come cosa divina la contempla".

[15] Giovanni Pietro Bellori, *Le vite de'pittori, scultori et architetti moderni*, Rome 1672, p. 11; ibid., pp. 146–147.

[16] Grassi / Pepe, Dizionario (see note 12), pp. 396–397.

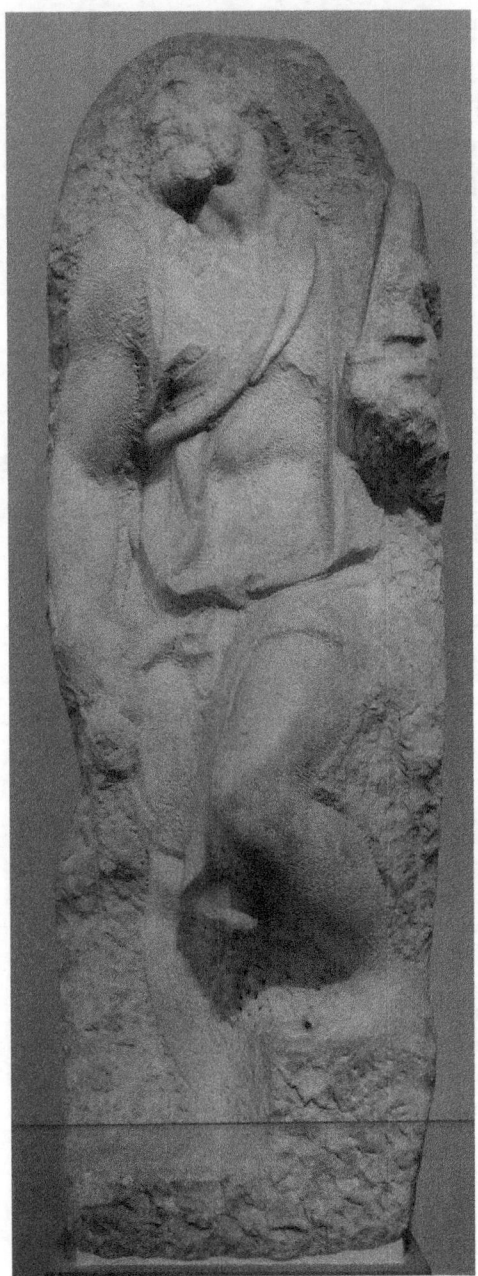

Fig. 13.2: Michelangelo, slave unfinished

Working traces thus bear testimony to the past and, above all, are a feature of unfinished work (fig. see 13.2). Consequently, visible working traces are a sign of incompleteness. However, they enable the beholder to participate in the process of production and to reconstruct the thoughts of the artist. Pliny wrote:

> It is also a very unusual and memorable fact that the last works of artists and their unfinished pictures [...] are more admired than those which they finished, because in them are seen the preliminary drawings left visible and the artists' actual thoughts.[17]

Moreover, Vasari's passages share a defensive quality in order to assure us that the unfinished factor should not make us view the works as being without value. Describing Michelangelo's Matthew or the Medici Madonna, he finds that in the *imperfezione* of the work we can see the *perfezione* of the complete form.[18] Furthermore, because of the visibility of the production process in the traces of the chisel, the sculptures of Michelangelo have "pedagogical value", as they show the correct way to extract a block without damaging it.[19] In any case, what it is exactly that is expressed in Michelangelo's *non-finito* is difficult to say. He certainly wished to complete each work he began and was unhappy when this did not happen. Ascribing an aesthetic value to the visible working traces in unfinished works is often the result of posthumous glorification of the artist. A passage in the biography of Michelangelo written by Condivi, commonly believed to be the artist's mouthpiece, expresses disapproval for unfinished work.[20] The only fault in Donatello, we are told, was that he did not polish his works enough, with the result that they look fine from afar but, when taken in up close, "lose their reputation". Today, an opposite view concerning the rough surfaces of Donatello, as expressed by Vasari, is much better known, and, as we have seen, the same is true for Michelangelo.[21]

---

[17] Pliny, *Natural History*, ed. by H. Rackham, Cambridge 1961, pp. 366–367: "illud vero perquam rarum ac memoria dignum est, suprema opera artificium imperfectasque tabulas [...] in maiore admiratione esse quam perfecta, quipppe in iis lineamenta reliquia ipsaeque cogitationes artificium spectantur".

[18] Creighton E. Gilbert, What is Expressed in Michelangelo's Non-Finito, in: *Artibus et historiae. An art anthology*, vol. 48 (2003), p. 57.

[19] Gilbert, Non-Finito (see note 18), p. 58.

[20] Ibid., p. 59.

[21] Nicolas Penny, Non-Finito in Italian fifteenth-century bronze sculpture, in: *Antologia di Belle Arti*, vols. 48–51 (1994), pp. 11–15; Michael Bockemühl, Vom unvollendeten zum offenen Kunstwerk. Zur Diskussion des non-finito in der Plastik von Michelangelo, in: *Studien zu Renaissance und Barock. Manfred Wundram zum 60. Geburtstag*, ed. by Michael Hesse and Max Imdahl, Frankfurt am Main / Bern / New York 1986, pp. 111–133.

When the painter Eugéne Delacroix wrote his journals in the 1850s, he praised Michelangelo among the geniuses that are sublime even while being "incorrect".[22] The imperfections of visible working traces can be perceived as perfect in this paradox due to historical distance. In the same years, John Ruskin justified Michelangelo's and others' unfinished works with a different version of praise of their effect: The rough chisel marks are admired because they set up lights and shade, thus producing a pictorial effect.[23] Lastly, Friedrich Hegel organized the evolution of the arts in three stages, evolving from the most material to the classical and finally to the spiritual. The first stage is most realized in architecture, the second in sculpture and the third, labelled romantic, is reserved to painting.[24] Coming from a Hegelian tradition, Michelangelo specialist Henry Thode suggests that Michelangelo's discomfort with the less spiritual character of sculptures led him to leave works in that medium unfinished in order to produce complete paintings.[25]

I will stop here with my investigation of unfinished sculptures, as the desired norm was a complete work. Whenever completion was lacking, it could commonly be linked to money problems, competition among promises, non-delivery of materials, or similar external factors. Consequently, the working traces that remain were unintentional. In order to understand them, they must be inserted in a meaningful context to reconstruct their messages.

However, works of art, especially sculptures, can also be characterized by working traces left behind intentionally by the artist during the process of production. The famous Roman baroque sculptor Gianlorenzo Bernini is known for his demonstration of sculptural "difficultas" applied to a subject matter that is particularly difficult for sculpture.[26] Sources for his carvings can be found in painting and his sculptures are narrative "sculpted paintings", intentionally transgressing the barriers separating the arts. Sculpture depicts substance in the physical as well as in the philosophical sense, and therefore it possesses greater validity than the imitation or even the depiction of

---

[22] Gilbert, Non-Finito (see note 18), p. 60.
[23] Ibid., p. 61.
[24] Ibid.
[25] Ibid.
[26] Rudolf Preimesberger, Themes from art theory in early works of Bernini, in: *Gianlorenzo Bernini. New aspects of his art and thought: A commemorative volume*, ed. by Irving Lavin, University Park 1985, pp. 1–18.

painting. Painting, however, is capable of imitating all of visible nature – movement, time, metamorphosis, fire, smoke, storm, and, above all, colour. If Bernini sought a *paragone* – a challenge – within painting, he assumes a common standpoint in Italian art theory, namely that imitation is all the more admirable when the means of imitation are far removed from the object to be imitated, as Galileo Galilei put it in 1612.[27]

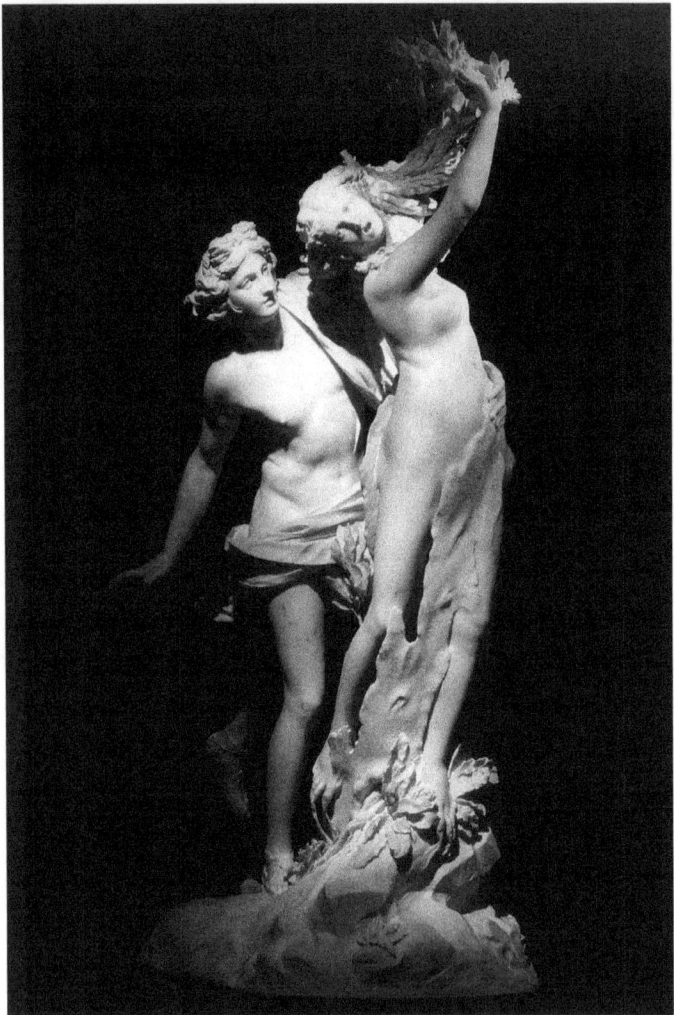

Fig. 13.3: Gianlorenzo Bernini, *Apollo and Daphne*

---

[27] Erwin Panofsky, *Galileo as a critic of the arts,* The Hague 1954.

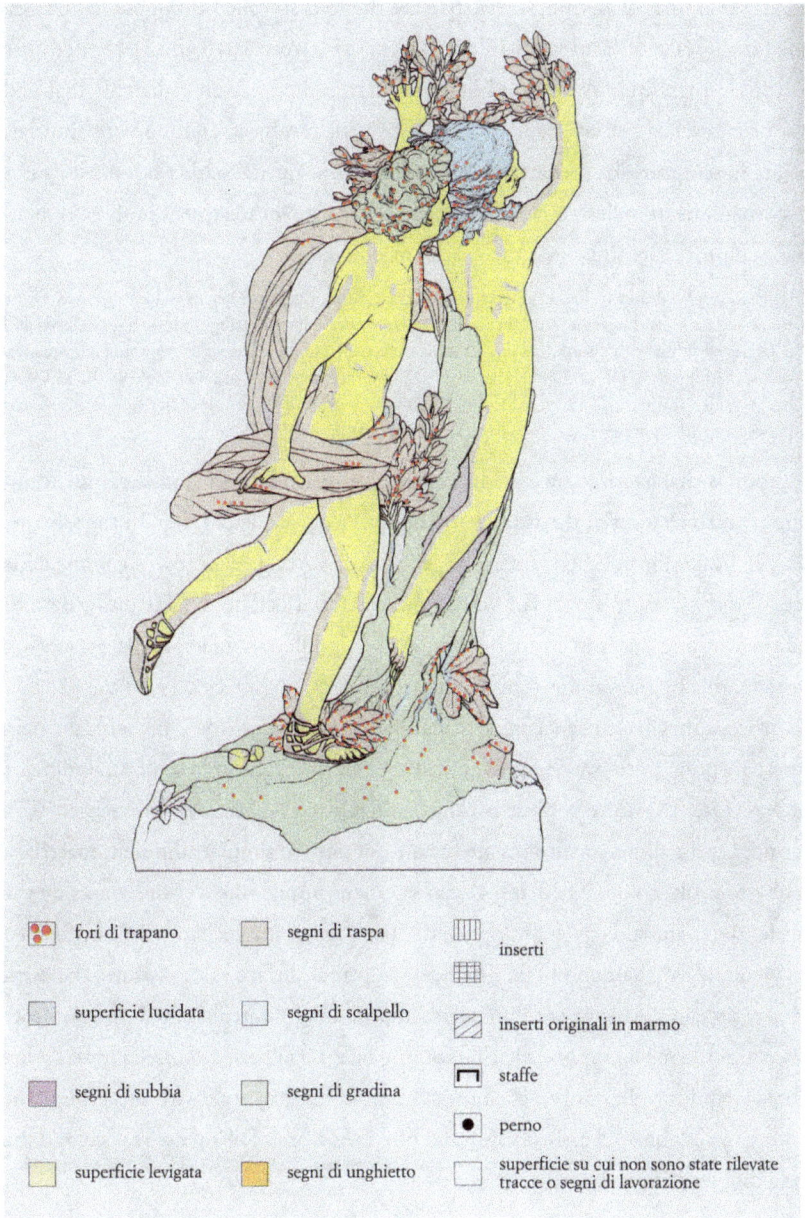

Fig. 13.4: Scheme of the different working traces left on the marble of *Apollo and Daphne*

Early examples of Bernini's new style are the four so-called Borghese sculptures, made for the Villa of Cardinal Scipione Borghese between 1618 and 1625. Bernini's last work, representing Apollo and Daphne, carries pictorialism to heights that had never been reached before (see fig. 13.3). The Ovidian subject, common in paintings, was rare in sculpture for reasons that can easily be imagined: Neither hot pursuits nor transformations from flesh to wood seemed appropriate for treatment in three-dimensional sculpture. Bernini chose the crucial moment:

> [J]ust as Apollo thinks he has achieved his goal, Daphne's fleeing form begins to be enveloped by the encircling bark; her fingers leaf out; her toes take root. Apollo has just caught up with his beloved and encircles her waist with a confident arm; but his facial expression indicates the beginning of awareness that something has gone wrong. Daphne seems ignorant of her transformation as she looks back over her shoulder, lips parted in fright. Daphne's hair swings around as a result of her sudden arrest and blows free with lightness.[28]

The group is characterized by a boldly contrasting differentiation and consequent mimetic characterization of the various marble surfaces (see fig. 13.4).[29] In the scheme, yellow indicates the polished parts, orange traces of *raspa*, green traces of *gradina*, blue traces of *scalpello*, purple traces of *subbia*, and red are drilled holes. Obviously, Bernini used the working traces to create the impression of different materials. The traces left on the marble by the various tools of the sculptor are no longer signs of the production process; they have been assigned their own aesthetic quality. Only with the help of these working traces was Bernini able to create a new version of sculptural mimesis that was closer to nature because it could represent every visible phenomenon. Without doubt, the different surfaces are meant not only to simulate different materials, but also to evoke colours. Perhaps we can say that, through the working traces on the marble, the material is overcoming itself. Hard, white marble stone is transformed into wood, leaves, hair and flesh. The new sculptural surface values witness the birth of a new style in the history of European sculpture. Bernini represented the transitory moment of the metamorphosis itself. Nothing like it had been attempted in sculpture before. Technically, Bernini reached the summit of his early style with this group. The working traces obtained artistic value and provided a basis for intense realism and the subtle differentiation of texture.

---

[28] Howard Hibbard, *Bernini*, London 1990, pp. 48–50.
[29] Anna Coliva (ed.), *Bernini scultore. La tecnica esecutiva*, Rome 2002, pp. 184–207.

In his representation of Pluto and Proserpina, Bernini had overcome the difficulties of rendering marble "as malleable as wax" – "pieghevole come la cera" – or, in his own and less elegant metaphor, as "pliable as pasta".[30] Nevertheless, the traces of the *subbia* around the fingers of Pluto are still visible in order to create a line of shadow to obscure the transition from the powerful hand to the soft flesh.

In the second and more elaborate edition of the *Lives of the Painters, Sculptors and Architects* from 1568, Giorgio Vasari writes:

> In the same city of Venice and about the same time there lived, as he still does, a painter called Jacopo Tintoretto, who has delighted in all the arts, and particularly in playing various musical instruments, besides being agreeable in his every action, but in the matter of painting swift, resolute, fantastic, and extravagant, and the most extraordinary brain that the art of painting has ever produced, as may be seen from all his works and from the fantastic compositions of his scenes, executed by him in a fashion of his own and contrary to the use of other painters [see fig. 13.5]. Indeed, he has surpassed even the limits of extravagance with the new and fanciful inventions and the strange vagaries of his intellect, working at haphazard and without design, as if to prove that art is but a jest. This master at times has left as finished works sketches still so rough that the brush-strokes may be seen, done more by chance and vehemence than with judgment and design.[31]

Vasari criticizes the fact that in Tintoretto's paintings the brush-strokes are still visible, even if the painter judged his work as finished. For the biographer, these assumed unfinished works were parodies of true art. Behind this estimation stands the famous antagonism between *disegno* and *colorito*, between the Romano-Tuscan and the Venetian tradition of painting.[32] The velocity of Tintoretto's works, with the consequences that the working traces remained visible, astonished Vasari on several occasions. On the other hand, the visible brush-strokes could also be interpreted as signs of the fast production process that characterized the work of the painter.

---

[30] Preimesberger, Themes (see note 26), p. 4.

[31] Giorgio Vasari, *Lives of the Painters, Sculptors and Architects*, trans. by Gaston du C., New York 1996, p. 509; Thomas Weigel, Tintoretto und das Non-Finito, in: *Die Virtus des Künstlers in der italienischen Renaissance*, ed. by Joachim Poeschke, Thomas Weigel and Britta Kusch-Arnold, Münster 2006, pp. 232–233.

[32] Weigel, Tintoretto (see note 31), p. 235.

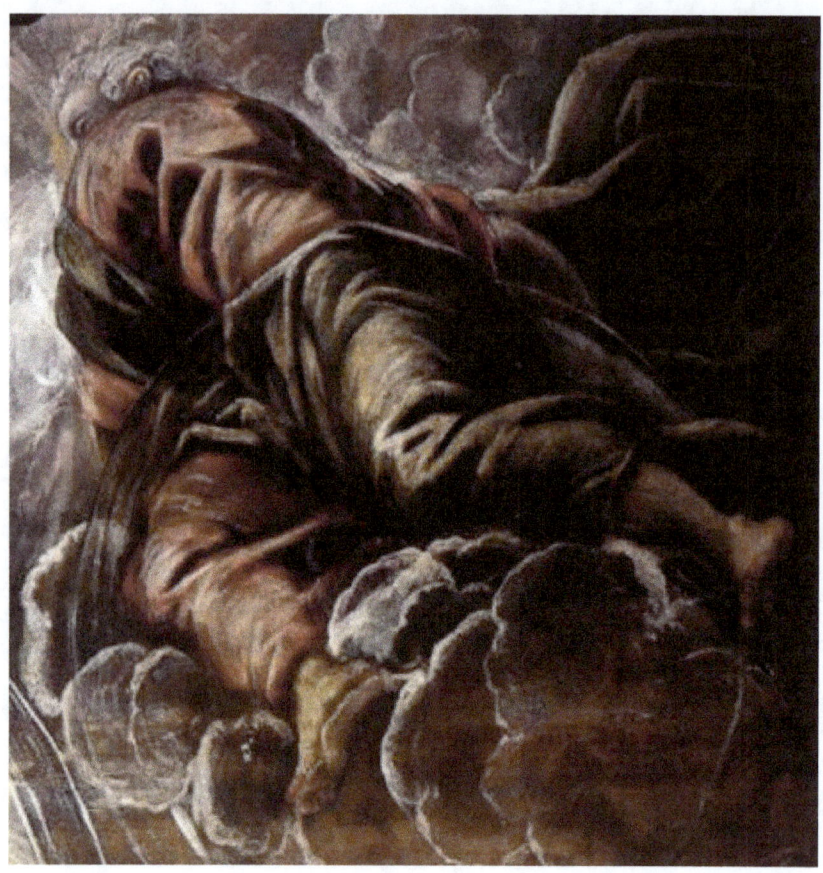

Fig. 13.5: Jacopo Tintoretto

In 1642, Carlo Ridolfi argues in his *Life of Tintoretto* that the visible working traces in the paintings of Tintoretto are determined by decorum. According to him, all works of the painter are done appropriate to the site – "proporzionato al sito".[33] Ridolfi extends Vasari's perspective, which focuses on the producer and the product with regard to the beholder. The visible working traces of the brush stroke lead to the appearance of the artwork as being determined by perception. We do not know if this has been the intention of Tintoretto, but it seems plausible. As early as in 1528, in his book *The Courtier – Il cortegiano –*, Baldassare Castiglione explains the

---

[33] Carlo Ridolfi, *Le meraviglie dell'arte*, Padua 1837, p. 202; ibid., pp. 240–241.

concept of *sprezzatura*, that is, the elegant and confident appearance of the courtier in his behaviour, speech and activities.[34] Castiglione uses the term for painting too. The counterpart of *sprezzatura* is the sketch-like, open and demonstrative *pennellata:* the brush-stroke – "una linea sola non stentata, un sol colpo di pennello, tirato facilmente".[35] The visible brush-stroke, or, in our context, the visible working trace, is thus a symbol of freedom and sovereignty.

But not only that, the challenges the artist faced from the 15th century onwards awakened emotions within his paintings. It seems that not only figures and their gestures and facial expressions complied to the duty of *movere*, but the visible brush-stroke was also transmitting emotions. Carlo Ridolfi writes: Tintoretto's "brush was a clap of thunder that struck down everybody with his lightning" – "era il suo pennello un fulmine, [...], che atterriva ogn'uno col lampo."[36] Working traces therefore have the power to stimulate feelings.

Finally, in 1914, Max Dvořák reinterprets Tintoretto's meaning.[37] He replaces the putatively optical concerns of impressionism with an emphasis on subjective inwardness, or enhanced spirituality. He argues that the painter's work,

> more than imitation [...] is an intensification of the magical interplay between spectator and the object, and this is the characteristic of the ultimate style of Tintoretto: a heightening of the means of painterly expression to a level of visionary representation of supernatural events.[38]

---

[34] Grassi / Pepe, Dizionario (see note 12), pp. 919–920; Axel Christoph Gampp, Sprezzatura. Pontormos Portraits und das höfische Ideal des Manierismus, in: *Manier und Manierismus*, ed. by Wolfgang Braungart, Tübingen 2000, pp. 221–250.

[35] Baldassare Castiglione, *Il Corteggiano*, ed. by Vittorio Cian, Florence 1929, p. 69: "Spesso ancor nella pittura una linea sola non stentata, un solo colpo di pennello tirato facilmente, di modo che paia che la mano, senza esser guidata da studio o art alcuna, vada per sé stessa al suo termine secondo la intenzione del pittore"; Valeska von Rosen, *Mimesis und Selbstbezüglichkeit in Werken Tizians. Studien zum venezianischen Malereidiskurs*, Emsdetten 2001, p. 324; Weigel, Tintoretto (see note 31), p. 245.

[36] Ridolfi, Meraviglie (see note 33), p. 207; Weigel, Tintoretto (see note 31), p. 246.

[37] Hans Aurenhammer, Max Dvořák, Tintoretto und die Moderne. Kunstgeschichte "vom Standpunkt unserer Kunstentwicklung" betrachtet, in: *Wiener Jahrbuch für Kunstgeschichte*, vol. 49 (1996), pp. 9–39.

[38] Matthew Rampley, *The Vienna School of Art History. Empire and the Politics of Scholarship, 1847–1918*, University Park 2013, p. 111; Max Dvořák, Tintoretto-Vortrag, cited in: Aurenhammer, Dvořák (see note 37), p. 24: "Dieser Ausdruck ist mehr als eine Nachahmung, ist eine Potenzierung des Zauberspiels, das sich zwischen dem Beschauer und dem Objekt abspielt, und diese Steigerung der malerischen Ausdrucksmittel bis zur visionären Expression, bis zum Übermenschlichen und Übernatürlichen, verbunden mit Kompositionen, die ebenfalls eine visionäre Darstellung von übernatürlichen Vorgängen sind, dies ist das Kennzeichen des letzten Stiles von Tintoretto."

For Dvořák, the history of art was now marked by the eternal struggle between material and spirit.[39] For him, impressionism signified a withdrawal from the material objectivity into the world of the inner spirit. The working trace thus overcame its own materiality.

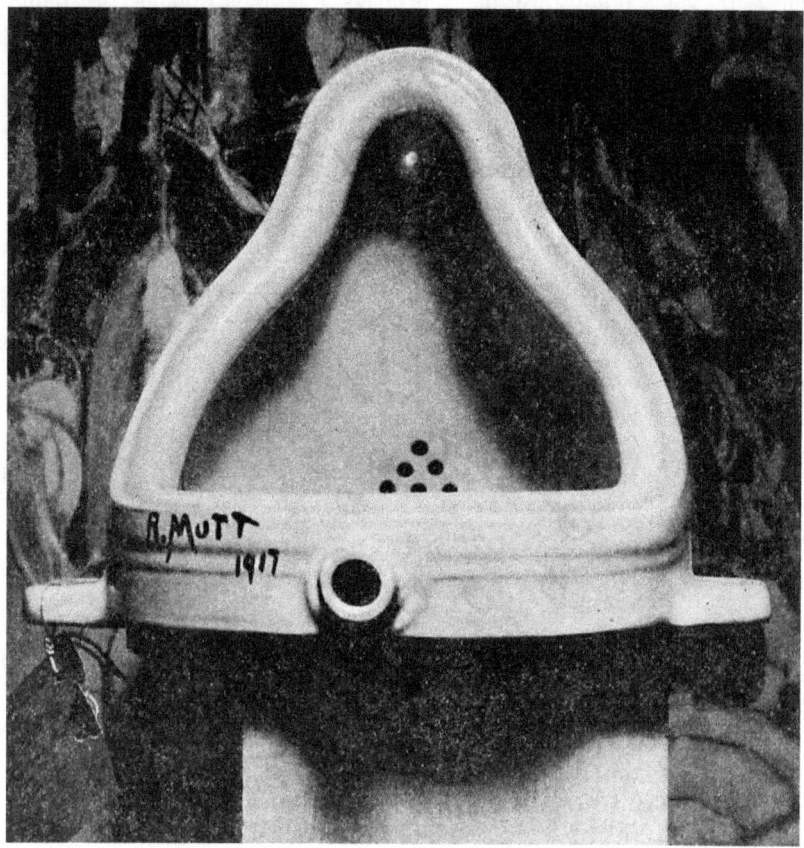

Fig. 13.6: Marcel Duchamp, *Fountain*

One of the most famous, or rather infamous, objects in the history of modern art is Marcel Duchamp's "Fountain" (see fig. 13.6). The work entered the history of art in April 1917 on the occasion of the first exhibition by the American Society of Independent Artists. "The Fountain", as it was declared by the majority, "may be a very

---

[39] Rampley, Vienna (see note 38), p. 111.

useful object in its place, but it is not an art exhibition, and it is, by no definition, a work of art."[40] The object was refused.

Duchamp himself described his "Fountain" as "ready-made".[41] The term indicates that, in his radically new definition of an artwork, not the forming or "un-forming" of the material were essential, but the concept of a finished object that is ready for use. Duchamp chose the industrial era and mass production as a central theme.[42] The mass-produced article of a urinal remained unchanged in form and material, only the signature "R. Mutt" certified the object as an artwork. Duchamp released the artist from manual labour and, instead, transformed an industrially produced and functional object into artistic material without "un-forming" or changing it.[43] Artistic production or working traces were no longer inherent parts of a work of art. What remains of the production process is the concept of detracting the utility of objects and emphasizing their purest form. In the concept of "ready-made" objects, material features have no creative value. The industrial product clashes with the conception of an artwork as an individually produced object.

In any case, Duchamp chose an object formed out of the primordial matter of artistic production, namely clay.[44] When Greek potter Butades invented sculpture, he formed portraits out of clay and burned them together with articles of daily use. From a material perspective, "The Fountain" can consequently be seen as sculpture. Duchamp thus carried a problem to extremes that had become obvious through industrialization: the divergence of artistic and non-artistic work.

I began my brief overview with the question what traces were. Talking about working traces, we should also ask what work is and which type of work leave traces. While there is no doubt that the products of Zuccari, Michelangelo, Bernini and Tintoretto are works of art, the artwork of Duchamp is a work of industrial production, and such products feature their own working traces. But as they do not result in artistic value, they are not important – at least in our context.

---

[40] Anonymous, His Art Is Too Crude for Independents, in: *The New York Herald*, April 14, 1917, p. 6.
[41] Monika Wagner, *Das Material der Kunst. Eine andere Geschichte der Moderne*, Munich 2002, p. 68.
[42] Ibid., p. 68.
[43] Ibid.: "Statt dessen interessiert Duchamps konzeptuelle Strategie, einen industriell produziert und funktional erscheinenden Gegenstand, ohne ihn zu „entformen" in Material der Kunst zu transformieren."
[44] Wagner, Material (see note 41), p. 70.

## Bibliography

Anonymous, His Art Is Too Crude for Independents, in: *The New York Herald*, April 14, 1917.

Aurenhammer, Hans, Max Dvořák, Tintoretto und die Moderne. Kunstgeschichte "vom Standpunkt unserer Kunstentwicklung" betrachtet, in: *Wiener Jahrbuch für Kunstgeschichte*, vol. 49 (1996), pp. 9–39.

Bellori, Giovanni Pietro, *Le vite de'pittori, scultori et architetti moderni*, Rome 1672.

Bockemühl, Michael, Vom unvollendeten zum offenen Kunstwerk. Zur Diskussion des non-finito in der Plastik von Michelangelo, in: *Studien zu Renaissance und Barock. Manfred Wundram zum 60. Geburtstag*, ed. by Michael Hesse and Max Imdahl, Frankfurt am Main / Bern / New York 1986, pp. 111–133.

Castiglione, Baldassare, *Il Corteggiano*, ed. by Vittorio Cian, Florence 1929.

Coliva, Anna (ed.), *Bernini scultore. La tecnica esecutiva*, Rome 2002.

D'Aquino, Tommaso, *La somma teologica*, Bologna 1985.

Gamiccia, Anna / Piantoni, Federica (eds.), *L'idea del Bello. Viaggio per Roma nel Seicento con Giovan Pietro Bellori*, 2 vols, Rome 2000.

Gampp, Axel Christoph, Sprezzatura. Pontormos Portraits und das höfische Ideal des Manierismus, in: *Manier und Manierismus*, ed. by Wolfgang Braungart, Tübingen 2000, pp. 221–250.

Gawoll, Hans-Jürgen, Spur, in: *Historisches Wörterbuch der Philosophie*, ed. by Joachim Ritter and Karlfried Gründer, Basel 1995, pp. 1550–1558.

Gilbert, Creighton E., What is Expressed in Michelangelo's Non-Finito, in: *Artibus et historiae. An art anthology*, vol. 48 (2003).

Grassi, Luigi / Pepe, Mario, *Dizionario die termini artistici*, Milan 1995.

Herrmann-Fiore, Kristina, Die Fresken Federico Zuccaris in einem römischen Künstlerhaus, in: *Römisches Jahrbuch für Kunstgeschichte*, vol. 18 (1979), pp. 35–112.

Hibbard, Howard, *Bernini*, London 1990.

Mahon, Denis, *Studies in Seicento Art and Theory*, London 1947.

Panofsky, Erwin, *Galileo as a critic of the arts*, The Hague 1954.

Penny, Nicolas, Non-Finito in Italian fifteenth-century bronze sculpture, in: *Antologia di Belle Arti*, vols. 48–51 (1994), pp. 11–15.

Plato, *Lysis Symposion Georgias*, ed. by W. R. M. Lamb, Cambridge 1961.

Plato, *Theaetetus Sophist*, ed. by Harold North Fowler, Cambridge 1961.

Pliny, *Natural History*, ed. by H. Rackham, Cambridge 1961.

Preimesberger, Rudolf, Themes from art theory in early works of Bernini, in: *Gianlorenzo Bernini. New aspects of his art and thought: A commemorative volume*, ed. by Irving Lavin, University Park 1985, pp. 1–18.

Rampley, Matthew, *The Vienna School of Art History. Empire and the Politics of Scholarship, 1847–1918*, University Park 2013.

Ridolfi, Carlo, *Le meraviglie dell'arte*, Padua 1837.

Vasari, Giorgio, *Lives of the Painters, Sculptors and Architects*, trans. by Gaston du C., New York 1996.

Von Rosen, Valeska, *Mimesis und Selbstbezüglichkeit in Werken Tizians. Studien zum venezianischen Malereidiskurs*, Emsdetten 2001.

Wagner, Monika, *Das Material der Kunst. Eine andere Geschichte der Moderne*, Munich 2002.

Weigel, Thomas, Tintoretto und das Non-Finito, in: *Die Virtus des Künstlers in der italienischen Renaissance*, ed. by Joachim Poeschke, Thomas Weigel and Britta Kusch-Arnold, Münster 2006.

Zuccari, Federico, Origine e Progresso dell'Accademia del Disegno di Roma, in: *Scritti d'arte di Federico Zuccari*, ed. by Detlef Heikamp, Florence 1961, pp. 1–99.

**Image Credits**

Fig. 13.1–13.3, 13.5: © Ralph Miklas Dobler.

Fig. 13.4: Anna Coliva (ed.), *Bernini scultore. La tecnica esecutiva,* Rome 2002.

Fig. 13.6: Photograph by Alfred Stieglitz, 1917.

# Traces in Sight. Aesthetic Production Dynamics by Nathalie Sarraute and Alain Robbe-Grillet
*Berit Callsen*

A trace only becomes so in sight. It includes tendencies both of back reference and announcement. This connection between trace, perception and retrospective-prospective production – which is the main subject of this paper – underlies the poetics of both Nathalie Sarraute and Alain Robbe-Grillet as a central motor in their creation of literary visuality.

The starting point of this paper is to compare the writing of these main figures of the *nouveau roman*, a literary movement created in France in the 1950s, which subverted conventional narrative elements, such as characters, time and place.[1] In several essays, Robbe-Grillet builds up the theoretical basis of the *nouveau roman*. Thus, in his well-known *Pour un nouveau roman* (1963), for instance, he underlines on the one hand the subversion of existentialism and so-called 'engaged literature', which was developed after 1945 by Albert Camus and Jean-Paul Sartre. On the other hand, he points out the importance of aspects of literary form for the *nouveau roman*. Both of these elements are immediately linked to each other, giving less importance to literary content.

Sarraute assumes an important role in the *nouveau roman* because her poetics of so-called 'tropisms' create a very peculiar way of innovating fiction by subverting conventional forms of writing. In contrast to Robbe-Grillet, who always refused introspective poetics, Sarraute focuses on psychical impulses by way of tropism movements. However, although they use different manners of implementing new literary procedures, both Robbe-Grillet and Sarraute prefer leaving behind forms of realistic narration.[2]

---

[1] Besides Sarraute and Robbe-Grillet, Michel Butor, Robert Pinget, Claude Simon, Jean Ricardou and Claude Ollier are important authors of the *nouveau roman;* cf. Brigitta Coenen-Mennemeier, *Nouveau roman,* Stuttgart / Weimar 1996, p. 7.

[2] On several occasions, critics have mentioned the differences that become obvious in this common motivation of Sarraute and Robbe-Grillet. Coenen-Mennemeier, for instance, sees "entgegengesetzte Pole einer gemeinsamen Erneuerungsfront"; cf. ibid., p. 26.

The differences evident in the work of Sarraute and Robbe-Grillet are linked, above all, by their respective ways of seeing, that is by notions of sight. This paper seeks to explore the relation between prospective or retrospective production characters of traces and a conceptual imprint of perception in two novels by Sarraute and Robbe-Grillet. For this purpose, it is essential on the one hand to investigate the quality of traces, that is, of the visual object, while, on the other, the respective forms of seeing will be brought into analytic focus.

## Dynamics of Appearance in Nathalie Sarraute

As mentioned before, tropisms[3] form the poetological centre of the entire literary work of Nathalie Sarraute. These ephemeral inner movements – Sarraute also calls them *'sous-conversations'* – can hardly be expressed by words; they just come into view for a moment and generate dynamics of visualization. That is, from the beginning, the focus is on making these inner movements visible, not on putting them into words.

At the same time, this crucial poetological assumption creates the starting point for interrelations between literature and the visual arts in the work of Sarraute. In many lectures and essayistic texts, Sarraute refers to the visual arts, declaring them a creative model for her writing.[4] In this argumentation, which – on a conceptual basis – makes, above all, abstract art a source of inspiration, as the aesthetics as well as the theoretical considerations of Paul Klee become an important reference. Thus, Sarraute often relates to the dictum Klee mentioned as a central conviction in his *Creative Confession* of 1920. In the text *Roman et réalité*[5], she quotes it as follows: "'L'œuvre d'art', disait Paul Klee, 'ne restitue pas le visible. Elle rend visible'".[6] Furthermore, in the interview "La littérature aujourd'hui", published in *Tel Quel* in 1962, as well as in

---

[3] The term 'tropisms' comes from biology and originally meant vegetable reactions to external stimuli such as heat or cold; cf. Coenen-Mennemeier, Roman (see note 1), p. 54.

[4] Ann Jefferson has already pointed out this interrelation between writing and visual arts in the work of Sarraute; she argues that painting becomes a crucial element of poetological considerations in her work (cf. Ann Jefferson, Les Fruits d'Or. Notice, in: Nathalie Sarraute, *Les Fruits d'Or. Œuvres Complètes,* Paris 1996, p. 2085). Rachel Boué sees a connection between a "poetics of negation" and modern art. She underlines the antimimetic focus of abstract art, giving room to a special work of deconstruction that Sarraute establishes on a discursive as well as on a narrative level (cf. Rachel Boué, *Nathalie Sarraute. La sensation en quête de parole,* Paris 1997, p. 54).

[5] This text is based on a lecture Sarraute held in 1959 at the University of Lausanne; cf. Jefferson, Fruits (see note 4), p. 2089.

[6] Nathalie Sarraute, *Roman et réalité. Œuvres Complètes,* Paris 1996, p. 1644.

the text *Les deux réalités* that appeared in *Esprit* in 1964, Sarraute quotes this central sentence.[7] In this she follows tendencies of strong references to Klee that started in the mid-fifties in France: Henri Michaux published his enthusiastic text "Aventures des lignes", inspired by the aesthetics of Klee, in 1954. In 1959, Pierre Klossowski translated the diaries of Klee into French and Merleau-Ponty referred to Klee as well as to the text of Michaux in his *L'œil et l'esprit* (1964). He claims, citing Michaux: "Jamais peut-être avant Klee on n'avait 'laissé rêver une ligne'".[8]

It is in relation, above all, to the following two aspects that Klee's statement becomes productive for the visual poetics of Sarraute: on the one hand, it illustrates the interrelation between literature and reality built on fiction that makes a new and unknown reality visible. On the other hand, the Klee's dictum provides a basis to describe tropism.

In *Les deux réalités,* Sarraute puts it like this:

> Ainsi, il y a dans la littérature un mouvement constant qui va du visible à l'invisible, du connu à l'inconnu, une constante transformation des formes. La réalité invisible devient une part de la réalité visible. Et, inversement, de nouvelles recherches conduisent à la découverte de nouvelles réalités encore inconnues.[9]

This attempt to represent invisible, its visualization, is connected to connotations of a process-related dynamic of appearance and formal changes. Moreover, it creates explorative gestures that cause a multiplication of realities and extensions of the visible.[10] Thus, by a process-related appearance, tropisms come into existence as a sort of priming. Here, the inner movements act as traces, announcing and visualizing themselves in textual space. Literary fiction that aims to investigate, describe and represent tropisms therefore operates in the frame of productive visuality, that is, it advances situations of appearance and is in turn exposed to them. This additionally creates special forms of seeing.

In the following, the relation between the vestigial character of the tropisms and their perception will be discussed in a more detailed way by analysing the novel *Les*

---

[7]  Ibid., p. 2090. The *Creative Confession* was translated into French in *Dans l'entremonde. Aquarelles et dessins de Paul Klee*, a catalogue with paintings and drawings by Klee published in 1957.

[8]  Maurice Merleau-Ponty, *L'œil et l'esprit*, Paris 1964, p. 74.

[9]  Nathalie Sarraute, Les deux réalités, in: *Esprit*, vol. 32, no. 329 (1964), p. 74.

[10]  This is why in *Roman et réalité* Sarraute defines literary work as an instrument of knowledge: "Sans doute, par cette recherche, par cet effort pour rendre visible un univers invisible, l'œuvre littéraire, comme toute œuvre d'art, est un instrument de connaissance" (Sarraute, Roman (see note 6), p. 1645).

*Fruits d'or*, published in 1963. Ann Jefferson points out that *Les Fruits d'or* forms a triptych relation with the novels *Entre la vie et la mort* (1968) and *Vous les entendez?* (1972), since all these texts focus on the process of production and reception of an aesthetic object.[11] *Les Fruits d'or* obtains a special position in this constellation because it applies a series of metatextual proceedings to the treatment of this issue. The plot, if we can call it that, is quite simple: A group of anonymous literary critics discusses positive and negative aspects of a novel entitled *Les Fruits d'or*, written by an author called Bréhier.

The critical statements refer directly to the structure and effects of the tropisms described in the book and, at the same time, are physically enwrought with these inner movements. Thereby, the metatextual commentaries provoke the appearance of the tropisms and, at the same time, call the attention of the characters to what is 'going to appear'. They generate a particular visual attitude to what is going to be configured in an oscillating movement between presence and significance. In his important study *Diesseits der Hermeneutik: Die Produktion von Präsenz* (2004), Hans Ulrich Gumbrecht describes these dynamics as an essential mechanism of the 'production of presence'.

The production of presence becomes a central part of what Gumbrecht calls "ästhetisches Erleben".[12] The main argument underlying this concept is that constitutive elements of this special mode of perception are in constant, but productive tension to each other:

---

[11] Jefferson, Fruits (see note 4), p. 1829.

[12] With the term "ästhetisches Erleben", and, accordingly, "Momente [...] der Intensität", Gumbrecht opens up an opposition to the concept of "ästhetischer Erfahrung" that, in his opinion, is near to aspects of interpretation and adscription of sense (Hans Ulrich Gumbrecht, *Diesseits der Hermeneutik. Die Produktion von Präsenz*, Frankfurt am Main 2004, p. 120; cf. Hans Ulrich Gumbrecht, *Präsenz*, Berlin 2012, p. 335). Nevertheless, the concept of "ästhetischer Erfahrung" is implemented in other theoretical positions: Küpper and Menke, for instance, refer to "ästhetischer Erfahrung" as a basic term of aesthetics (Joachim Küpper / Christoph Menke (eds.), *Dimensionen ästhetischer Erfahrung*, Frankfurt am Main 2003, p. 7). Kern connects it to a failed understanding (Andrea Kern, Zwei Seiten des Verstehens. Die philosophische Bedeutung von Kunstwerken, in: *Literatur als Philosophie – Philosophie als Literatur*, ed. by Eva Horn, Bettine Menke and Christopf Menke, Munich 2006, p. 379). Fromm shapes it explicitly in relation to perception, experience and thinking as a process-related concept (Waldemar Fromm, *An den Grenzen der Sprache. Über das Sagbare und das Unsagbare in Literatur und Ästhetik der Aufklärung, der Romantik und der Moderne*, Freiburg im Breisgau / Berlin 2006, p. 71), and for Seel aesthetic experience is an intensive way of aesthetic perception, that becomes incident (Martin Seel, *Die Macht des Erscheinens*, Frankfurt am Main 2007, pp. 57–58).

> Präsenz und Sinn treten [...] stets zusammen auf und stehen immer in einem Spannungsverhältnis zueinander. Es gibt keine Möglichkeit, sie kompatibel zu machen oder sie im Rahmen einer 'ausgewogenen' phänomenalen Struktur zusammenzubringen.[13]

These aspects of tension and moreover of simultaneity and incompatibility do not only present characteristics of the relation between presence and sense in 'aesthetic experience'. In addition, they also form a constant oscillation between these aspects in the aesthetic object.[14] Furthermore, instability is created because phenomena of presence elude their conservation. Therefore, Gumbrecht defines them as ephemeral.[15]

The metatextual commentaries in *Les Fruits d'or* create an expectation for processes of appearance and incidence around the traces of tropism. Through this, they become part of a special modus of seeing that would be near to 'aesthetic experience'. At this juncture, the substantial and material character of the tropisms is crucial, just as their fading and ephemeral character. This is shown in the following quotation:

> Dans un instant cela va surgir [...] une substance coule, se répand [...]. Et voilà que dans ces mots, dans ces phrases apparaît comme un à peine perceptible gonflement... cela palpite doucement... Il se décide, il s'éclaircit la voix... mais les mots, dès qu'il les prononce, pareils à des bulles qu'on envoie dans un air trop lourd, s'amenuisent, se réduisent, il ne reste presque rien, il n'y avait rien...[16]

It can be seen that tropisms underlie words, or what is going to be put into words; they invade them by their special dynamic and deforming effects. Formal changes appear then as processual elements of a vestigial manner, according to how language fails or at least becomes fragmentary and incomplete.

As shown in the quotation, tropisms are produced as moving substances, announcing their appearance by subtle spatial grasps; consequently, these inner movements frame a presence of appearance. In this connection, oxymorons like a "flowing substance" create an oscillation between form and formlessness, and, above all, between presence and sense, which, for its part, establishes an indeterminable status of the tropisms. Through this, the inner movements generate an 'event character' related to

---

[13] Gumbrecht, Hermeneutik (see note 12), p. 126. In another part of his study, Gumbrecht specifies: "Und Schweigen steht in Zusammenhang mit der Stummheit der Dinge, die mit jener Stummheit präsent sind, die ihre Präsenz bewirkt. Andererseits gibt es kein Aufscheinen von Sinn, das nicht zu einer Verminderung des Gewichts der Präsenz führte" (p. 110). In reference to terminological indeterminacy that Seel identifies in aesthetic objects, we can say: What we see during aesthetic perception cannot be signified in a conceptual way.

[14] Cf. also Gumbrecht, Präsenz (see note 12), pp. 341–342.

[15] Gumbrecht, Hermeneutik (see note 12), p. 427.

[16] Nathalie Sarraute, *Les Fruits d'Or. Œuvres Complètes*, Paris 1996, pp. 574–591.

terminological gaps. This relation between the event of appearance and a positively measured lack of words can be considered a crucial aspect of how aesthetic perception is defined in philosophical aesthetics.

Martin Seel, for instance, explored the concept of aesthetic perception in recent times as a kind of particular visual attitude. He argues that speechlessness and processes of appearance are crucial elements of this special mode of perception.[17] Seel claims: "In der ästhetischen Wahrnehmung [...] ereignet sich eine Affirmation des begrifflich und praktisch Unbestimmbaren".[18] On another occasion he specifies:

> Der ästhetischen Wahrnehmung [...] kommt es nicht auf die Fixierung eines *Soseins*, sondern auf ein Spiel von *Erscheinungen* an – wir nehmen die empirische Welt im Glanz ihrer konstitutiven *Unterbestimmtheit* wahr.[19]

Here, the process of appearance is linked directly to a perception without words, which does not operate in discursive logic. Thus, aesthetic perception in itself connects a productive form of terminological indeterminacy with processes of appearance.[20] This perceptual mode is then based on the causal nexus of these elements. In the visual poetics of Sarraute, it becomes the starting point of seeing tropisms.

Furthermore, tropisms do not only appear but also reappear in different situations of the plot. Thus, in another part of the text, we read again: "La substance invisible se coule, s'adapte parfaitement... elle prend forme, je la vois... grêle... en effet... assez gauche..."[21]

---

[17] For Seel, aesthetic perception is indeed a special mode of seeing: "Etwas in seiner sinnlichen Erscheinung zu vernehmen – so könnte man das allgemeine Verfahren sinnlicher Wahrnehmung charakterisieren. Die ästhetische Wahrnehmung ist ein spezieller Modus dieser Wahrnehmung. Sie unterscheidet sich durch eine besondere Polung des Sehens" (Martin Seel, *Ästhetik des Erscheinens*, Frankfurt am Main 2003, p. 50).

[18] Ibid., p. 38.

[19] Seel, Macht (see note 12), p. 14.

[20] Wolfgang Welsch also indicated the connection between appearance and speechlessness in aesthetic perception: "Denn Wahrnehmung als Aisthesis bedeutet die Stätte, an der Erscheinungen – jenseits von Subjekt und Objekt – in besonders intensiver Weise ihr Erscheinen vollziehen" (Wolfgang Welsch (ed.), *Die Aktualität des Ästhetischen*, Munich 1993, p. 378). He adds: "Gerade im merkwürdigen Zustand, in dem die Begriffe nicht greifen und die Worte versagen oder gar noch nicht verfügbar sind, erfahren wir die Nähe des Erscheinenden. Doch sobald wir es in den Kontext von 'Etwas als Etwas' stellen, ordnet es sich ein in den unendlichen Kontext der Zeichen und verschwindet" (ibid., p. 382).

[21] Sarraute, Fruits (see note 16), p. 606.

Substance, materiality and form(lessness) become elements of a process that deals with spatialization and, above all, with visualization. Consequently, the text implements dynamics of appearances that come into view.

The permanent movement of the tropisms produces traces and heterogeneous forms; this formal variety goes from a rhythmic vibration to a flow and seems to include line textures, as shown in the following quotation:

> Et soudain, c'est comme un effluve, un rayonnement, une lumière... je distingue mal sa source restée dans l'ombre... Cela afflue vers moi, se répand... Quelque chose me parcourt... c'est comme une vibration, une modulation, un rythme... c'est comme une ligne fragile et ferme qui se déploie, tracée avec une insistante douceur... c'est une arabesque naïve et savante... cela scintille faiblement... cela a l'air de se détacher sur un vide sombre... Et puis la ligne scintillante s'amenuise, s'estompe comme résorbée et tout s'éteint...[22]

It becomes clear once more that the appearance process of tropisms is a gradual one; here, the production of presence and the laying of traces in terms of visuality take place in a spatial distance of three dots. At the same time, textual gaps work as echo chambers where tropisms move constantly, appearing and reappearing from different directions of nowhere. Thus, they become visible as pushing and room-filling events. The following fragmentations of textual flow are not measured as deprivation at all, but rather create space for contingent movements of appearance and generate productive visuality. Breaking up the textual corpus thereby reinforces visual perception.

Accordingly, traces of tropism are built up by processes of substantialization and appearance as well as by a certain 'event character' and speechlessness; but, above all, tropisms create a responsive way of seeing. This special perceptual mode has been described and theorized both by Dieter Mersch and Bernhard Waldenfels.

Dieter Mersch argues that a responsive way of seeing is an expectant perception with a receptive and accessible gesture, waiting for something to appear. This responsive attitude is the main aspect of *aisthesis*.[23] Mersch claims: "Alles Wahrnehmungsgeschehen wurzelt in *Aisthesis*. *Aisthesis* bezeichnet die Empfänglichkeit für Anderes, deren Struktur nicht intentional, sondern responsiv bestimmt ist".[24] At the same time, this definition extends phenomenological approaches to perception, since intentional

---

[22] Ibid.

[23] Mersch uses the term '*Aisthesis*' as a synonym for 'aesthetic perception'.

[24] Dieter Mersch, *Ereignis und Aura. Untersuchungen zu einer Ästhetik des Performativen*, Frankfurt am Main 2002, p. 53.

structures are without primary function here.²⁵ What is at the centre of this kind of perception then?

It opens a space in which to focus on the indeterminable:

> Statt dessen wäre daran zu erinnern, daß Wahrnehmungen stets einen privilegierten Zugang zum Nichtkonstruierten, einem gleichermaßen Unbeherrschten wie Unbeherrschbaren unterhalten: Unverfügbarkeit des Daß, der Andersheit, die entgegenkommt.²⁶

Perception is thus exposed to something active and becomes congruent with the "Gewahrung dessen, was sich von sich her zeigt, als nicht festzuhaltendes Ereignis einer Präsenz und zugleich Aufscheinen einer unaufhebbaren 'Blöße' ohne […] Bestimmtheit".²⁷

Responsive seeing registers the indefinable and advances the event character of an active visual object, shaping it. Such a responsive perceptual attitude is also at the starting point for an exploration of silence:

> Freigelegt werden so Wegbahnen einer Gewahrung, die sich dem öffnet, was nicht gesagt oder repräsentiert werden kann, was in Erscheinung tritt, wo die Sprache schweigt. *Aisthesis* im eigentlichen Sinne bedeutet die Sensibilität für solche Augenblicke.²⁸

Thus, noticing the appearance is immediately linked to a view behind language.

Bernhard Waldenfels frames perception in terms of responsive seeing as well. He underlines that it is defined as "ein Sehen, das sich von den Dingen anregen und einnehmen lässt".²⁹ Terms of "Pathos" and "Widerfahrnis"³⁰ express the very notion of perception Waldenfels has in mind. On another occasion, he puts it like this: "Bilder fallen ins Auge".³¹ The potential for action is then located in the object of perception itself; consequently, it seems to be independent from the act of seeing and acts on it instead. At this point, some connections to the conceptual imprint of aesthetic perception, as Dieter Mersch has defined it, also become evident.

---

[25] Cf. also ibid., p. 15.

[26] Ibid., p. 43.

[27] Dieter Mersch, Aisthetik und Responsivität. Zum Verhältnis von medialer und amedialer Wahrnehmung, in: *Wahrnehmung und Medialität*, ed. by Erika Fischer-Lichte et al., Tübingen / Basel 2001, p. 293.

[28] Mersch, Ereignis (see note 24), p. 44.

[29] Bernhard Waldenfels, Sinne und Künste im Wechselspiel. Modi ästhetischer Erfahrung, Berlin 2010, p. 207.

[30] Bernhard Waldenfels, Verkörperung im Bild, in: *Logik der Bilder. Präsenz – Repräsentation – Erkenntnis*, ed. by Richard Hoppe-Sailer, Claus Volkenandt and Gundolf Winter, Berlin 2005, p. 31.

[31] Bernhard Waldenfels, Von der Wirkmacht und Wirkkraft der Bilder, in: *Movens Bild. Zwischen Evidenz und Affekt*, ed. by Gottfried Boehm, Birgit Mersmann and Christian Spies, Munich 2008, p. 47.

In *Les Fruits d'or*, interior elements come into view as material substances and forms, emerging constantly from nowhere and creating contingent spatial movements; thus, they contain active potential. Consequently, they frame a process of appearance that in the end has no reference but becomes incident. Responsive seeing, as Mersch and Waldenfels put it, precedes these processes of appearance; thereby, visual perception is expecting what comes into view. In this connection, seeing becomes waiting for appearance.

### Dynamics of Deciphering in Alain Robbe-Grillet

It is in particular the later 1970s works of Alain Robbe-Grillet that explore the relation between writing and visuality. A characteristic of these works, which are part of the so-called *nouveau nouveau roman*[32], is the exploration between literature and the visual arts. This interrelation aims at a special exploration of literary visuality. In doing so, Robbe-Grillet focuses, above all, on the aesthetics of Belgian surrealist painter René Magritte.[33]

Aspects of precarious visuality, which underlie the aesthetics of Magritte, have been at the centre of art historical research for many years. These positions often focus on the *mise en abyme* structures that Magritte used in a lot of his pictures. Stoltzfus, for instance, sees here the mechanism of a "subversion picturale qu'opère Magritte".[34]

---

[32] Zeltner-Neukomm argues that the novel *Dans le labyrinthe*, published in 1959, is already part of the *nouveau nouveau roman* (Gerda Zeltner-Neukomm, *Im Augenblick der Gegenwart. Moderne Formen des französischen Romans*, Frankfurt am Main 1974, p. 43). Barilli (Renato Barilli, Neutralisation et différence, in: *Robbe-Grillet. Analyse, Théorie*, ed. by Jean Ricardou, Paris 1975, p. 394) and Blüher (Karl Alfred Blüher (ed.), *Robbe-Grillet zwischen Moderne und Postmoderne. Nouveau Roman, Nouveau Cinéma und Nouvelle Autobiographie*, Tübingen 1992, p. 9) support this position. Hempfer distinguishes between *nouveau nouveau roman* and *Tel Quel* novel, with the first demonstrating a lower degree of self-referential structures (Klaus W. Hempfer, *Poststrukturale Texttheorie und narrative Praxis. Tel Quel und die Konstitution eines Nouveau nouveau romans*, Munich 1975, p. 170).

[33] Nevertheless, Robbe-Grillet related to a wide variety of phenomena of visual arts. Thus, from 1971 onwards, he published his so-called 'picto-romans' almost once a year; these novels are based on different interrelations between image and text and establish dialogues with several painters and photographers like Robert Rauschenberg, Paul Delvaux, David Hamilton and Irina Ionesco (Jean-Jacques Brochier, *Alain Robbe-Grillet. Qui sui-je?*, Lyon 1985, p. 156).

[34] Ben Stoltzfus, Robbe-Grillet et Magritte. La femme, le miroir et les liaisons dangereuses, in: *Alain Robbe-Grillet. Balises pour le XXIe siècle*, ed. by Roger-Michel Allemand and Christian Milat, Ottawa 2010, p. 188. Here, Stoltzfus refers to the paintings *La belle captive* and *Les liaisons dangereuses* and adds: "sont des toiles d'une réalité impossible et, en niant le réalisme, elles deviennent l'image même de la peinture" (p. 190).

This procedure leads to a certain "undecidability of perception", as Stoltzfus argues in another context.[35] This briefly exposed interpretation of one of the main aesthetic principles implemented by Magritte implies a paradoxical concept of visuality.[36] Pictures thereby become a basis for precarious experiences of seeing. Consequently, seeing acquires the status of a precarious action.

It is at this point that the aesthetics of Magritte build up a poetological programme for uncertain visuality in the writing of Robbe-Grillet. Thus, the connection between literature and the visual arts is not so much linked to concrete images, nor is it localized in text-image connections. It is rather based on a conceptual treatment of perception arising from the field of a diffuse seeing that Magritte applies in his work. Therefore, the reference to the surrealist painter is a homological one. Seeing, as pre-formed in the aesthetics of Magritte, becomes a leading poetological principle in the literary representation of precarious seeing in the later works of Robbe-Grillet.

The novels *La belle captive* (1975) and *Topologie d'une cité fantôme* (1976) are conceptualized in reference to numerous pictures of Magritte, and they were written and published when text theory by *Tel Quel* had already gained momentum.[37] Even though both texts were published in different years, they can almost be read as one text, as they include congruent passages and intratextual references – namely the same protagonists and settings.

In the novel *Topologie d'une cité fantôme* (1976), handwritings, engravings and numerical sequences appear on architectonic fragments and papers, referring apparently to things passed and faded. These traces invite the eye of the observer to decipher and to reconstruct, which means to read and to search; but traces are often deceiving, since they only strengthen their visual and material aspect and thereby, finally, subvert actions of reading and reconstruction.

---

[35] Ben Stoltzfus, La Belle Captive. Magritte's Surrealism, Robbe-Grillet's Metafiction (2005), http://www.imageandnarrative.be/inarchive/surrealism/stoltzfus.htm (13/04/2014).

[36] On another occasion, Stoltzfus establishes an interrelation between the structures of *trompe l'œil* and the aesthetics of the *nouveau nouveau roman*: "Pour Magritte, l'art n'est pas le miroir de la réalité, mais la réalité du miroir et, comme le disait Jean Ricardou, le *nouveau roman* n'est pas le récit d'une histoire, mais l'histoire d'un récit. Cet art souligne les mises en abyme, l'ambiguïté et la contradiction, rejetant ainsi la mimesis et créant un nouvel aperçu du monde" (ibid., p. 183).

[37] Based on theoretical positions forwarded mainly by Jacques Derrida, Michel Foucault, Julia Kristeva and Roland Barthes at the beginning of the 1960s, *Tel Quel* developed theoretical aspects concerning the concept of *écriture*. Writing, then, is described as a functional modus that refers to itself in its productivity.

In the novel, different sequences and places of action as well as different temporal notions appear: the search for traces takes place in theatres, subterranean catacombs and prisons as well as on different time levels in the past and present. However, there is one main setting: a landscape of ruins.

On the whole, the text establishes a series of situations characterized by the link between perception and writing; consequently, it only generates episodes of iconographic writings and does not advance coherent and chronological plot sequences. Within this process, an architectonical fragment is transformed, as labels, walls and papers with different writing traces come into view. Consequently, seeing becomes reading traces or a failing process of deciphering, of creating an uncertain perception, as prefigured by the aesthetics of Magritte.

First, the focus is on signs of writings, following different constellations:

> Sur l'affiche, on peut lire le mot 'Règlement' imprimé à la partie supérieure, en lettres capitales romaines de très grande taille, et quatre chiffres du même corps –1, 2, 3, 4– dans la marge de gauche, en tête de chacun des paragraphes qui, à l'inverse, ont été composés en caractères minuscules, ce qui les rend tout à fait indéchiffrables; un cinquième paragraphe apparaît encore, tout en bas, mais le nombre 5 qui devrait figurer là dans la marge est complètement masqué par la tête d'un des personnages.[38]

In this situation, detailed description of the iconographic imprint of writing and the exact disposition of letters and numbers contrasts with the difficulty of reading and deciphering them; furthermore, the content of the rules remains diffuse.

In another situation, words seem to be elements of architecture; they are like stones bearing fragmented inscriptions. Here, the remains of an ancient city are transformed into haptic codes:

> Ici, les vestiges d'un texte gravé en latin permettent de lire les deux mots …NAVE AD… ; le reste est effacé par le temps. Mais la phrase se reconstitue sans peine, grâce au nom de DAVID qui apparaît un peu plus bas, dans ces mêmes caractères dont la géométrie étirée semble dater du bas empire, donnant le sens approximatif: vide elle va sur un navire / vers l'azur divin de david /.[39]

As reading the signs becomes a process of deciphering traces, visual perception again implies a very uncertain activity. By constantly encountering gaps, this precarious process of reading can nearly reconstruct senses underlying the iconographic signs.

Furthermore, the iconographic focus obtains a particular presence in the materiality of the text: Following a *mise en abyme* structure, there appear slashes, capital

---

[38] Alain Robbe-Grillet, *Topologie d'une cité fantôme,* Paris 1976, p. 18–19.
[39] Ibid.

letters and blank positions. All these elements are mechanisms that lead the eye of the reader to focus on the spatial disposition of letters. Thereby, the reproduction of inscriptions introduces a certain dynamic of signs into the text that determines forms of seeing on the receptive level too.

The constellation of uncertain perception becomes still more intensive in the second half of the text, since an inversion and loss of signs is implemented. Furthermore, precarious seeing results from different forms of illegible letterings. In the following quotations, for instance, the narrator's eye focuses on some missing characters in the name of a fashion boutique: "[J]e remarque une fois de plus la boutique de confection pour communions et mariages dont l'enseigne 'Aux Vanités Divines' n'a encore perdu que deux de ses lettres".[40] In other situations, forms of blurred letters appear on paper: "Il y a sans doute quelque chose d'écrit sur cette page quadrillée de fines lignes bleues, mais le texte est à l'intérieur et personne, pour le moment, ne peut le déchiffrer".[41] And on wet paper, the diffuse characters become even more intense: "Il y avait, flottant dans le clapotis, des feuilles de papier rectangulaires au format des anciens cahiers d'école, avec des traces d'une écriture bleue déclavée, pâlie, brouillée, sans doute illisible".[42] The loss of letters and different forms of blurring subvert the reading of traces; hence, deciphering is hindered and activated at the same time.

In other situations, character traces implement a proper dynamic in the text, creating a special focus on visual perception. In the following quotation, for instance, the dynamic gesture of the writing trace is suggested as serial production:

> une lettre G de couleur rouge vif.
> Cette lettre donne la série suivante, à laquelle d'ailleurs on devait s'attendre:
> vanadé – vigie – navire
> danger – rivage – devin
> nager – en vain – carnage
> divan – vierge – vagin
> gravide – engendra – davida
> et il est aisé de voir, d'après la disposition des consonnes, que le nom complet de cet enfant serait en fait David G.[43]

---

[40] Robbe-Grillet, Topologie (see note 38), p. 194.
[41] Ibid., p. 70.
[42] Ibid., p. 100.
[43] Ibid., p. 49.

The sign becomes the motor of this paragraph and the letter G a *'générateur'* that seems to be inspired by Ricardou's paradigm of textual productivity.

It was in the 1970s that Ricardou began to draw up his theory of so-called *générateurs*. In his *Pour une théorie du nouveau roman*, he marked a crucial distinction between production and use, that is, between the "rôle producteur des mots (le nom propre s'y révèle comme signe dégagé du signifié autoritaire qui occulte communément l'aptitude productrice du signifiant) par opposition à leur fonction strictement utilitaire".[44] This opposition itself forms a basic mechanism of the *générateurs*. A few years later, Ricardou specifies in his *Nouveaux problèmes du roman*:

> Produire, nous le savons, c'est mettre en œuvre une matière. S'agissant du texte, cette matière est principalement le langage, entendu, non plus comme moyen d'expression, mais bien comme matière signifiante. Produire, nous le savons, c'est transformer une matière.[45]

Here, language is reduced to its materiality and production defined as a process of material transformation.

Gaps, incomplete writings and illegible series of signs are just a few aspects that become visible traces in the novel, acting like a multiplication of *générateurs;* these elements incite a process of deciphering and subvert it at the same time. During this ambiguous process, the connection between seeing and writing is suggested as an option of loss, since the writing traces coming into view do not only lead the eye, but cause occasions of precarious perception. Thereby, writing turns into action. The paradigm of writing thus becomes the motor of the text and makes perception a process of deciphering, which includes haptic sensations. On the whole, seeing is shaped as a constant research in the novel. This movement of research is made even more intense and complex by the shifting and transforming dynamics of signs. According to the visualization of blurred writing traces, the poetics of Robbe-Grillet generate situations of precarious visuality.

Overall, through the comparison of the poetics of Sarraute and Robbe-Grillet, it has been possible to identify some differences with regard to the relation between trace, visual perception and production. Thus, the concept of trace entails different poetological implications for both authors.

---

[44] Ricardou, Jean, *Pour une théorie du nouveau roman,* Paris 1971, p. 11.
[45] Ricardou, Jean, *Nouveaux problèmes du roman,* Paris 1978, p. 16.

In fact, both tropisms and writings are active elements and both of these literary figures are finally conceptualized beyond relations of reference. However, tropisms and writing traces generate different perceptual attitudes and different forms of visuality in the compared novels. In this regard, an anticipating and prospective production status of tropisms, shaped as a construction of traces, differs from a retrospective mode of reading traces where the production process is already finished. Thereby, the potential for action and production of traces is considered prospective on the one hand and defined as retrospective on the other; this means it causes forms of productive and, accordingly, precarious visuality.

According to this, visual perception is shaped as noticing an appearance or as a failed process of deciphering. Thus, there exists a relation of cause and effect between the way of seeing and what is seen; this causal nexus is crucial for the visual poetics of Sarraute and Robbe-Grillet. The argumentation behind this special relation between process and object of perception was based on an interdisciplinary theoretical toolbox that connected recent approaches from a philosophy of presence (Gumbrecht) with new ideas from philosophical aesthetics (Seel and Mersch) and perspectives of phenomenology (Waldenfels). All these have the fact in common that both perception processes and visual objects are defined as performative aspects. Notions of action and production thus underlie the different theoretical approaches, helping to shape visual poetics as a writing that is constantly in dynamic processes.

## Bibliography

Barilli, Renato, Neutralisation et différence, in: *Robbe-Grillet. Analyse, Théorie*, ed. by Jean Ricardou, Paris 1975, pp. 391–408.

Blüher, Karl Alfred (ed.), *Robbe-Grillet zwischen Moderne und Postmoderne. Nouveau Roman, Nouveau Cinéma und Nouvelle Autobiographie*, Tübingen 1992.

Boué, Rachel, *Nathalie Sarraute. La sensation en quête de parole*, Paris 1997.

Brochier, Jean-Jacques, *Alain Robbe-Grillet. Qui sui-je?*, Lyon 1985.

Coenen-Mennemeier, Brigitta, *Nouveau roman*, Stuttgart / Weimar 1996.

Fromm, Waldemar, *An den Grenzen der Sprache. Über das Sagbare und das Unsagbare in Literatur und Ästhetik der Aufklärung, der Romantik und der Moderne*, Freiburg im Breisgau / Berlin 2006.

Gumbrecht, Hans Ulrich, *Diesseits der Hermeneutik. Die Produktion von Präsenz*, Frankfurt am Main 2004.

Gumbrecht, Hans Ulrich, *Präsenz*, Berlin 2012.

Hempfer, Klaus W., *Poststrukturale Texttheorie und narrative Praxis. Tel Quel und die Konstitution eines Nouveau nouveau romans*, Munich 1975.

Jefferson, Ann, Les Fruits d'Or. Notice, in: Nathalie Sarraute, *Les Fruits d'Or. Œuvres Complètes*, Paris 1996, pp. 1827–1836.

Kern, Andrea, Zwei Seiten des Verstehens. Die philosophische Bedeutung von Kunstwerken, in: *Literatur als Philosophie – Philosophie als Literatur*, ed. by Eva Horn, Bettine Menke and Christoph Menke, Munich 2006, pp. 57–79.

Küpper, Joachim / Menke, Christoph (eds.), *Dimensionen ästhetischer Erfahrung*, Frankfurt am Main 2003.

Merleau-Ponty, Maurice, *L'œil et l'esprit*, Paris 1964.

Mersch, Dieter, *Ereignis und Aura. Untersuchungen zu einer Ästhetik des Performativen*, Frankfurt am Main 2002.

Mersch, Dieter, Aisthetik und Responsivität. Zum Verhältnis von medialer und amedialer Wahrnehmung, in: *Wahrnehmung und Medialität,* ed. by Erika Fischer-Lichte et al., Tübingen / Basel 2001, pp. 273–299.

Ricardou, Jean, *Nouveaux problèmes du roman,* Paris 1978.

Ricardou, Jean, *Pour une théorie du nouveau roman,* Paris 1971.

Robbe-Grillet, Alain, *Topologie d'une cité fantôme,* Paris 1976.

Robbe-Grillet, Alain, Warum und für wen ich schreibe, in: *Robbe-Grillet zwischen Moderne und Postmoderne. Nouveau Roman, Nouveau Cinéma und Nouvelle Autobiographie,* ed. by Karl Alfred Blüher, Tübingen 1992, pp. 17–64.

Sarraute, Nathalie, *Les Fruits d'Or. Œuvres Complètes,* Paris 1996.

Sarraute, Nathalie, *Roman et réalité. Œuvres Complètes,* Paris 1996.

Sarraute, Nathalie, Les deux réalités, in: *Esprit,* vol. 32, no. 329 (1964), pp. 72–75.

Sarraute, Nathalie, La littérature aujourd'hui, in: *Tel Quel,* vol. 9 (1962), pp. 48–53.

Seel, Martin, *Ästhetik des Erscheinens,* Frankfurt am Main 2003.

Seel, Martin, *Die Macht des Erscheinens,* Frankfurt am Main 2007.

Stoltzfus, Ben, La Belle Captive. Magritte's Surrealism, Robbe-Grillet's Metafiction (2005), http://www.imageandnarrative.be/inarchive/surrealism/stoltzfus.htm (13/04/2014).

Stoltzfus, Ben, Robbe-Grillet et Magritte. La femme, le miroir et les liaisons dangereuses, in: *Alain Robbe-Grillet. Balises pour le XXIe siècle,* ed. by Roger-Michel Allemand and Christian Milat, Ottawa 2010, pp. 183–191.

Waldenfels, Bernhard, *Sinne und Künste im Wechselspiel. Modi ästhetischer Erfahrung,* Berlin 2010.

Waldenfels, Bernhard, Verkörperung im Bild, in: *Logik der Bilder. Präsenz – Repräsentation – Erkenntnis,* ed. by Richard Hoppe-Sailer, Claus Volkenandt and Gundolf Winter, Berlin 2005, pp. 17–34.

Waldenfels, Bernhard, Von der Wirkmacht und Wirkkraft der Bilder, in: *Movens Bild. Zwischen Evidenz und Affekt,* ed. by Gottfried Boehm, Birgit Mersmann and Christian Spies, Munich 2008, pp. 47–63.

Welsch, Wolfgang (ed.), *Die Aktualität des Ästhetischen,* Munich 1993.

Zeltner-Neukomm, Gerda, *Im Augenblick der Gegenwart. Moderne Formen des französischen Romans,* Frankfurt am Main 1974.

# The (Im-)Possibility of Tracing Labour.
# On Jean-Luc Moulène's *Objets de Grève*[1]
*Friederike Sigler*

When French artist Jean-Luc Moulène looked at the June 5, 1987 issue of the *International Herald Tribune,* he must have been as irritated as all other readers for its lack of pictures. Instead, the newspaper was riddled with white rectangles that, upon closer examination, turned out to be empty picture frames. There were even the usual captions below the rectangles, but they only pointed to a curious void. An editor's note on the front page of the issue revealed it was not done for artistic purposes, as could have been imagined at a first glance, but rather due to a strike on behalf of the picture editors, who protested against cuts in working hours.

The issue of the *International Herald Tribune* reminded Moulène of an object he had already come across some years earlier: a pack of French *Gauloises* cigarettes, noticeably distinguished from ordinary packs of the brand. Glaring red in appearance, it featured black letters underneath its logo, saying "fabriquées par les travailleurs en lutte" – made by workers on strike. As with the *International Herald Tribune,* the original version had been modified to make people aware of the workers' strike by way of this deviation. Over the course of a 1999 exhibition, Moulène begins looking further into the matter and finds out that both objects derive from a custom of workers voicing their criticism of working conditions by including it in a limited number of their own (mis-)produced goods.[2] He tracks down additional strike objects, takes pictures of them and shows them in different number and constellation once as *24 Objets de Grève* in 1999 and again as *Trente-neuf Objets de Grève* a year later (1999/2000).[3] Aside from the *International Herald Tribune* issue, the equally modified pack of *Gauloises* and other things, the photo spread includes a pipe featuring three eights, pleading in favour of eight hours each reserved for work, spare time and sleep; the 'Chomageo-

---

[1] The text was translated from German by Sven Ondrazek. The author would like to thank Sven Ondrazek for his translation as well as Dietmar Rübel for his remarks.

[2] He begins his research as part of an exhibition in the Galerie Noisy-le-Sec (Seine-Sainte-Denis), titled *24 Objets de Grève Présentés par Jean-Luc Moulène* (1999). Cf. Paolo Magagnoli, Moulène, Rancière and *24 Objets de Grève*: Productive ambivalence or reifying opacity?, in: *Philosophy of Photography*, vol. 3, no. 1 (1999). p. 156.

[3] The second version was first shown in the Musée du Bassin Houllier Lorrain, La Petite-Rosselle in Forbach. Cf. ibid.

poly', a Monopoly for the unemployed; the 'Parfum de solidarité', a perfume bottle with the words "Touche pas a mon emploi"; the Nina Ricci dress 'La Stromboli'; and children's shoes in red and black, the colours of revolution.⁴

What to make of these deviations then? What do the empty rectangles of the *International Herald Tribune*, the inscription on the pack of *Gauloises* and the three eights on the pipe signify? Are they traces of a strike, of non-production and non-labour, or are they not rather traces of labour and production?

## Labour as Practice of Resistance

Jean-Luc Moulène's *Objets de Grève* are samples of an established industrial workers' practice, known under the term 'homer' in English and 'la perruque' in French.⁵ Within this practice, workers mostly produce individual objects with small modifications that set them apart from the commodities they were actually supposed to be. This includes, for example, bedside lamps, vases or tools. The aim is to showcase the workers' know-how, manual skills and creativity – attributes which do not come into effect in official work processes, as these inversions demonstrate.⁶ However, these objects are usually not the products of strike, which means that although Moulène's objects may be part of this practice, they constitute an exception within it, appearing here and there, every once in a while and in no comprehensible manner. This is mainly due to them – and this is of particular importance – being produced during official working hours: "A 'homer' is an artifact that a worker produces using company tools and materials outside normal production plans but at the workplace and during workhours."⁷ To get hold of the practice of homers, the category of labour becomes an effective feature of distinction since they are defined by their production at work, but "outside of the organization's [official] production".⁸ For this reason, they are often in a legal grey area, as law mostly prohibits activities not contributing to official work as well as the

---

4  *Bin beschäftigt*, exh. cat. GAK Gesellschaft für aktuelle Kunst, Bremen 2007, pp. 74–79.

5  Michel Anteby, Factory "Homers". Understanding a Highly Elusive, Marginal, and Illegal Practice, in: *Sociologie du Travail*, Annual English Language Edition, vol. 48 (2006), p. 24. As Anteby emphasizes, it is a practice that is transregional on the one hand, but also entails regional features, which are often overlooked in the attempt of a definition.

6  Magagnoli, Moulène (see note 1), p. 156.

7  Anteby, Homers (see note 4), p. 22.

8  Robert Kosmann, cited after ibid., p. 23.

use of materials and tools for non-official purposes. This legally precarious situation is part of the reason for historian Michel Anteby to speak of a "silent practice".[9] Workers give only scant information about their homers, even in retirement, when they are no longer bound by legal constraints.[10] This is aggravated by the fact that homers are only produced on a one-off basis, after which they usually disappear again immediately. They are not intended for public consumption, after all, but for private use, or, as the English term emphasizes, for use 'at home'. In that regard, Moulène's strike objects take a similar approach, as they are equally manufactured in single to small numbers and – with the exception of the 'strike issue' of the *International Herald Tribune* – fade into invisibility subsequent to their appearance. However, while the status of these strike objects, which, as objects 'of' strike, are the product of objectionable working conditions; while these can at once be identified as partaking in a practice of resistance, the status of homers is controversially discussed. Do they constitute an act of resistance too or are they not rather gimmicks beyond resistance?

In contrast to Moulène's strike objects, homers initially remain within the context of labour, as Michel de Certeau notes in his book on *The Practice of Everyday Life*:

> La perruque is the worker's own work disguised as work for his employer. It differs from pilfering in that nothing of material value is stolen. It differs from absenteeism in that the worker is officially on the job. La perruque may be as simple a matter as a secretary's writing a love letter on 'company time' or as complex as a cabinetmaker's 'borrowing' a lathe to make a piece of furniture for his living room.[11]

They are neither produced to support a strike, nor to represent the precarious working conditions on a symbolic level. At the same time, being produced "outside the official production plan", they have a status, which can hardly be included in the regular working schedule in its adherence to the prevailing economy of time. Studies specifically refer to the uncertain status of such deviations, but only to make the case for them 'not' partaking in a practice of resistance. Thus, homers are described as processes of "self-determined work", as a "non-position" and as products of creative and aesthetic quality, that is, as works which (in themselves) lack the potential for resistance.[12]

---

[9] Ibid., p. 23.

[10] Anteby tried to find out more about the practice through interviews with former workers, but was often confronted with silence and refusal in doing so. Cf. Anteby, Homers (see note 4).

[11] Michel de Certeau, *The Practice of Everyday Life*. Berkeley / Los Angeles 1984.

[12] Anteby, Homers (see note 4), pp. 34–35.

That these are attributes, which are usually not asked for in the context of industrial labour; that there is a dichotomy between the works and the sphere they come from; indeed, that creative and aesthetic processes in particular may take on the potential for resistance, both de Certeau and Jacques Rancière took note of, the latter in his early study on the *Proletarian Nights*.[13]

Rancière looks back at 1830s France and traces workers who engage in literary pursuits in their spare time, which often means by night. Writing poems, short stories and books, they are creative and intellectual – two qualities that, as already mentioned, have no place in industrial labour. Although they do not necessarily address the 'oppressed working life', such aesthetic processes are ultimately far more dangerous than workers singing songs of the revolution, that is, workers who openly speak out against their working and living conditions[14], as the practice of the 'Proletarian Nights' does not constitute an opposition, but adopts practices and aspects of cultural knowledge, which are usually reserved for the bourgeoisie.[15] As such, this appropriation changes their status and identity as workers and aligns them with those of the class dominating them. Instead of confronting them directly, they secretly sneak in to impinge upon the structures like a parasite. This process is the result of the classic separation of labour and non-labour, regulated as it is by space and time. Traditionally, 'leisure', the spare time after work, is the space for creativity and self-determination. Homers on the other hand try to create this space during the time reserved for work. Creative and aesthetic processes are thus brought into action at work, which has the consequence, according to Michel de Certeau, that the order which determines production and labour is suspended for the moment. In this stretch of time, workers determine their time on their own – not by doing "nothing", however, but rather by "divert[ing] time" to do something else.[16] In this comparison, the resistant qualities of homers become apparent, for to be creative and to produce for one's own purposes, in these examples, means to indulge in an activity that is contrary to labour and thus

---

[13] Jacques Rancière, *Proletarian Nights. The Worker's Dream in Nineteenth-Century France,* London / New York 2012.

[14] Jacques Rancière, Interview with Lawrence Liang (2009), http://kafila.org/2009/02/12/interview-with-jacques-ranciere (10/08/2014).

[15] Ibid.

[16] De Certeau, Practice (see note 10), p. 25.

no labour to begin with. That is why homers emerge as products of an activity, which is bound to other categories of 'productivity' than those of industrial labour. Strictly speaking, then, it is indeed a form of striking if by striking as such we mean to stop working and indulge in non-labour. Even if, in the case of homers, their form of strike does not entail an aura of rebellion or violence, the slowdown of normal work, the procrastination and the undermining of the established production logic are already a form of resistance. In the words of Werner Hamacher, these short moments of being otherwise occupied have a "depositing" quality. For brief periods of time, production is shut off. Homers are thus a type of "afformatives"[17], a short neglecting, abandoning and delaying. They are part of a production, which is no longer directed towards something, but, on the contrary, "against anything that has the character of a positing, an institution, a representation, or a program."[18] They are produced for the sake of production. Their uselessness disables all "positing" parameters for the moment and renders them visible thereby. By way of this "depositing", homers not only manage to suspend production briefly, but also to uncover the mechanisms under which work is carried out and which configure labour.

It becomes clear then that resistant qualities are inscribed to homers although they are not produced for the sake of a strike. For this reason, their form of resistance does not necessarily seem to hinge on the purpose of their production. It rather raises the question whether it is not the objects themselves, which are on strike and whether it is not a similar case with Moulène's strike objects, which, in contrast to homers, explicitly emerge out of a strike and specifically address it as such.

## Objects on Strike (Marx)

Both homers and Moulène's strike objects differ from other commodities of their kind through small deviations. Strike slogans are printed onto packs of *Gauloises* and a bottle of perfume, children's shoes have abnormal colours, and the Nina Ricci dress suggests a sense of drama, which is unusual in this brand. Consequentially, they are unsalable as commodities, as they are unique items, not to be integrated into the never-ending production line. Thanks to these deviations, they are also useless in the context of

---

[17] Werner Hamacher, Afformative, Strike, in: *Cardozo Law Review*, vol. 13, no. 4. (1991), pp. 1133–1157.
[18] Ibid., p. 1140.

any economic commodity logic, as they are basically robbed of their use value: The cigarettes cannot be smoked, the tickets not be validated, and the fake bank notes not be used as payment. As a result, they seem to be in resistance against that which Marx calls commodity form.

According to Marx, commodities appear to us per se "as a complex of two things"[19], because they unite two forms of value: use value and exchange value. Use value, the 'usefulness' of an object, is an intrinsic part of every product created through human labour. In capitalism, however, the object gains an additional exchange value. Value is now determinable by other measures, such as money. As a result, the two forms of value are put in direct competition with each other. At the moment of an objecting becoming a commodity, its use value, which determines its function and usefulness, is superseded by its exchange value, putting it on the same level with all other commodities of equal exchange value – regardless of their function and use. Through this shift, then, use value only comes in second, or, to be more exact, the price of a commodity always occupies centre stage in capitalism, as only the price guarantees the creation of surplus value for different use values. Neither homers nor Moulène's strike objects, however, can withstand this dictum – or it is rather the dictum that cannot withstand the objects. Indeed, it looks as if their use value cannot be abstracted because the objects all but refuse to become commodities. Through their modifications, that is, their deviations, they become useless, which means that, from the point of view of capitalist logic, they become 'production failures'. They cannot fulfil the basic condition for being commodities – their usefulness – and, for this reason, are resistant to a 'revaluation' towards exchange value and commodity form, meaning that they are effectively on strike against it.

A Marxist reading of Moulène's strike objects reveals a further component of particular relevance to the issue of labour. One effect of a commodity being "a complex of two things" is its approach to the production of use value. According to Marx, labour is first of all

---

[19] Karl Marx, *Capital. A Critique of Political Economy*, Vol. I: *The Process of Capitalist Production*, Chicago 1909, p. 48.

human action with a view to the production of use-values, appropriation of natural substances to human requirements; it is the necessary condition for effecting exchange of matter between man and Nature; it is the everlasting Nature-imposed condition of human existence, and therefore is independent of every social phase of that existence, or rather, is common to every such phase.[20]

In a capitalist society, however, use value is abstracted, resulting in an equal abstraction of – and that is the crux of the matter in this context – commodity-oriented labour. Whereas a focus on use value would still yield "concrete useful forms of labour", an orientation towards exchange value only appears as "a mere congelation of homogeneous human labour".[21] The "transcendent" character of commodity is thus implied in its very nature,

> Simply because in it the social character of men's labour appears to them as an objective character stamped upon the product of that labour; because the relation of the producers to the sum total of their own labour is presented to them as a social relation, existing not between themselves, but between the products of their labour.[22]

It is only through this *quid pro quo* that commodities turn into illusions, fetishes, "social things whose qualities are at the same time perceptible and imperceptible by the senses"[23], so that production and production-oriented labour are absent in the essence of commodities. Through the strike of the objects against their becoming commodities, this process of the abstraction of labour is compromised and subverted. Because the strike objects are produced through means of labour, but do not meet the standard of commodities owing to their nature as defective products, they reveal that form of labour, which usually disappears in the process of becoming commodities. Defective as they are, the strike objects are traces of a form of labour, which can never obtain presence in the commodities themselves. They lay bare that they work, that they are products of work and that they have been worked on. By striking against the disappearance of labour, they render it visible in the first place.

If it becomes visible, however, the question arises how this type of labour presents itself. In the case of Moulène's strikes objects, for example, labour presents itself as precarious. Although their production is ultimately based on a call for the improvement of working conditions to a state which does no longer fall into the category

---

[20] Marx, Capital (see note 18), pp. 204–205.

[21] Ibid., p. 45.

[22] Ibid., p. 83.

[23] Marx, Capital (see note 18).

of the precarious – and which would move labour back into invisibility –, it is only through this precarious element, the resulting dissatisfaction of the workers and their emancipatory efforts that such strike objects can be produced in the first place and recognized as such. This precarious dimension is revealed in homers too, albeit only on the assumption that self-determined work stands above heteronomous work and that creative and artistic work is the better form of labour, as the bourgeois aesthetics of autonomy set to establish.[24] In this sense, they are expressions of a form of labour, which does not tolerate defective products, disregards manual skills and suppresses moments of subjective creativity in its machinery. In other words, they are expressions of a form of labour, which in Marx would be a typical example of alienation and exploitation, for the capitalist mechanism, causing labour to become invisible, deprives workers of the product of their work. Homers on the other hand distinguish themselves from the production of commodities by being products of self-determined work, not subjected to alienation because they remain in the possession of their makers. As this comparison shows, then, not all forms of labour are the same. It rather becomes apparent that labour is divided into several categories and also, as will become clearer in the following, marked by major changes during the twentieth century in particular.

Labour and the Image:
On Subversive Energies and the Ghost of Capitalism

An essential aspect, which has not yet been taken into account in discussions about traces of labour, is that it is not the strike objects themselves which are put on display, but photographs of these objects. If one were to define the role of Moulène, who first selected which objects were to be photographed and exhibited, he could be referred to as a collector, for the compiling and correlating of the objects immediately imbues them with similarities and gives them an order, thus fulfilling the parameters of a collection. Of particular note is that Moulène draws on objects that have not been made for exhibition purposes. The strike objects were only supposed to attract atten-

---

[24] See, for example, Martin Jörg Schäfer, *Die Gewalt der Muße. Wechselverhältnisse von Arbeit, Nichtarbeit, Ästhetik*, Zürich / Berlin, 2013. p. 24: "Since the establishment of an autonomous aesthetic theory in the late eighteenth century, artistic productivity is often seen as a privileged form of labour, free from outside constraints, and therefore perhaps no form of labour to begin with or presenting alternatives to existing forms of labour by being a better one." Transl. by Sven Ondrazek.

tion for a limited amount of time before they, homer-like, disappeared again from the public eye. Moulène, however, compiles them, transfers them to the museum and puts them on display, thus detaching them from their original context and bestowing upon them a new attention. Doing that, Moulène's handling of the objects resembles the role of the collector, as Walter Benjamin describes it in a number of his works. Being characterized by collecting things which are "detached from all [their] original functions"[25], Benjamin's collector indeed "does not emphasize their functional utilitarian value – that is, their usefulness – but studies and loves them as the scene, the stage, of their fate".[26] Within such a collection, the objects adopt a special quality: As historical remains, "once they are thrown out of their orbit", they begin "to send signals of their most subversive potentiality".[27] A similar strategy can be observed in the practice of so-called 'history workshops', which established themselves in the 1970s to tell stories of the everyday lives of those who are usually not given a voice[28], drawing special attention to the 'oppressed' and commonly ignored working-class environment in particular. Against this backdrop, Moulène's strategy of compiling and displaying can be described as a 'history from below', told not by human agents, but by way of things and pictures. As both a collection and such a history from below, the photo spread becomes the voice of the negated in history, speaking out in favour of self-determined and better forms of labour as well as, in equal measure, against those, which are precarious and alienating. As traces of strike and thus of precarious labour, the objects are subject to a resurrection within the collection. Originally doomed to fade into invisibility, they now demand their actuality. This, of course, raises the question which role the picture of an object can play in this context with regard to its relation to the object itself. Can a photograph uphold the material subversiveness of the latter or does it erase any traces of labour?

It is here that a look back at the curious history of photography would help to give a satisfying answer. Ever since the first attempts at defining the medium ontologically,

---

[25] Walter Benjamin, *The Arcades Project,* Convolute H1a,2, Cambridge 1999, p. 204.

[26] Walter Benjamin, *Illuminations,* New York 1968, p. 60.

[27] Giulio Schiavoni, Zum Kinde, in: *Benjamin Handbuch. Leben – Werk – Wirkung,* ed. by Burkhardt Lindner. Stuttgart / Weimar 2011, p. 375. Transl. by Sven Ondrazek.

[28] Hannes Heer / Volker Ullrich (eds.), *Geschichte entdecken. Erfahrungen und Projekte der neuen Geschichtsbewegung,* Hamburg 1985.

its status between representation and autonomous image, between trace of reality and image of such a trace has been an object of debate.[29] Particularly in recent years, an end of photography has been increasingly pronounced on account of its 'loss of referent' and its resulting loss of authenticity.[30] Owing to digitalisation and its consequent replacement of analogue imaging procedures in particular, photography is said to have lost its claim to be considered a trace of reality. However, such a process cannot be observed in the case of Moulène's *Objets de Grève*. The collection-like character of the photo spread alone withstands such proclamations. The strike objects were produced between 1969 and 1999 and thus entail a historical component, which the photograph is not able to erase. What is more, the individual histories of the objects may only be partially told in Moulène's work, but they are described and historicised in detail in contemporaneously published photo series, such as *Les Cahiers du Musée National d'Art Moderne* (2000).[31] Likewise, there is no exhibition catalogue, which would leave out the history of the strike objects in favour of their pictures.[32] It rather seems as if the original context of any given object is given the same weight as the photographs themselves. In their presentation, reception and historical continuity, the objects manage to reveal their defiance of bowing to a dictum of death without comment. In the sense of Roland Barthes, it could be said that they become "specters"[33] between past and present, life and death; that is, in the medium of photography, they are present as both what has been and what is. Emphasising the aspect of labour once again, the referents strike against turning into a mere representation and claim a presence that goes beyond or rather retreats from that fate. Moulène thus usurps photography and its status of being in-between and allows the strike objects not only to be objects that strike against becoming commodities and the consequent fading of labour into invisibility, but also objects that strike against becoming photography in form. Instead of letting itself be reduced to the status of representation, the referent, to quote Bar-

---

[29] Peter Geimer, Das Bild als Spur. Mutmaßung über ein untotes Paradigma, in: *Spur. Spurenlesen als Orientierungstechnik und Wissenskunst*, ed. by Sybille Krämer, Frankfurt am Main 2007, pp. 95–97.

[30] Ibid.

[31] Magagnoli, Moulène (see note 1), p. 156.

[32] *Bin beschäftigt*, exh. cat. GAK Gesellschaft für aktuelle Kunst, Bremen 2007; *Valeurs croisées*, exh. cat. Les Ateliers de Rennes – Biennale d'art contemporain, 2008.

[33] Roland Barthes, *Camera Lucida: Reflections on Photography*, New York 1981, p. 14.

thes again, "adheres"³⁴ as a resistance, which does not fully manage to overcome the pictorial and representational nature of photography, but accompanies the medium precisely as such a resistance, "adheres" to it and shows itself under certain conditions.

Still, the question of the relation between object and photograph should also be raised from the perspective of the economic conditions of production and of the term of labour that is to be derived from them. After all, the strike objects have been made in the vein of industrial labour and, if viewed as part of the tradition of homers, are paradigmatic of this form of production. Since at least the 1970s, of course, industrial forms of production have significantly decreased in importance. Put into motion by an outsourcing and mechanisation of production, deindustrialisation processes have led to industrial production being extensively curbed and replaced by new forms of labour. Instead of material production, the tertiary sector now focuses on "immaterial production"³⁵, on account of which the strike objects do not represent the current surplus value. They rather signify a paradigm, which has long been on the wane. However, that this shift towards an immaterialisation of production conditions is inherent to Moulène's photo spread, the striking relationship between 'objectness' and 'imageness' makes particularly clear, since photographs can be more than just pictures of their referents. Indeed, they have qualities that constitute realities of their own. Taking such qualities as a starting point, Horst Bredekamp shows that images can have performative effects in his *Theorie des Bildakts* ("Theory of the Image Act").³⁶ As such, numerous examples attest to a "force of images", the "form-inherent *potentia*"³⁷; that is, an image activity, which refuses to be reduced to the status of an 'image'. Performativity takes on a special role in the current service sector too if one assumes that the shift from material to immaterial production lends integral substance to the image. In advertising, for example, it becomes manifest that economic immaterialisation is more concerned with the affects an image can produce than with the object to be sold.³⁸ Images excite affects, not unlike the ideal worker in our service society does

---

[34] Barthes, Camera (see note 32), p. 6.

[35] Maurizio Lazzarato, Immaterial Labour, in: *Radical Thought in Italy*, ed. by Paolo Virno and Michael Hardt, Minneapolis 1996, pp. 132–146.

[36] Horst Bredekamp, *Theorie des Bildakts. Frankfurter Adorno-Vorlesungen 2007*, Berlin 2010.

[37] Ibid. p. 55. Transl. by Sven Ondrazek.

[38] Michael Hardt, Affective labor, in: *boundary 2*, vol. 26, no. 2 (1999), pp. 89–100.

within economic production. That is why images can also engage in affective, that is, immaterial labour. Within the economic sphere, as a result, they obtain the character of commodities and thus also certain object-like qualities – which is a process Moulène is quite familiar with through his previous career as advertising photographer. By not exhibiting the actual strike objects, then, but only pictures of them, Moulène reveals the double meaning of the pictorial. Again, images and, in this case, photographs are no longer only representations of their referents, but materialise themselves through performative acts of positing. In Moulène's photo spread, this shift becomes even clearer through the use and peculiar transparency of the acrylic glass, into which the photographs are embedded. The acrylic glass impairs the familiar pictorial nature of photography by eliminating materiality in favour of illusion. Its opacity makes it impossible to fixate the picture and conceive of it as a mere image. Evoking rather an impression of plasticity, the image thus defies two-dimensionality and lays claim to a space that goes beyond it. In other words, it does not open up a space within itself, as would be the case, for example, in the painterly tradition of Alberti. It is no window on the world, which constitutes itself in the depth of the image. Moulène's pictures open up a space, which confronts their recipients and, viewed as an "exit from the image"[39]; specifically demands an 'objectness'. The pictures thus become objects. They are reified and become items or articles in terms of a commodity logic, which means they become potential commodities. The oscillation between the knowledge of the two-dimensionality of the pictures on the one hand and their spatial impression on the other illustrates their performative effect and the shift in meaning from object to image – as well as, in turn, from image to object. Still, does that suffice to say these images are on strike? Can they be called strike objects?

In contract to industrial workers who strike by voicing their criticism of working conditions on individual objects, it appears that the possibility of striking in the service sector is subject to several limitations. This becomes particularly apparent when looking at the difference between the two. Work on strike objects, just as work on homers, is categorised as a form of non-labour, since the objects do not create a surplus value due to their defectiveness. Analogous to the dichotomy between art and labour, which was solidified during the late eighteenth century, creative and self-determined

---

[39] Laszlo Glozer, *Westkunst. Zeitgenössische Kunst seit 1939*, Cologne 1981. Transl. by Sven Ondrazek.

work corresponds to non-labour and, as such, to the practice of strike as well. Labour is only made visible by way of a suspension of official work through non-labour, that is, through strike. Strike as such as well as the strike objects are thus traces of labour, which would usually not show themselves. However, while the workers are producing their strike objects, their form of labour has long been on the wane. Labour is now no longer to be understood as production in the material sense. It is rather the production of immaterial qualities, of relations, networks and ideal means of communication; and, as Maurizio Lazzarato notes, it is now also work on oneself: "What modern management techniques are looking for is for 'the worker's soul to become part of the factory'. The worker's personality and subjectivity have to be made susceptible to organization and command."[40] If labour in the 21st century, then, no longer proceeds by producing objects – can there still be strike objects in the first place? In the service sector at any rate, creative and self-determined work can no longer breed resistance. After all, if current theories of labour are to be believed, it is precisely those qualities, which have distinguished artists from workers for centuries that have now become a prerequisite for the new ideal type of worker. According to these theories, this becomes clearest in how the new work models tend to occupy a worker's whole life, thus blurring the boundaries between labour and non-labour. At the same time, full devotion to work has long become mandatory and, in the context of biopolitical mechanisms of governing, a prerequisite for the constitution of the subject. Labour indeed means work on the subject, and the subject-status is only constituted through labour, which means one has to work to become a subject. In a sense, labour has become the "antinomy of modernity".[41] Of course, if everything can become a form of labour and if every worker is constantly engaged in it, it seems difficult to search for its traces. After all, it seems as if it can no longer be concretely determined in the first place. This raises a multitude of questions, not the least of which concerns which activities are to be considered part of it and which not. In this age of immaterial labour, one might also wonder which form a strike could possibly take at all. If labour becomes the prerequisite for the constitution of the subject, what would one strike against?

---

[40] Lazzarato, Labour (see note 34), p. 133.
[41] Timo Skrandies, ArbeitsloseR, in: *What Can a Body Do? Praktiken und Konfigurationen des Körpers in den Kulturwissenschaften*, ed. by Netzwerk Körper, Frankfurt am Main 2012, p. 22. Transl. by Sven Ondrazek.

Becoming a subject? The entire feasibility of a strike seems to be put into question – and with it the existence of strike objects. What form would they take? Could they still be produced if workers no longer made 'any' objects? Jean-Luc Moulène's photo spread finds itself right in the middle of that uncertainty. By turning his objects into images, which in our current age use their performative qualities for the purpose of economic valorisation, thus enabling them to be reified, Moulène shows how strike objects and homers have long been on the wane. On the other hand, however, the assumption that images too can become strike objects, which the title of the photo spread already implies – it is called *Objets de Grève* and not *Photographies des Objets de Grève* after all –, makes clear that images as products of immaterial labour can also be objects of precarious labour. Still, the production of the original strike objects no longer seems to offer itself as an opportunity for tracing labour. If anything, this is reserved for the arts.

# Bibliography

Anteby, Michel, Factory "Homers". Understanding a Highly Elusive, Marginal, and Illegal Practice, in: *Sociologie du Travail,* Annual English Language Edition, vol. 48 (2006), pp. 22–38.

Barthes, Roland, *Camera Lucida. Reflections on Photography,* New York 1981.

Benjamin, Walter, *The Arcades Project,* Cambridge / London 2002.

Benjamin, Walter, Unpacking My Library. A Talk about Book Collecting, in: Walter Benjamin, *Illuminations,* New York 1969, pp. 59–67.

*Bin beschäftigt,* exh. cat. GAK Gesellschaft für aktuelle Kunst, Bremen 2007.

Bredekamp, Horst, *Theorie des Bildakts. Frankfurter Adorno-Vorlesungen 2007,* Berlin 2010.

De Certeau, Michel, *The Practice of Everyday Life,* Berkeley / Los Angeles 1984.

Magagnoli, Paolo, Moulène, Rancière and *24 Objets de Grève*: Productive ambivalence or reifying opacity?, in: *Philosophy of Photography,* vol. 3, no. 1 (2012), pp. 155–171.

Geimer, Peter, Das Bild als Spur. Mutmaßung über ein untotes Paradigma, in: *Spur. Spurenlesen als Orientierungstechnik und Wissenskunst,* ed. by Sybille Krämer, Frankfurt am Main 2007, pp. 95–120.

Glozer, Laszlo, *Westkunst. Zeitgenössische Kunst seit 1939,* Cologne 1981.

Hamacher, Werner, Afformative, Strike, in: *Cardozo Law Review,* vol. 13, no. 4 (1991), pp. 1133–1157.

Hardt, Michael, Affective labor, in: *boundary 2,* vol. 26, no. 2 (1999), pp. 89–100.

Heer, Hannes / Ullrich, Volker (eds.), *Geschichte entdecken. Erfahrungen und Projekte der neuen Geschichtsbewegung,* Hamburg 1985.

Lazzarato, Maurizio, Immaterial Labour, in: *Radical Thought in Italy,* ed. by Paolo Virno and Michael Hardt, Minneapolis 1996, pp. 132–146.

Marx, Karl, *Capital. Critique of Political Economy, Vol. I: The Process of Capitalist Production*, Chicago 1909.

Rancière, Jacques, *Proletarian Nights. The Worker's Dream in Nineteenth-Century France*, London / New York 2012.

Rancière, Jacques, Interview with Lawrence Liang (2009), http://kafila.org/2009/02/12/interview-with-jacques-ranciere (10/08/2014).

Schäfer, Martin Jörg, *Die Gewalt der Muße. Wechselverhältnisse von Arbeit, Nichtarbeit, Ästhetik*, Zürich / Berlin 2013.

Schiavoni, Giulio, Zum Kinde, in: *Benjamin Handbuch. Leben – Werk – Wirkung*, ed. by Burkhardt Lindner, Stuttgart 2011, pp. 373–385.

Skrandies, Timo, ArbeitsloseR, in: *What Can a Body Do? Praktiken und Konfigurationen des Körpers in den Kulturwissenschaften*, ed. by Netzwerk Körper, Frankfurt am Main 2012, pp. 19–25.

*Valeurs croisées*, exh. cat. Les Ateliers de Rennes – Biennale d'art contemporain, 2008.

# Labour and Its Aftermath, or: On the Difficulty of Catching Oneself in the Act of Doing 'What Artists Do'

*Katja Gentric*

*Seipone* by Lerato Shadi and *The 370 Day Project* by Willem Boshoff: Two artistic actions, written and performed biographical notes, invented almost 30 years apart, serve as case studies for our enquiry into the strange and paradoxical 'difficulty' of any attempt at delimiting the production process from its antecedents and its consequences. As to the unlikelihood of 'catching oneself in the act', the paradox appears to be twofold: It is almost impossible not to leave any 'fingerprints' while engaging in any action, and any attempt to call to mind bygone action necessitates quite considerable material organization. The difficulty seems to be how to put the finger on action itself, how to prolong the tension of the lived event for it to be able to be remembered as a 'work' of 'art'. Likewise, it remains an incongruity to endeavour isolating the production process within the complexity of the socio-economic, political and historical whole it is inextricably embedded in; in our case: the recent history of South Africa.

For an entire year, or, more precisely 370 days, every single action carried out by Willem Boshoff should be understood as pertaining to the project. The herculean task is commenced on September 12, 1982 and ended on September 18, 1983. In preparation of this one-year feat, the artist had designed a system of cryptic signs, equivalents for the kinds of actions he would be likely to encounter, and started collecting samples of wood from 370 different species of trees. Every morning from September 12, 1982 onwards, he cuts rectangular signs into oblong blocks of wood[1] representing his tasks for the day. During the day, these planned actions have to be carried out, and, in the evening, circular motifs, evaluating their success or failure, are engraved as a right-hand column into the same wood.[2] Apart from the impressive amount of work done during this period, the only physical remains of the project are the sculpted tokens covered in cryptic circular and square symbols and inserted into as many slots in a cabinet constructed for this purpose: a result with definite aesthetic qual-

---

[1] Each block measures 24 x 4,8 x 1cm.

[2] Willem Boshoff, *Die Ontwikkeling en Toepassing van Visuele Letterkundige Verskynsels in die Samestelling van Kunswerke*, Johannesburg 1984, pp. 73–85.

ity, but a very unusual form of sculpture. The artist furthermore religiously collects the carvings and waste material generated during the woodworking sessions, storing them in a drawer added for this purpose at the bottom of the cabinet. Hidden under the carvings are two notebooks, where the artist wrote down, legible in red ink, the actual tasks undertaken. He also invented a *'Dagspreuk'*, a sort of motto for the day. These notebooks are to remain jealously hidden from view: The creator's secret? The secret dissident? A resistance fighter in hiding?[3]

The most spectacular task the artist impedes himself with is the obligation to run a training run of 10km a day in preparation of the Ultramarathon of 87.7km: The 'comrades' run every year on May 31, 1983 between Durban and Pietermaritzburg.[4] Another block is worked on in the maternity ward, on the day his son is born. One of the first wooden tokens is made on an aeroplane, on his return trip from the Venice Biennale and *Documenta 7* in Kassel. Boshoff remembers having planned his daily runs during his stay in Kassel to coincide with the granite monoliths and trees planted by Joseph Beuys as part of the project *7000 Eichen*.[5] Beuys seems a possible spiritual predecessor of Boshoff's artistic attitude.[6] In order to be flexible enough to work in such diverse conditions, Boshoff designed a carrying bag, storage for all his tools. The bag can be opened in any place circumstances might impose. Boshoff refers to the carving sessions as meditation, the menial task accompanying and calming his thoughts, a process of interiorization. The cryptic signs constitute an intentionally contrived, inscribed trace. However, the actual 'work' of art is not the carving (done early in the morning or late at night) but the activities carried out in the interval – most of them very banal tasks of daily life: drinking Coca-Cola in an unprecedented place or drawing lines on the ceiling, travelling, running… Boshoff states the ambi-

---

[3] In another project, *Bangboek* (1977–1981), Boshoff invents a cryptic writing system and rewrites the notes he has taken as a conscious objector to military service. The slippage between artistic dissidence and political resistance will interest us in more detail on the question of 'labour' in a South African context (cf. Hayden Proud, Experiments under Constraint, in: *Visual Century*, vol. 3, ed. by Mario Pissarra, Johannesburg 2011, pp. 129–155). Boshoff's personal resistance becomes evident in the fact that he produces an art that is against everything the state would have expected of him. The National Party was an advocate for a resolutely realistic figurative style while conceptual art practices are very little known in the South Africa of the 1980s and not in the least encouraged, as they were indeed considered suspect.

[4] Ivan Vladislavić, *Willem Boshoff*, Johannesburg 2005, p. 34.

[5] Boshoff, in discussion with the author, Washington 2012.

[6] Jean-Philippe Antoine, *La traversé du XX<sup>e</sup> siècle. Joseph Beuys, l'image et le souvenir*, Dijon 2011.

tion to "be" a work of art.[7] His activity is aimed not at an object being produced but at himself: The actions he undertakes are intended to make himself discover certain character traits (*'deugdes'* in Afrikaans) as, for example, patience, perseverance, or unflinching loyalty to one's task. Boshoff remembers his bewilderment with art practices of the 1960s. During the above-mentioned trip to Europe, Boshoff made contact with Herman Nitsch. Highly impressed by the personality of Nitsch, but at pains to reconcile the non-conformist practices of Actionism with the ideals of art-making generally accepted in South Africa, Boshoff admits that he sets out on the *370 Day Project* with the feeling of "not knowing" and wanting to "teach" himself what art might be.[8] For the actions, the actual activities he invented for himself, he implemented a tripartite classification system: He distinguishes 'obligations' and 'recreations', which is to be expected in 20th century society[9], but the third category is more intriguing and unexpected, as it consists of 'sacrifices'. Reading the very ample written comments, the questioner discovers that this notion pertains to the idea of the creator's sacrifice in relinquishing his creation, having to confront it with public questioning, a vertiginous moment when his vulnerability is brought home to him. This implies not only that the artist might have preferred sustaining secrecy, but also that he has a feeling of not being recognized by society.[10]

More recently, from 2006 onwards, another young artist from South Africa, Lerato Shadi, has been performing a series of actions that are as demanding as those carried out by Willem Boshoff in 1983. By now, performances have become part of a standard if not classical vocabulary of artistic practices. The art-going public discusses Lerato Shadi's interventions not because of their unusualness but because of their personal depth and sincerity.

---

[7] Willem Boshoff, Parrots kiss like this, interview with Paul Jorgensen and Charity Ellis (1998), http://www.onepeople.com/intArtists/artists/bosinterv.html (25/01/2015), edited version published by R. N. Casper and C. Hawkey, Massachusetts 2002, pp. 54–55. Even though Boshoff does not know the work of Filliou, this idea resonates with the latter's *Galerie Légitime* (1968).

[8] Katja Gentric, *Willem Boshoff. Monographie d'artiste et Catalogue*, Ph.D. thesis, Dijon 2013, p. 237; Boshoff, Parrots (see note 7).

[9] Coincidence or not, the system of "poetical economics" proposed by Filliou advocates art as "a form of organization of leisure"; cf. Robert Filliou, *Lehren und Lernen als Auffuehrungskuenste. Teaching and Learning as Performing Arts*, ed. by Kaspar König, Cologne 1970, p. 77.

[10] Proud, Experiments (see note 3), pp. 129–155.

Lerato Shadi's personal journal, *Seiphone*, is a performance executed from June 27–30, 2012 at the Alpha Nova Kulturwerkstatt and the Galerie Futura Kunstfabrik in Berlin and from July 28–30 at the Stevenson Gallery in Johannesburg. The first phase, during which, using a pencil, Shadi writes her biography on a white wall, lasts four hours. The next four hours are spent rubbing out the written text word for word, line for line. What has been recorded four hours before gets removed as it is being read. The project is conceived according to a precise rhythm and makes allowance for equal phases of resting and writing.[11] The same cycle of writing, effacing and resting is carried out three times. The final evidence of the labour of several days is contained in the pencil dust and wooden carvings, as a result of sharpening the pencils, the grey rests of rubber, and, finally, a (relatively) clean wall.[12]

The significant detail here is the fact that Shadi, like Boshoff, writes a personal diary. She does not invite an art public during the performance phase of writing, effacing and rewriting, which is nevertheless documented in images by one solitary photographer.[13] The photographs do not keep a record of the written words: These are known to the artist only. Shadi remarks the importance of writing her life's story free from the fear of being judged, not measuring the confidences she is disclosing against "public opinion".[14] She calls the work *Seipone*, mirror: The artist reflects herself in her life story. Once the work is completed, the gallery is opened to the public. Finding themselves faced by an empty wall bearing traces of writing and effacing, spectators are then told that what was formerly written here was a biography. Shadi imagines that the spectator mirrors himself in what she has written. What he imagines Shadi's personal secrets to be would depend on his own life experience. This is a work about the process of writing and effacing, about the form of mediation, but more impor-

---

[11] Lerato Shadi, email, November 18, 2014: "The Berlin performance was done over 4 days, one day writing the next day erasing then repeating the process. The Joburg performance was done over 24 hours 8 hours performing 8 hours sleep and 8 hours performing. The 8 hours consisted of 4 hours writing and 4 hours erasing."

[12] Lerato Shadi, personal website, http://www.lerato-shadi.net (25/01/2015), with documentary photographs taken during the performance.

[13] Both artists turn out to be quite weary of keeping a tangible or photographic 'proof' of their actions, which is true for a great number of 'conceptual' artists; cf. Catherine Strasser, *Du Travail de l'Art. Observation des œuvres et analyse du processus qui les conduit,* Paris 2006, p. 152.

[14] Lerato Shadi, telephone interview, November 7, 2014.

tantly about lived experience, which is told and imagined, but not communicated. Invited to speak about her work, Shadi draws attention to the process in the first place:

> The prevailing theme in my current body of work deals with absence and presence, subject and object and their transformation through performance. I use elements such as concentration, breath, tension and duration to reflect this research in my œuvre. Knitting, installation, video and sound are some of the mediums I have used to record my current investigations.[15]

Several common criteria link the work of Shadi to Boshoff. However, looking at them in dialogue form, reciprocal and with other artists, an essential shift in attitude becomes apparent. The first common denominator is the fact that they both obey an intricate system of constraints. Their reasoning is meticulously measured in time and in the physical dimensions their actions take. Their actions are guided by premeditation, or even premonition, and then carried out to the last detail: The artist has elaborated a programme that functions like a script, a scenario for the day to come. The programmatic approach is not an exclusive prerogative of these two artists only, but has always been present in artistic practices[16] and has seen an increase in popularity during the 1960s. In connection with the work of Boshoff and Shadi, a few names come to mind as though they bore a family resemblance. During his visit to Europe in 1982, Boshoff spent time with Herman Nitsch. The latter designs elaborate partitions of his actions that may involve hundreds of participants and are carried out over a long time-span: *Das Sechstagespiel* (1998).[17] A one-year action concerned with gesture closely related to current events is the series *Lakonikon* by Pia Lindman.[18]

The second coincidence between Boshoff and Shadi is that, at first glance, both artistic projects depend on an impressive quantity of work for their success. Intuitively, the onlooker rates the artist's endurance as self-sacrifice. Common belief has it that the artist must have 'something more' than ordinary humans and shows this status by his determination in a self-imposed super-human task. Several exhibitions have recently challenged this preconceived idea in order to unpack its reasoning, which is as old as the idea of the 'melancholic' mind-set of artistic nature. In 2005, Jean

---

[15] Shadi (see note 11).

[16] Cf. i. a. Strasser, Travail (see note 13), pp. 41–68.

[17] Herman Nitsch, *Das Sechstagespiel des Orgien Mysterien Theaters Prinzendorf, 3. – 9. August 1998*, ed. by Otmar Rychlik, Ostfildern 2003.

[18] *Lakonikon, Black Square, The New York Times Project* (2004); cf. Barbara Formis, Refaire le deuil. Les gestes des autres, in: *Gestes à l'œuvre. De l'incidence* éditeur, ed. by Barbara Formis, Cherbourg-Octeville 2008, pp. 169–185.

Clair, curated the exhibition *Mélancolie, Génie et Folie en Occident* in Paris. Albrecht Dürer's *Melancholia I* has become emblematic for this questioning[19]; it becomes a synonym for the humanistic mind-set, measuring time and matter and meditating on the creative process in deep turmoil and self-contradiction over the fate of being a creator. Somewhere along the construction of the self-perception of the artist, the link has been made between creative genius and the idea of suffering for art, an idea driven home by numerous self-portraits in the vein of Saint Sebastian: The artist as misunderstood by 'ordinary' humans. The idea of the martyr is accentuated and complicated in South-African artistic thinking.[20] Consequently, this attitude needs to be put into perspective. The guiding notion is still the same: The idea of 'work', or rather its socio-political counterpart, 'labour'. The complexity of this notion in the present context will oblige us to move back and fourth several times – work in dialogue form.

From a European point of view, the tautological and solipsistic nature of the melancholic attitude has come under critique and is actively negated by recent art-critical writing. Barbara Polla and Paul Ardenne curated the exhibition *Working Men, Art contemporain et Travail* in 2008. Demonstration of dexterity or of the super-human task of creation is unmasked for ridicule and impertinence in the context of post-Fordist society.[21] A strong aspect of feminist opposition to this mind-set is probably best exemplified by Nathalie Djurberg's "Just because you are suffering doesn't make you Jesus" (a video from 2005).[22] Catherine Strasser, in a series of essays "On the work of art: Observation of artworks and analysis of the processes that drive them", claims that artists' attitudes towards work have in a certain way anticipated what work will come to signify for society and, by the same token, are an indicator of the course it might take in years to come.[23] Her chapter on Meret Oppenheim, Lygia Clark, Orlan Lea Lublin and Gina Pane looks at artists taking the body as tool and as material, referring to it as an alphabet of a new language for which vocabulary and syntax are still

---

[19] Peter-Klaus Schuster, Melancholia I. Dürer et sa postérité, in: *Mélancolie. Génie et folie en Occident*, exh. cat., ed. by Jean Clair, Paris 2005, pp. 90–104.

[20] Gentric, Boshoff (see note 8), pp. 168–170.

[21] Paul Ardenne / Barbara Polla (eds.), *Working Men. Art Contemporain et Travail*, Brussels 2008, pp. 69–71, 139–143.

[22] Eugen Blume et al., *Schmerz, Kunst + Wissenschaft*, exh. cat., Berlin 2007.

[23] Strasser, Travail (see note 13), pp. 9–10.

to be invented.²⁴ She identifies an "economics of process"²⁵ parallel to the economics of the object produced.

At this stage, let us draw attention to one incidence of call and response between theoretical arguments on the question of production and process in art analysed for the ambivalent status of the artist as producer and his place in society. Walter Benjamin, in 1934, within a socialist understanding of the word 'producer', looks at the conditions under which the artist's work might be regarded as work of common interest (*'Gemeinwesen'*).²⁶ Benjamin lists possible declinations of the relationship between the artist-producer and the state, expressing the difficulty of artistic intervention to be autonomous from short-lived social 'trends', but still remain an asset for society. Sixty years later, Hal Foster writes "The artist as ethnographer"²⁷ as an updated answer to Benjamin. Foster's text has since become key for the discourse of contemporary art at odds with cultural spheres hitherto unattended. Readings of this text all too often overlook the fact that Foster means to warn of an uncritical approach, mistaking an investigative *modus operandi* for original experimentation, which is what Benjamin had referred to as the 'laboratory'. The dialogue has since been taken up by a long list of art-critical texts referring to diverse notions of pre- or post-production.²⁸ Little known to the international academic discourse, this debate has a South-African variant in a programmatic text written by Albie Sachs: "Preparing ourselves for Freedom,

---

[24] Ibid., p. 153. One work by Lea Lublin, *My Son* (1968), is of particular interest in the current discussion. Lublin's participation in the *Salon de Mai 1968* consists of living the daily chores of a mother tending her seven-month-old son. Lublin analyses this gesture in terms of artistic language and the relationship between spectator and artist. Boshoff has shown in 1983 that this gesture is not exclusive to feminist discourse; cf. pp. 139–175.

[25] Ibid., p. 11.

[26] Benjamin shows the complexity of the idea of the autonomy of the artist at times when the artist is persuaded to conduct production in the interest of class struggle. He warns of the danger of superficial lip service to class-issues and argues for necessity of a radical renewal of artistic attitude: "Sie sehen bestätigt, dass es die Literarisierung aller Lebensverhältnisse ist, welche allein den rechten Begriff vom Umfange dieses Schmelzvorgangs gibt, so wie der Stand des Klassenkampfes die Temperatur bestimmt, unter der er – mehr oder weniger vollendet – zustande kommt"; cf. Walter Benjamin, Der Autor als Produzent. Ansprache im Institut zum Studium des Faschismus in Paris, am 27. April 1934, in: *Medienästhetische Schriften*, ed. by Detlev Schöttker, Frankfurt am Main 2002, p. 241.

[27] Hal Foster, The Artist as Ethnographer, in: *The Return of the Real. The Avant-Garde at the End of the Century*, London 1996, pp. 171–203.

[28] Nicolas Bourriaud, *Postproduction*, New York 2002.

Culture and the ANC Constitutional Guidelines".[29] Sachs's text, as that of Benjamin, warns of the impoverishing effect that it would mean not to be weary of the slippage between cultural practices and political ideology. In the present context, let us consider not only the role of the artist as producer or as participant in the production chain: Artists have gone beyond this question and made lucid contributions in analysing the signification of the meaning of 'work' as socio-political activity: 'labour'. Drawing on their own experience of working as activity, artists fathom the anthropological, economic, politically motivated and historical baggage of this notion.

We need both history and artistic experimentation in tandem in order to understand Shadi and Boshoff. In their case, artistic action questioned as 'labour' takes on a radically problematic tone: Aware of the fact that both Boshoff and Shadi are South-African, the spectator links them to the tragic political situation of their country. During the 1960s and continuing until 1994, the name of their country, South Africa, is notorious for reports of brutal police interventions and mass action by the labour force in major cities. In media society, the country is associated with such names as 'Sharpeville', the township where a massacre of 69 demonstrators took place on March 21, 1960, or Soweto, the township where police interventions claimed an unconfirmed death toll in 1976. After the democratic elections of 1994, we might have thought that these atrocities would be a problem of the past, but recently South Africa has sadly added another item to this list – August 16, 2012 – at the Platinum mine of Marikana: 34 deaths as immediate result of police shootings. The events of the struggle against apartheid looked at form within the specialized field of visual studies and gave rise to the publication *Images of Defiance,* which conducts an analysis of the very rich visual production accompanying the campaigns of the trade unions. The collection of posters documents a strife for political rights and social and economic justice going hand in hand with arrests of trade union leaders, strikes, 'stayaways', boycotts, confrontations with well-armed police forces, a state of emergency, and police raids of trade union headquarters. While political parties are banned, trade unions are a makeshift, but simultaneously the most powerful means of organizing

---

[29] Albie Sachs, Preparing Ourselves for Freedom. Culture and the ANC Constitutional Guidelines, in: *Spring is Rebellious,* ed. by Ingrid de Kok and Karen Press, Cape Town 1990.

resistance against an unjust and fascist state.[30] Achille Mbembe unflinchingly analyses the ideology underlying the segregated system of interdependence between labour and economical power in racial terms:

> as a potential commodity form, black life and labour were not only needed but also valued for their industrial utility. But the specifics of the commodity form and the particulars of the market in which blacks were forced to circulate were predetermined by a logic of productive expenditure that was the key underpinning of a racialized institution of private property. [...] In a context in which the control of native bodies had become a new frontier of capital accumulation, the assumption was that expending black life for the sake of profit was a necessary sacrifice – a sacrifice that could be redeemed because it served as the foundation of civilization.[31]

The Gold Rush, the colonial period, the apartheid system and recent post-apartheid economically driven confrontations had disastrous consequences that still shape everyday life in South Africa. The story of European colonial expansion is closely linked to the quest for mineral wealth, which in turn is linked to the organization of the labour force. Seeing that the most discriminatory part of the apartheid system was motivated by the ambition of insuring the presence of the workforce, needed to exploit the gold-mines efficiently, the symbols of this trade have repeatedly found their way into contemporary South-African art-making: The shovel and wheel-barrow appear in works by Gavin Younge, Willy Bester and Moshekwa Langa.[32] Each of these works drives home most efficiently the idea of work, compensation, and exploitation within the South-African mining system. Robin Rhode's *Spade,* made of gold, has a handle of charcoal, which can be used as a drawing instrument.[33] This ridiculously luxurious spade, with a charred handle, is consuming itself in order to be used. Even though the examples named were chosen for their illustrative nature, it needs to be specified that the same artists have elsewhere commented on their artistic agency with political intent.[34] What these works have in common is the conviction of the necessity of resis-

---

[30] Emilia Potenza et al., *Images of Defiance. South African Resistance Posters of the 1980s,* Sunnyside 2004; cf. also the website of the South-Africa Labour and Development Research Unit, http://saldru.lib.msu.edu/dvd4/Foreign%20Firms%20in%20SA%20Germany%201988%20-%201993.pdf (04/01/2014), which holds a large collection of press clippings.

[31] Achille Mbembe, Zero World, in: *The Rise and Fall of Apartheid,* ed. by Okwui Enwezor and Rory Bester, New York 2013, p. 66.

[32] Gavin Younge, *Work Men's Compensation* (1981); Willy Bester, *Poverty Driven* (2002); Moshekwa Langa, *Babylonia* (2009).

[33] *My Joburg. Guide de la scène artistique,* exh. cat., Lyon 2013, p. 177.

[34] Gavin Younge, *Resistance Register* (1975/76); Moshekwa Langa, *The Mountains of My Youth – A Novel* (1997); Robin Rhode, *Untitled (Bits and Pieces)* (2004).

tance in a given political context. In Apartheid South Africa, counter-culture thinking has ample injustice to oppose. While cultural production is expected to represent the state, or at least some kind of cultural identity of some nation, many South African artists have a deeply ambivalent relationship with the state.[35]

Both artists singled out for our present argument, Boshoff and Shadi, have shown their awareness of the deep ambivalence of the thematic cluster of 'labour': Willem Boshoff made a work with the title *Cheap Labour* in 2004 and Lerato Shadi performed *Hema* in 2007.[36] Both artists regularly emphasize the socio-political preoccupation of their work[37], all the while being constantly at pains to go beyond preconceived ideas by breaking the question into elemental gestures of everyday life. Their attitude corresponds to what Jacques Rancière has termed "aesthetics of politics and politics of aesthetics intertwined".[38]

*Cheap Labour* is the antithesis of the earlier super-human task of the *370 Day Project*. The artist works with found objects: seven worn shovels, one for each day of the week – no day for 'recreation' in this case – and delegates the task of adding inscriptions ('MON', 'TUE', 'WED', 'THU', 'FRI', 'SA', 'SUN') to an assistant. The shovels are exhibited leaning against the wall. The work is explained in the press release written by Boshoff in preparation for the exhibition *Nonplussed*. Boshoff references global capitalism, where the notion of 'work' has lost all value, where the labourer works under impossible conditions and is exploited without scruples. The 'work' having been invested into the seven shovels of *Cheap Labour* is not that of the artist (the genius is most definitely not the sufferer here) – it is the work of a long line of anonymous labourers, made present through some conceptual sleight of hand in the title: "Cheap Labour".

Lerato Shadi performs *Hema (Or six hours of out breath captured in 792 balloons)* in 2007. The six-hour performance is documented by filmed images, edited by the artist to produce a six-minute video. Shadi is seated on a plinth set up amidst the

---

[35] For a list of the very diverse reasons to support or to contest the cultural embargo, cf. Mario Pissara, Isolation, Distance and Engagement. South African art and artists in the international sphere, in: *Visual Century*, vol. 3, ed. by Mario Pissarra, Johannesburg 2011, pp. 181–203.

[36] A second work with a comparable attention to the process of production is *Mosako wa Nako* (2014).

[37] Willem Boshoff, *Press release for Nonplussed*, 2004; Shadi (see note 14).

[38] "Les paradoxes de l'art politique"; cf. Jacques Rancière, *Le spectateur émancipé*, Paris 2008, pp. 56–92.

central staircase of an open-space publicity agency. We see her blowing up balloons, filling them with the breath of six hours. The immaculate whiteness of the building, the window partitions through which we see the employees at their desks, the glass lifts going up and down in a regular motion, members of the staff on their way upstairs or downstairs, balloons slowly drifting through the air while they bounce downwards from one floor to the next, reflected images in the windows; every element in the video enhances the breathing rhythm. The office space seems to inhale and exhale with the performer in its midst. As time goes by, the agency is filled with light and colourful air containers. Employees are playing with them as they invade their desks and photocopying-machines. Eventually, everything goes still as members of the staff leave one by one at the end of the day until the last balloon is blown and the workspace has gone to rest.

Artists throughout the 20th century have given quite extensive attention to the minute details of their every action.[39] Breathing, the most intimate gesture, in Shadi's setup is inextricably caught up with the public sphere. We can imagine the artist entirely filled, replete with the most intimate interiority, by her breath. But air and breath are also evasive, all-encompassing and intangible. The breathing rhythm seems to be measuring our time, our life. Breathing is one of the most democratic activities: All are concerned by this elemental need.

The sequence of the works mentioned, the *370 Day Project, Seipone* and *Hema*, is resolutely turned away from object production in any sense. They reflect on everyday gestures, carried out for the activities in and for themselves. The material consequences of these works, however, leave the art critic with a complex paradox to disentangle. The art world has been much intrigued with the notion of the possibility or impossibility of 'immaterial' art. This utopia needs to be understood within the context of 1960s philosophical movements of counterculture, the beginning of ecological discourse and anti-system thinking in the context of resistance to the Vietnam War.[40] While it is generally held that preoccupation in conceptualist art practices has shifted from the consideration of the object to that of the idea, this assumption has been revised

---

[39] E. g. Bruce Nauman or Vito Acconci; cf. Gentric, Boshoff (see note 8), pp. 134, 152, 310, 344.

[40] This notion is clearly expressed in the later writings by Lucy Lippard and Ursula Meyer; cf. Gentric, Boshoff (see note 8), pp. 393, 396.

from the position of art production in countries far removed from the mainstream. Thus, Luis Camnitzer points out that art adopting a conceptual *modus operandi* has followed a particularly pertinent line of thought in newly industrialized countries:

> Few third world countries escaped the experience of revolution, military takeover, or internal armed conflict [...] and where there was absence of real politics and a free press, students, artists, and other intellectuals were often the only citizens who spoke on behalf of the people. As before, the need for an urgent response to a social and political conditions encouraged artists in the Soviet Union, South Korea, China, and parts of Africa to abandon formalist or traditional art practices for conceptualist art. [...] Art's role as catalyst, as stand-in for forbidden speech as exemplification of systems of thought and belief, and as vehicle for dissent became central. [...] In countries with repressive political regimes, dematerialization broke the stranglehold of the state in relation to the display of art. What's more, 'idea art' was easier to slip by the censors.[41]

In this configuration it seems natural to speak of a "move from the object to the *conduct* of art".[42] Simultaneously, there is strong interest for a "material reality for the conceptual position".[43] Although artists have repeatedly played with the idea of an 'immaterial' art that would resist being included in the market, avoiding accumulation of monetary value, most of these attempts have led artists to admit to the quite considerable material effort involved in bringing this alleged 'immateriality' about.[44] Let us suggest that these artists have instead laid the finger on a fundamental question: They have experienced the fact that any gesture encounters resistance, taking action means going against the flow. The encounter with material resistance is inevitable; it means leaving traces, inscribing an imprint.

Extensive thought on the question of this cluster of ideas can be found in the writings of Georges Didi-Huberman, following in the footsteps of Aby Warburg, Carl Einstein and Walter Benjamin.[45] The initial text on this subject was written for the exhibition *L'Empreinte* in 1997. From the outset, Didi-Huberman positions traces or

---

[41] Louis Camnitzer / Jane Farves / Rachel Weiss (eds.), *Global Conceptualism. Points of Origin, 1950s–1980s*, exh. cat., New York 1999, pp. vii–viii.

[42] Ibid., p. viii.

[43] Mari Carmen Ramírez, cited in: ibid.

[44] Gentric, Boshoff (see note 8), pp. 90, 191, 249, 323–324.

[45] The dialectical notion of 'Aura und Spur' is of crucial relevance to our present discussion; Didi-Huberman more closely defines the notion of the "image dialectique" – "image dans laquelle passé et le présent se dévoient, se transforment se critiquent mutuellement pour former quelque chose que Benjamin nommait *constellation*, une configuration dialectique de temps hétérogènes"; cf. Georges Didi-Huberman, *La Ressemblance par Contact. Archéologie Anachronisme et Modernité de l'Empreinte,* Paris 2008, p. 13.

imprints within the vocabulary of the flux of time and memory. He remarks that in the vocabulary of human science, imprints or traces are conceptualized as a paradigm but not as a process, a mode, which he suggests, that art history and artists might be able to fill in. Even a gesture in dance – commonly expected to be nothing more than an ephemeral movement of the body in space – has an impact. Didi-Huberman puts it this way: "[O]n dérange la terre en la percutant" ("We disturb, or ruffle, the earth when we make contact").[46] More recently, Didi-Huberman has reconsidered the question. This time, the centre of his interest has moved to the remembering body. Past gestures are not effaced from memory, which induces a state of call and response with events long gone by.[47] The body is political. This need not be repeated and is emphatically so in the South African and post-colonial context.[48]

Lerato Shadi puts this question differently but essentially means the same. She follows a line of thought questioning stereotypes attached to bodies by the collective, be they politically or socially induced. Her most urgent and most persistent endeavour is to get beyond the preconceived idea. But, she remarks, in order to be overcome, the stereotype needs to be acknowledged, just as the history that made it come about.[49]

After *Cheap Labour* and *Seipone*, Boshoff and Shadi went on to artistic interventions even less concerned with material production. Lerato Shadi, in *u'titled*[50], goes as far as implying that inventing a title for her performances is not the artist's task alone. She invites spectators to start conversations in any chosen language. Shadi impecca-

---

[46] Ibid., p. 21.

[47] Didi-Huberman on Ahron Appelfeld: "une sorte de mémoire corporelle où remuent, où refluent des images"; cf. Georges Didi-Huberman, *Essayer Voir*, Paris 2014, p. 16. Later (p. 76), he links this same notion to the knock-out blow in boxing "et c'est bien ce nœud dialectique – image avec temps, corps avec histoire – qui donne sa nécessité au dire" about history and bodily presence in tandem as "dialectical interweaving". The "body's memory" is also referred to by Strasser in her analysis of "corporalité" (body-embeddedness) as a subject in action art; cf. Strasser, Travail (see note 13), p. 17. In the context of the work of Gina Pane, Strasser maintains that "quand le travail n'a pas pour finalité la production d'objets mais qu'il ne les rejette pas non plus, le jouet fournit au corps agissant une alternative. Il en conservera la mémoire au même titre que la 'cicatrice intérieure'", an "internal scar"; cf. p. 153.

[48] Mbembe, Zero (see note 31); John Peffer, *Art and the End of Apartheid*, London 2009, pp. 41–72: In a chapter with the title "Becoming Animal, the tortured body during Apartheid", Peffer seems to speak of the body in terms of its political expressivity.

[49] Shadi (see note 14).

[50] Bordeaux, November 27, 2013.

bly answers in her mother tongue, Setswana. This exchange is a most sophisticated remark on translatability or the inherent translation process in all human expression. Even though Shadi does not record her performance, the camera (simultaneously projecting the image, but not recording it, capturing the words she writes with rapidly disappearing black ink on black paper) is there to prove beyond any doubt the intrinsically mediated condition of her encounters with the public. Shadi thinks of the ephemeral nature of this exchange as a preliminary drawing, a provisional moment.[51]

Willem Boshoff moved on to instances where the presence of the artist is the main concern. Learning by heart disused words, plants threatened by extinction, or names of victims, he insures their survival through his mnemonic activity. While they are not incarnated in any artistic material form, these gardens inhabiting Boshoff's head would paradoxically disappear without a trace were it not for his bodily existence. They have no reality outside the artist's memory.

The quaint nature of Boshoff's conceptual approach is that he takes aspects of conceptual discourse literally, which results in an original fictive approach.[52] His work is ostensibly non-figurative and motivated by conceptualist reasoning, but also inextricably immersed in the manipulation of matter. Boshoff has gone so far as to design the vast *Blind Alphabet Project,* a still incomplete series started in 1994. Today it counts up to more than 500 sculptures, meant to be apprehended by touch and not by sight, representing a 'morphological' vocabulary. Lerato Shadi's contributions come too late to be in danger of being classified as 'conceptualist', their concern for material traces not needing to be explained away: pencil-carvings, transformed rubber matter, knitted objects of quite considerable size, 792 balloons... These works accept that any activity entails transformation – even though everything is done to avoid 'production' in the traditional sense of the word.

The ambivalent relationship between artistic action and the object produced has been minutely analysed by Barbara Formis whose initial thesis was the disappearance of action the moment the object appears. In a later essay revisiting the vocabulary pertaining to artistic activity, creativity, performativity and production, she moved on to evaluating the notion of gesture in dance or art-making as the essential act, an

---

[51] Lerato Shadi, in discussion with the author, Bordeaux, November 25–29, 2012.

[52] Gentric, Boshoff (see note 8), pp. 756–811, suggesting the *370 Day Project* as a possible case of auto-fiction.

act that crystalizes the indiscernibility between art and life.[53] Having re-read Georges Didi-Huberman and Walter Benjamin for the South African context, we might dare to add that this is possibly a question of the indiscernibility of artistic activity and the everydayness of history: history being acted out one day at a time and by beings intervening individually and collectively in their time, be it in intimacy or in public.

This is what brings us back to our initial remarks, putting into doubt the modalities according to which action can be remembered as a 'work' of art, especially in Shadi and Boshoff's case, where actions are linked in a most intimate way to everyday living. Paradoxically, while the object it produces effaces ephemeral gesture, gesture seems to capsize in the trace it leaves. Deformed matter witnesses the process; the material trace vouches for action having encountered an obstruction. Not sure whether she acted wisely in collecting the pencil carvings, what their status is, or whether she should even admit having archived them, Lerato Shadi nevertheless safe-keeps fragments of rubble as survivors as eye-witnesses of her action. These carvings do not illustrate or document the actual activity in any way. The artist did not put her intentionality into the creation of these bits of matter: They were 'not expected'. Arriving as a by-product, as an undesired side effect, they speak of the action, and only that. The unintentional object is accepted as a compromising morsel, left on a crime scene after the deed was done.

The back-and-forth (the call and response) between the two artists' working methods crystallizes the possibility of traces that continue transmitting the 'living tension' of labour or action. The *corpus delicti* comes about as though the artist had been caught in the act. It constitutes material evidence of investment of work beyond the time-span covered by action. A fundamental shift has taken place in artistic work. Freed of the obligation of producing a 'work of art' in the form of an object or artefact and, likewise, freed of the expectation of providing an 'immaterial' art practice, these works install a call and response with history and with the future. These projects go far beyond the impressiveness of the artistic work and investigate the indiscernibility between art and gesture in everyday life, the interlinked coexistence of action and matter.

---

[53] Barbara Formis, *Esthétique de la vie ordinaire*, Paris 2010.

## Bibliography

Antoine, Jean-Philippe, *La traversé du XXe siècle. Joseph Beuys, l'image et le souvenir,* Dijon 2011.

Ardenne, Paul / Polla, Barbara (eds.), *Working Men. Art Contemporain et Travail,* Brussels 2008.

Benjamin, Walter, Der Autor als Produzent. Ansprache im Institut zum Studium des Faschismus in Paris, am 27. April 1934, in: *Medienästhetische Schriften,* ed. by Detlev Schöttker, Frankfurt am Main 2002, pp. 231–247.

Blume, Eugen et al., *Schmerz, Kunst + Wissenschaft,* exh. cat., Berlin 2007.

Boshoff, Willem, *Die Ontwikkeling en Toepassing van Visuele Letterkundige Verskynsels in die Samestelling van Kunswerke,* Johannesburg 1984.

Boshoff, Willem, Parrots kiss like this, interview with Paul Jorgensen and Charity Ellis (1998), http://www.onepeople.com/intArtists/artists/bosinterv.html (25/01/2015), edited version published by R.N. Casper and C. Hawkey, Massachusetts 2002, pp. 54–55.

Boshoff, Willem, *Press release for Nonplussed,* 2004.

Bourriaud, Nicolas, *Postproduction,* New York 2002.

Camnitzer, Louis / Farves, Jane / Weiss, Rachel (eds.), *Global Conceptualism. Points of Origin, 1950s–1980s,* exh. cat., New York 1999.

Clair, Jean (ed.), *Mélancolie. Génie et Folie en Occident,* exh. cat., Paris 2005.

Didi-Huberman, Georges, *Essayer Voir,* Paris 2014.

Didi-Huberman, Georges, *La Ressemblance par Contact. Archéologie Anachronisme et Modernité de l'Empreinte,* Paris 2008.

Filliou, Robert, *Lehren und Lernen als Auffuehrungskuenste. Teaching and Learning as Performing Arts,* ed. by Kaspar König, Cologne 1970.

Formis, Barbara, Refaire le deuil. Les gestes des autres, in: *Gestes à l'œuvre. De l'incidence* éditeur, ed. by Barbara Formis, Cherbourg-Octeville 2008, pp. 169–185.

Formis, Barbara, *Esthétique de la vie ordinaire*, Paris 2010.

Foster, Hal, The Artist as Ethnographer, in: *The Return of the Real. The Avant-Garde at the End of the Century*, London 1996, pp. 171–203.

Fourie, Abrie (ed.), *Mine*, exh. cat., Berlin 2013.

Gentric, Katja, *Willem Boshoff. Monographie d'artiste et Catalogue*, Ph.D. thesis, Dijon 2013.

Mbembe, Achille, Zero World, in: *The Rise and Fall of Apartheid*, ed. by Okwui Enwezor and Rory Bester, New York 2013, pp. 66–70.

*My Joburg. Guide de la scène artistique*, exh. cat., Lyon 2013.

Nitsch, Herman, *Das Sechstagespiel des Orgien Mysterien Theaters Prinzendorf, 3. – 9. August 1998*, ed. by Otmar Rychlik, Ostfildern 2003.

Peffer, John, *Art and the End of Apartheid*, London 2009.

Perriol, Véronique, *Conceptions du langage verbal en Art. De Fluxus à l'art conceptuel*, Ph.D. thesis, Paris 2006.

Pissara, Mario, Isolation, Distance and Engagement. South African art and artists in the international sphere, in: *Visual Century*, vol. 3, ed. by Mario Pissara, Johannesburg 2011, pp. 181–203.

Potenza, Emilia et al., *Images of Defiance. South African Resistance Posters of the 1980s*, Sunnyside 2004.

Proud, Hayden, Experiments under Constraint, in: *Visual Century*, vol. 3, ed. by Mario Pissara, Johannesburg 2011, pp. 129–155.

Rancière, Jacques, *Le spectateur émancipé*, Paris 2008.

Recht, Roland, L'homme sans qualités. Robert Filliou, in: *Point de fuite. Les images des images des images: Essais critiques sur l'art actuel 1987–2007,* Paris 2009, pp. 145–157.

Schimmel, Paul, Leap into the Void. Performance and the Object, in: *Out of Actions,* London 1999, pp. 97–100.

Strasser, Catherine, *Du Travail de l'Art. Observation des œuvres et analyse du processus qui les conduit,* Paris 2006.

Sachs, Albie, Preparing Ourselves for Freedom. Culture and the ANC Constitutional Guidelines, in: *Spring is Rebellious,* ed. by Ingrid de Kok and Karen Press, Cape Town 1990.

Schuster, Peter-Klaus, Melancholia I. Dürer et sa postérité, in: *Mélancolie. Génie et folie en Occident,* exh. cat., ed. by Jean Clair, Paris 2005, pp. 90–104.

Shadi, Lerato, personal website, http://www.lerato-shadi.net (25/01/2015).

Shadi, Lerato, http://www.lerato-shadi.net/_files/LShadi_DocCV.pdf (25/01/2015).

Shadi, Lerato, e-mail, November 18, 2014.

Shadi, Lerato, telephone interview, November 7, 2014.

South-Africa Labour and Development Research Unit (website), http://saldru.lib.msu.edu/dvd4/Foreign%20Firms%20in%20SA%20Germany%201988%20-%201993.pdf (04/01/2014).

Vladislavić, Ivan, *Willem Boshoff,* Johannesburg 2005.

# About the Authors

**Daniel Blanga-Gubbay** studied philosophy at the Venice University of Architecture, got his PhD on the notion of gesture in philosophy at the Universities of Palermo and Valencia and held a postdoctoral position at the postgraduate school "Materiality and Production" at Heinrich Heine University Düsseldorf from 2012–2014. He currently teaches at the Royal Academy of Fine Arts in Brussels, where he also runs the think tank Aleppo and works as dramaturge for the Kunstenfestivaldesarts.

**Berit Callsen** studied Spanish and South American literature and got her PhD on the continuities of aisthetic poetics in French and Mexican literature from 1963–1984. She is currently a research assistant at the University of Würzburg.

**Noémie Chardonnens** studied French medieval literature in France and Switzerland, got her PhD on intertextual loans and repetitions in the *Roman de Perceforest* in 2014 and was a visiting scholar at the postgraduate school "Materiality and Production" at Heinrich Heine University Düsseldorf the same year. She currently teaches at the University of Lausanne.

**Nicole De Brabandere** does her PhD on habitual embodied experience and scripted action through research at the Zürich University of the Arts. She regularly exhibits and presents her work in the form of artistic research in both artistic and academic contexts.

**Ralph-Miklas Dobler** is professor of art history and media studies at the Munich University of Applied Sciences. He was a research assistant at the Bibliotheca Hertziana – Max-Planck-Institute in Rome from 2004–2015 and associate professor and acting chair of art history at the University of Bonn in 2015. His main research fields are the history and theory of Baroque art, 20th century architecture and urban planning, photography and mass media.

**Joseph S. Freedman** is professor of history at Alabama State University and has been a guest professor at the Universities of Halle-Wittenberg (2004), Munich (2006) and Coimbra (2009). His main research field is early modern academic philosophy with special emphasis on Central Europe.

**Katja Gentric** studied fine arts at the National Superior School D'Art in Dijon and got her PhD on the work of Willem Boshoff at the University of Burgundy. She published several articles on contemporary African art and helped organize numerous exhibitions in Paris.

**Akos Hermann** does his PhD at the Saint-Louis University of Brussels and is an affiliate of the Centre Prospéro research group on language, image and cognition. His main research focuses on questions of history, memory and language in the works of Walter Benjamin and Jacques Derrida.

**Dawid Kasprowicz** was a research assistant at the Institute for Modern German Literature and Media Studies at the University of Hagen from 2012–2013. He is currently a PhD student at the DFG-funded Institute of Advanced Study on Media Cultures of Computer Simulation at Leuphana University Lüneburg.

**Claudia Mongini** studied physics at the University of Turin, got a PhD on chaos theory and neuroscience and engaged in philosophy and the fine arts in Vienna, both in her theoretical research and her artistic practice. She is currently doing a PhD on the intersections between contemporary artistic and scientific modalities of production at the University of Paris 8.

**Veronica Peselmann** is an art historian and does her PhD on material and compositional shifts in 19th century painting at the Free University of Berlin.

**Claudio Rozzoni** got his PhD on aesthetics and the theory of art at the University of Palermo and developed two postgraduate research programmes on the notion of image at the University of Milan. He was a visiting scholar at the Husserl Archive at the University of Cologne and is currently a postdoctoral researcher at the New University of Lisbon, focussing on the philosophical significance of the film image.

**Elisabeth Ruchaud** studied art history at the École du Louvre in Paris and got her PhD in medieval history and art at the Paris School for Advanced Studies in the Social Sciences and the Humboldt University in Berlin in 2011. From 2012–2014, she held a postdoctoral position at the postgraduate school "Materiality and Production" at Heinrich Heine University Düsseldorf. She currently teaches at the Catholic University of Paris and the École du Louvre.

**Louis Schreel** studied philosophy at the University of Leuven and held a doctoral fellowship at the postgraduate school "Materiality and Production" at Heinrich Heine University Düsseldorf from 2012–2015. He is a currently doing his PhD on the immanent sublime in the aesthetics of Gilles Deleuze at the University of Antwerp.

**Friederike Sigler** studied art history at the Universities of Marburg and Berlin and held a doctoral fellowship at the postgraduate school "Materiality and Production" at Heinrich Heine University Düsseldorf from 2012–2014. She is currently a research assistant at the Dresden Academy of Fine Arts.

**Katharina Thurmair** does her PhD on matter and materiality in French Symbolism at the Ludwig Maximilian University of Munich. There, she is also a free art researcher and research assistant.

**Francesca Valentini** studied modern and contemporary art history and currently holds a doctoral fellowship at the a.r.t.e.s. Graduate School for the Humanities Cologne and a research doctorate in philosophy at the Ca' Foscari University of Venice. Her main research fields are the representation of time-based art and its ontology, artists' publications (1960s–2000s) and the concept of immateriality in the visual arts.

www.ingramcontent.com/pod-product-compliance
Lightning Source LLC
Chambersburg PA
CBHW050200230526
45470CB00001B/178